TERRORISM

Also by Walter Laqueur

TERRORISM

WALTER LAQUEUR

Little, Brown and Company — Boston - Toronto

Second Printing

T 09/77

Library of Congress Cataloging in Publication Data

Laqueur, Walter, 1921–
  Terrorism.

  Bibliography: p.
  Includes index.
  1. Terrorism. I. Title.
HV6431.L36   301.6'33   77–4872
ISBN 0–316–51470–5

Designed by Susan Windheim

PRINTED IN THE UNITED STATES OF AMERICA

Introductory Note

Terrorism, one of the most widely discussed issues of our time, is also one of the least understood. Its recent manifestations have been described in countless books, monographs, articles, plays, novels, films on all possible levels of sophistication; terror has fascinated the metaphysicians as much as the popular novelists. This essay grew out of a study of guerrilla warfare, and the conclusion that urban terrorism is not a new stage in guerrilla warfare, but differs from it in essential respects, and that it is also heir to a different tradition. It was not my purpose to deal with the problems of the response to terror nor to describe in detail various recent terrorist movements; this has been done elsewhere in great detail and with competence. Instead I have aimed at hitherto neglected aspects which are of key importance — the doctrine of systematic terrorism, the sociology of terrorist groups, current interpretations of terrorism, its common patterns, motives and aims and lastly the efficacy of terrorism.

This is the third part of a study on guerrilla warfare and political terrorism; it was helped by a generous grant on the part of the Thyssen Foundation. I would like again to mention the research assistance provided by Kimbriel Mitchell all along and the editorial help by Aviva Golden, Janet Langmaid and Bernard Krikler.

In the course of my work I had to consult experts on questions of detail ranging from the history of explosives to terrorism in the Turkish novel and the origins of anarchism in Argentina. I would like to express my thanks to all of them for their help and patience.

Cambridge, Mass. April 1977

Contents

TERRORISM

1

The Origins

Terrorism has long exercised a great fascination, especially at a safe distance, but it is not an easy topic for discussion and explanation. The fascination it exerts (Shelley's "tempestuous loveliness of terror") and the difficulty of interpreting it have the same roots: its unexpected, shocking and outrageous character. War, even civil war, is predictable in many ways; it occurs in the light of day and there is no mystery about the identity of the participants. Even in civil war there are certain rules, whereas the characteristic features of terrorism are anonymity and the violation of established norms.

Terrorism has always engendered violent emotions and greatly divergent opinions and images of it. The popular image of the terrorist some eighty years ago was that of a bomb-throwing alien anarchist, disheveled, with a black beard and a satanic (or idiotic) smile, fanatic, immoral, sinister and ridiculous at the same time. Dostoevsky and Conrad provided more sophisticated but essentially similar descriptions. His present-day image has been streamlined but not necessarily improved; it certainly has not been explained by political scientists or psychiatrists called in for rapid consultation. Terrorists have found admirers and publicity agents in all ages. No words of praise are fulsome enough for these latter-day saints and martyrs. The terrorist (we are told) is the only one who really cares; he is a totally committed fighter for freedom and justice, a gentle human being forced by cruel circumstances and an indifferent majority to play heroic yet tragic roles: the good Samaritan distributing poison,

St. Francis with the bomb. Such a beatification of the terrorist is grotesque, but terrorism cannot be unconditionally rejected except on the basis of a total commitment to nonviolence and nonresistance to evil. Killing, as Colonel Sexby pointed out some three hundred years ago, is not always murder and armed resistance cannot always proceed in open battle according to some chevalresque code: *"Nein, eine Grenze hat Tyrannenmacht . . . zum letzten Mittel, wenn kein anderes mehr verfangen will, ist ihm das Schwert gegeben"* (No, tyranny does have a limit, and as a last resort, one has the sword if nothing else avails). Schiller's famous statement of the *ultima ratio* of free men facing intolerable persecution has been invoked by generations of rebels against tyranny. But for every Wilhelm Tell there have been many self-appointed saviors of freedom and justice, impatient men, fanatics and madmen invoking the right of self-defense in vain, using the sword not as the last refuge but as a panacea for all evils, real or imaginary. Patriotism has been the last refuge of many a scoundrel, and so has been the struggle for freedom. Horse thieves in Latin America used to claim political motives for their actions as a safeguard against being hanged. The study of terrorism is not made any easier by the fact that most terrorists have been neither popular heroes in the mold of Wilhelm Tell nor plain horse thieves but both these as well as many other things. It is a moot point whether Burke was right when he said that one only had to scratch an ideologue to find a terrorist, but it is certainly not true that scratching a terrorist will necessarily reveal an ideologue.

The interpretation of terrorism is difficult for yet other reasons. Even over the last century the character of terrorism has changed greatly. This goes not only for its methods but also for the aims of the struggle and the character of the people that were and are involved in it. Only two generations divide Sofia Perovskaya and Emma Goldman from Ulrike Meinhof and Patty Hearst, yet morally and intellectually the distance between them is to be measured in light years. The other difficulty is equally fundamental: unlike Marxism, terrorism is not an ideology but an insurrectional strategy that can be used by people of very different political convictions.

Yet terrorism is not merely a technique. Those practising it have certain basic beliefs in common. They may belong to the left or the right; they may be nationalists or, less frequently, internationalists, but in some essential respects their mental makeup is similar. They are often closer to each other than they know or would like to admit to themselves or others. And as the technology of terrorism can be mastered by people of all creeds, so does its philosophy transcend the traditional dividing lines between political doctrine. It is truly all-purpose and value-free.

Terrorism is not, as is frequently believed, a subspecies of guerrilla (or "revolutionary") warfare and its political function today is also altogether different. "Urban guerrilla" is indeed urban, but it is not "guerrilla" in any meaningful sense of the term; the difference between guerrilla and terrorism is not one of semantics but of quality. This study grew out of a dissatisfaction with many of the current attempts to explain and interpret political terrorism, both on the popular and academic level.* According to widespread belief, the main features of contemporary terrorism are, very briefly, as follows:

1. Terrorism is a new, unprecedented phenomenon. For this reason its antecedents (if any) are of little interest.

2. Terrorism is one of the most important and dangerous problems facing mankind today.

3. Terrorism is a response to injustice; if there were political and social justice, there would be no terrorism.

4. The only known means of reducing the likelihood of terrorism is a reduction of the grievances, stresses and frustration underlying it.

5. Terrorists are fanatical believers driven to despair by intolerable conditions. They are poor and their inspiration is deeply ideological.

6. Terrorism can occur anywhere.

The intention of this study is not to refute misconceptions; for this purpose a mere juxtaposition of theories with the known facts about terrorism would be sufficient. My aim is to have a fresh look at the

---

*Elsewhere in this study I have commented on the difficulties involved in agreeing on a comprehensive definition of terrorism. Such a definition does not exist nor will it be found in the forseeable future. To argue that terrorism cannot be studied until such a definition exists is manifestly absurd. Even now, three decades after the end of the Fascist era the controversies about its character continue but the contemporaries had to confront Fascism anyway on both the theoretical and practical level. I have refrained, on the whole, from using the currently fashionable term "revolutionary terrorism"; many terrorist groups, past and present, were not at all revolutionary, including some which stressed their revolutionary orientation.

whole phenomenon. This presents certain difficulties of methodology: some terrorist movements have been exceedingly well documented; for every member of the Baader-Meinhof group or the Symbionese Liberation Army there have been several books and articles. The same is true, incidentally, for an infinitely more important movement, the *Narodnaya Volya*. On the other hand, many other terrorist groups have hardly attracted any attention at all; they have never become known outside the country in which they operated or they have been forgotten. To write a "world history" or provide a "general theory" of political terrorism is a hopeless undertaking; I have concentrated, therefore, on the main stages in the development of terrorism and terrorist doctrine and on its essential features and cardinal problems.

The terms "terrorism" and "terrorist" are of relatively recent date; the meaning of terrorism was given in the 1798 supplement of the Dictionnaire of the Académie Française as *système, régime de la terreur*.[1] According to a French dictionary published in 1796, the Jacobins had on occasion used the term when speaking and writing about themselves in a positive sense; after the 9th of Thermidor, "terrorist" became a term of abuse with criminal implications.[2] It did not take long for the term to reach Britain; Burke, in a famous passage written in 1795, wrote about "thousands of those hell hounds called terrorists" who were let loose on the people. Terrorism at the time referred to the period in the French Revolution broadly speaking between March 1793 and July 1794 and it was more or less a synonym for "reign of terror." Subsequently it acquired a wider meaning in the dictionaries as a system of terror. A terrorist was anyone who attempted to further his views by a system of coercive intimidation.[3] Even more recently, the term "terrorism" (like "guerrilla") has been used in so many different senses as to become almost meaningless, covering almost any, and not necessarily political, act of violence. According to one of the arguments frequently used against the study of political terrorism, many more people have been killed throughout history, and more havoc has been wrought, as the result of crimes committed by governments than by terrorism from below. This is not in dispute, but the present study is concerned not with political violence in general or with the inequities of tyranny but with a more specific phenomenon.

No definition of terrorism can possibly cover all the varieties of terrorism that have appeared throughout history: peasant wars and labor disputes and brigandage have been accompanied by systematic terror, and the same is true with regard to general wars, civil wars, revolutionary wars, wars of national liberation and resistance movements against foreign occupiers. In most of these cases, however, terrorism was no more than one of several strategies, and usually a subordinate one. My concern in the present study is with movements that have used systematic terrorism as their main weapon; others will be mentioned only in passing. It is generally believed that systematic political terrorism is a recent phenomenon dating back to the last century. This is true in the sense that the "philosophy of the bomb" as a doctrine is indeed relatively new. Yet it hardly needs to be recalled that there have been many systematic assassinations of political enemies throughout history. Like Molière's bourgeois, who had talked prose all along, there have been terrorists (and terrorist movements) *avant la lettre*. Many countries have had their Sicilian Vespers or St. Bartholomew's nights; foes, real and imaginary, were eliminated by Roman emperors, Ottoman sultans, Russian tsars and many others.

Terrorism "from below" has emerged in many different forms and out of such various motivations as religious protest movements, political revolts and social uprisings. One of the earliest known examples of a terrorist movement is the *sicarii*, a highly organized religious sect consisting of men of lower orders active in the Zealot struggle in Palestine (A.D. 66–73). The sources telling of their activities are sparse and sometimes contradictory, but it is known from Josephus that the *sicarii* used unorthodox tactics such as attacking their enemies by daylight, preferably on holidays when crowds congregated in Jerusalem. Their favorite weapon was a short sword *(sica)* hidden under their coats. In the words of the expert in De Quincey's club considering murder as a fine art: "Justly considering that great crowds are in themselves a sort of darkness by means of the dense pressure, and the impossibility of finding out who it was that gave the blow, they mingled with crowds everywhere . . . and when it was asked, who was the murderer and where he was — why, then it was answered *'Non est inventus'.* "[4] They destroyed the house of Ananias, the high priest, as well as the palaces of the Herodian dynasts; they burned the public archives, eager to annihilate the bonds of moneylenders and to prevent the recovery of debts. They are also mentioned in Tacitus and in the rabbinical authorities as having burned granaries and sabotaged Jerusalem's water supplies. They were the extremist, nationalist, anti-Roman party and their victims both in Palestine and the Egyptian diaspora were the moderates, the Jewish peace party. Some authorities claim that they had an elaborate doctrine, the so-called fourth philosophy, something in the nature of a Jewish protestantism according to whose tenets God alone was considered as the Lord; political allegiance was refused to any earthly power; and priests were rejected as intermediaries. Others regarded the *sicarii* as a movement of social protest intent on inciting the poor to rise against the rich. Josephus doubted their idealistic motivation and claimed that they were *listai,* robbers, out for personal gain and manipulated by outside forces, with patriotism and the demand for freedom as a mere ideological cloak.[5] But even Josephus admits that there was a frenzy of religious expectation among them, an inclination to regard martyrdom as something joyful and a totally irrational belief after the fall of Jerusalem that, as the sinful regime was no longer in authority, victory over the Romans was possible and also that God would reveal Himself to His people and deliver them. Such qualities were not that common among ordinary *listai.*

A similar mixture of messianic hope and political terrorism was the prominent feature of a much better known sect — the Assassins, an offshoot of the Ismailis who appeared in the eleventh century and were suppressed only by the Mongols in the thirteenth. The Assassins have fascinated Western authorities for a long time and this interest has grown in recent times, for some of the features of this movement remind one of contemporary terrorist movements. Based in Persia the Assassins spread to Syria, killing prefects, governors, caliphs and even Conrad of Montferrat, the Crusader King of Jerusalem. They tried twice to kill Saladin but failed. Their first leader, Hassan Sibai, seems to have realized early on that his group was too small to confront the enemy in open battle but that a planned, systematic, long-term campaign of terror carried out by a small, disciplined force could be a most effective political weapon.[6] They always operated in complete secrecy; the terrorist fighters *(fidaíin)* were disguised as strangers or even Christians.[7] The Assassins always used the dagger, never poison or missiles, and not just because the dagger was considered the safer weapon: murder was a sacramental act. Contemporary sources described the Assassins as an order of almost ascetic discipline; they courted death and martyrdom and were firm believers in a new millennium. Seen in historical perspective, the terrorist struggle of the Assassins was a fruitless attempt by a relatively small religious sect to defend its religious autonomy (and way of life) against the Seljuqs who wanted to suppress them. But the means they used were certainly effective for a while, and the legends about the Old Man from the Mountain deeply impressed contemporaries and subsequent generations.

Secret societies of a different kind existed for centuries in India and the Far East. The Anglo-Indian authorities denied the existence of the Thugs until Captain (subsequently Major General) William Sleeman studied the subject and ultimately destroyed the sect. The Thugs strangled their victims with a silk tie; Europeans were hardly ever affected, but otherwise their choice of victims was quite indiscriminate. Its devotees thought the origin of Thuggee was derived from an act of sacrifice to the goddess Kali. It had a fatal attraction. In the words of Feringea, a captured Thug: "Let any man taste of that *goor* [sugar] of the sacrifice, and he will be a Thug, though he knows all the trades and has all the wealth in the world. . . . I have been in high office myself and became so great a favorite wherever I went that I was sure of promotion. Yet I was always miserable when away from my gang and obliged to return to Thuggee."[8] The Thugs had contempt for death. Their political aims, if any, were not easily discernible; nor did they want to terrorize the government or population.

In a survey of political terrorism the phenomenon rates no more than a footnote. The same applies to the more militant secret societies in China that existed among river pirates and the outlaws in the hills as well as among respectable city dwellers. Each society had its "enforcer," usually a trained boxer. Some engaged in criminal extortion; there were hired killers among them, selling themselves to the highest bidder. The societies ran gambling houses and smuggled salt. Some of the more important societies also had distinct political aims: they were anti-Manchu and loathed foreigners.[9] They were behind the Boxer Rebellion and helped Sun Yat-sen in the early days of his career. The "Red Spears" of the 1920s combined politics with exercises such as deep breathing and magic formulas, rather like the counterculture of the 1960s. But politics was only one of their many activities and in this respect they resemble more the Mafia than modern political terrorist movements.[10]

The interest of the Ku Klux Klan in politics was perhaps more pronounced, but it was still not in the mainstream of terrorist movements. It is not always remembered that there was not one Klan, but three, which did not have much in common with each other. The first Klan, a product of the Reconstruction period, was a secret, violent association, proscribing recently emancipated Negroes. The second Klan (ca. 1915–1944) also stood for white supremacy, but at the same time it campaigned for a great many other causes such as patriotism and attacked bootleggers, crapshooters and even wife-beaters. With all the ritual mumbo-jumbo around the Great Wizard, it became very much part of establishment politics in the South, both on the local and state level. It also engaged in various business enterprises, such as dealing in emulsified asphalt for road construction. The second Klan was in fact an incorporated society, whose history ends in April 1944, not with a dramatic shoot-out with the police but with a federal suit for $685,000 in delinquent income tax. As a result its charter had to be surrendered and the Klan went out of business.[11]

Compared with the *sicarii* and Assassins, with Thugs, Red Spears and the Ku Klux Klan, contemporary terrorist groups seem to belong to another species altogether. For the starting point to the study of modern political terrorism one clearly has to look elsewhere and this takes one back to the Wilhelm Tell syndrome. Political assassinations of leading statesmen were relatively infrequent in the age of absolutism, once the religious conflicts had lost some of their acuteness. There was solidarity between monarchs whatever their personal differences or the clashes of interest between them; they would not normally have thought of killing one another. The idea of regicide also had temporarily gone out of fashion — with a few notable exceptions. This changed only after the French Revolution and the rise of nationalism in Europe. Outside Europe there were cases of political murder, as there had been since time immemorial, but these belonged, *grosso modo,* to the tradition of dynastic quarrels or clashes between rival groups fighting for power or of military coups or the actions of fanatics or madmen.

Systematic terrorism begins in the second half of the nineteenth century and there were several quite distinct categories of it from the very beginning. The Russian revolutionaries fought an autocratic government in 1878–1881 and again in the early years of the twentieth century. Radical nationalist groups such as the Irish, Macedonians, Serbs or Armenians used terrorist methods in their struggle for autonomy or national independence. Lastly, there was the anarchist "propaganda by the deed," mainly during the 1890s in France, Italy, Spain and the United States. The few assassinations in France and Italy attracted enormous publicity, but they were not really part of a general systematic strategy. The character of terrorism in the United States and Spain was again different inasmuch as it had the support of specific sections of the population. In the United States there was working-class terrorism such as practiced by the Molly Maguires and later by the Western Union of Mineworkers. In Spain there was both agrarian terrorism and industrial terrorism. Seen in historical perspective the various manifestations of terrorism, however different their aims and the political context, had a common origin: they were connected with the rise of democracy and nationalism. All the grievances had existed well before: minorities had been oppressed, nations had been denied independence, autocratic government had been the rule. But as the ideas of the enlightenment spread and as the appeal of nationalism became increasingly powerful, conditions that had been accepted for centuries became intolerable. However, the movements of armed protest had a chance for success only if the ruling classes were willing to play according to the new rules and this precluded violent repression. In short, terrorist groups could hope to tackle only nonterrorist governments with any degree of confidence. This was the paradox facing modern terrorism, and what was true with regard to repression by old-fashioned authoritarian regimes applied, *a fortiori,* to the new style totalitarian systems of the twentieth century.

Of all these movements the *Narodnaya Volya* was the most important by far, even though its operations lasted only from January 1878 to March 1881. The armed struggle began when Kovalski, one of its members, resisted arrest; it continued with Vera Zasulich's shooting of the governor general of St. Petersburg and reached a first climax with the assassination of General Mezentsev, the head of the Third

Section (the Tsarist political police) in August 1878. In September 1879 Alexander II was sentenced to death by the revolutionary tribunal of the *Narodnaya Volya*. Even before, in April of that year, Solovev had tried to kill the tsar, but this had been a case of failed private initiative. Further attempts were no more successful; they included an attempt to blow up the train in which the tsar traveled and the explosion of a mine in the Winter Palace. Success came on 1 March 1881, paradoxically after most of the members of the group had already been apprehended by the police. This was the apogee of the terror and also its end for more than two decades.

The second major wave of terrorism was sponsored by the Social Revolutionary Party and opened with the assassination in 1902 of Sipyagin, the minister of the interior, by Balmashev. The year before, Karpovich, a young nobleman, had shot Bogolyepov, minister of education. The Social Revolutionaries carried out a mere three major *attentats* in 1903 (including the killing of the governors Obolenski and Bogdanovich) and two in 1904, but the number rose to fifty-four in 1905 (the year of the war with Japan), eighty-two in 1906 and seventy-one in 1907. After that the number dwindled rapidly — three in 1908, two in 1909, one in 1910.[12] The most striking assassination was that of Plehve, minister of the interior and the strong man of the regime, in a Petersburg street in 1904. The next year Kalyayev killed the Grand Duke Serge Aleksandrovich. The last spectacular assassination, that of Stolypin in the Kiev Opera House in 1911, was again the act of an individual, probably a double agent; it took place after the fighting organization of the Social Revolutionaries had ceased to exist. Some minor sporadic incidents apart, there was no individual terror after 1911. There was a third, much smaller wave of political terror after the Bolshevik coup in November 1917; it was directed partly against Communist leaders — Uritski and Volodarski were killed and Lenin wounded — but also against German diplomats and military commanders in an attempt to sabotage the peace negotiations between Russia and Germany. The Communist authorities suppressed this challenge to their rule without great difficulty.

The achievements of Irish terrorism have been much less striking, but it has continued, on and off, for a much longer period. There have been countless ups and downs ever since the emergence, partly due to agrarian unrest, of the United Irishmen in 1791. The policy of open force in the 1860s was an unmitigated failure. The activities of the Dynamiters in the 1870s and 1880s resulted in one spectacular operation, the Phoenix Park murders. After that there followed several decades of calm, with new upsurges in 1916, 1919–1921, before the Second World War and then again in the 1970s.

Armenian terrorism against Turkish oppression began in the 1890s but was shortlived and ended in disaster because the Armenians faced an enemy less patient and good-natured than did the Irish. Further terrorism occurred in the 1890s and again after 1918 in the form of assassinations of some individual Turkish leaders who had been prominently involved in the massacres of the First World War. This terrorist tradition has continued sporadically to the present day; political leaders and church dignitaries have been killed by their opponents and in 1975 there was a new upsurge of terrorism with the murder of the Turkish ambassadors in Vienna and Paris and of the first secretary of the Turkish embassy in Beirut.

At the very time that the Armenian terrorists first launched their operations, another separatist organization directed against the Turks, the Macedonian IMRO led by Damian Gruev, came into being. First an underground, civilian propagandist society, it turned after a few years into a military movement, preparing both for systematic terror and a mass insurrection.[13] The mass insurrection (*Ilin Den*) was a catastrophe, yet the Macedonians were more fortunate than the Armenians, inasmuch as they did have allies and as Macedonia was not part of the Turkish heartland. But Macedonia did not gain independence; in 1912–1913 it was redistributed between Greece, Bulgaria and Serbia. IMRO continued its struggle from the Petrich district in Bulgaria; some of its operations were directed against Yugoslavia but, in fact, it became a tool of successive Bulgarian governments. In the decade between 1924 and 1934 the number of its own members (and Bulgarian oppositionists) who perished in internecine struggles considerably exceeded the casualties it inflicted on its enemies. By the time a new Bulgarian government suppressed IMRO in the mid-1930s, it had only the name in common with the organization founded four decades earlier.

Among other nationalist terrorist groups that appeared before the First World War were the Polish socialists and some Indian groups, particularly in Bengal.[14] In both cases the terrorist tradition continued well after independence had been achieved. Nehru and others had warned against terrorism and there is no doubt that the sectarian character of the terror, even though limited in scope, further poisoned the relations between the communities and contributed to the partition of India in 1947. In Poland organized terror continued for more than a decade after the First World War in the eastern territories among the Western Ukrainians, who turned against the Warsaw government when their demands for autonomy were ignored.

The high tide of terrorism in Western Europe was the anarchist "propaganda of the deed" in the 1890s. The exploits of Ravachol, Auguste Vaillant and Emile Henry between 1892 and 1894 created an enormous stir, and because the bomb throwing by individuals coincided with a turn in anarchist propaganda favoring violence, the impression of a giant international conspiracy was created, which in actual fact never existed. Ravachol was in many ways an extraordinary villain, a bandit who would have killed and robbed even if there had been no anarchist movement in France; Vaillant was a Bohemian and Emile Henry an excited young man. An analysis of the statistics of urbanization in nineteenth-century France would not add much to the understanding of their motives. The public at large was fascinated by the secret and mysterious character of the anarchist groups; anarchists, socialists, nihilists and radicals were all believed to be birds of one feather. Governments and police forces who knew better saw no reason to correct this impression.

There were a great many attempts on the lives of leading statesmen in Europe and America between the 1880s and the first decade of the twentieth century. Presidents Garfield and McKinley were among the victims; there were several unsuccessful attempts to kill Bismarck and the German emperor; French President Carnot was assassinated in 1894; Antonio Canovas, the Spanish prime minister, was murdered in 1897, Empress Elisabeth (Zita) of Austria in 1898 and King Umberto of Italy in 1900. But inasmuch as the assassins were anarchists — and quite a few were not — they all acted on their own initiative without the knowledge and support of the groups to which they belonged. It was conveniently forgotten at the time that there had been a long tradition of regicide, and attempted regicide, in Europe and that there had been countless attempts to kill Napoleon and Napoleon III. As a contemporary observer, who had little sympathy for anarchism, noted: "It is difficult to assign to them [the anarchists] any participation in the various outrages, notably the assassination of rulers."[15]

Psychologically interesting, the *ère des attentats* was of no great political significance. By 1905 the wave of attacks and assassinations outside Russia had abated; there were further spectacular happenings in Paris and London in the years just before the outbreak of World War I, such as the exploits of the Bonnot gang and of groups of Poles and Latvians (Peter the Painter) in London's East End. But the motive of these groups was predominantly self-gain and the importance of the anarchist admixture, which did exist, was usually exaggerated. There were, to summarize, no systematic terrorist campaigns in Central and Western Europe. They did exist on the fringes of Europe, in Russia, the Balkans and, in a different form, in Spain.

Labor disputes in the United States had been more violent than in Europe almost from the beginning. The story of the Molly Maguires in the 1870s is only one of several such historical episodes; the group was identified at the time, quite wrongly, with Communism.[16] It was, of course, not a matter of Communism but of the traditional violence displayed by a group of Irishmen transplanted to a new continent and feeling itself discriminated against and exploited. But it fought not only mine owners but also fellow workers of Welsh and German extraction. There was also the Haymarket Square bombing in 1886 and many other bloody incidents involving factory police on the one hand and militant coal miners and steelworkers on the other. Again, the killing of Governor Frank Steunenberg of Idaho in 1905 was not an isolated incident; the IWW did not deny that it had been inspired by the "Russian struggle." There was the bombing by the MacNamara brothers of the Los Angeles Times Building in 1910 and other such incidents now remembered only by historians specializing in the byways of the American labor movement. But terrorism in the United States was limited in scope and purpose; there was no intention of overthrowing the government, killing the political leadership or changing the political system.

Spain was the other country in which systematic terrorism was a factor of some political importance. Political violence had been rampant in Spain throughout the nineteenth century, notably during the

Carlist wars. The emergence of the working class movement, very much under Bakuninist influence, was accompanied by a great deal of fighting; in the trade unions terrorism became endemic. There was also rural violence, especially in the provinces of southern Spain such as Andalusia. Like France, Spain had its *ère des attentats* in the 1890s but, unlike France, there was a resurgence in 1904–1909 and again during World War I and after. There were all sorts of anarchists, but the most militant group, the FAI, became the dominant force. Among its leaders, Buenaventura Durruti (1896–1936) was the most outstanding ("We are not afraid of ruins").[17] This terrorism was politically quite ineffective except that it caused a great deal of internecine struggle inside the left and that it contributed to the fatal events of 1936–1939. Catalonia was the main scene of terrorism up to and including the civil war. In the later stages of the Franco dictatorship the center of gravity shifted to the Basque region, but there separatism was the main driving force, sometimes, as in Ulster, appearing under a Marxist veneer. Terrorist anarchism radiated from Spain to Latin America, especially to Argentina; Barcelona had its tragic week in 1909 and Buenos Aires' *Semana Tragica* took place a decade later.[18] Durruti shot the Archbishop of Saragossa and the indefatigable Simon Radowitsky killed the Buenos Aires chief of police.

Up to the First World War terrorism was thought to be a left-wing phenomenon, even though the highly individualistic character of terrorism somehow did not quite fit the ideological pattern. But neither the Irish nor Macedonian freedom fighters, neither the Armenian nor Bengali terrorists were socialist or anarchist in inspiration. The "Black Hundred" was certainly a terrorist organization, but its main purpose was to fight the Russian revolution, engage in anti-Jewish pogroms and, generally speaking, to assassinate the leaders of the liberal-democratic opposition to Tsarism. The "Black Hundred" constituted the extreme right in Russian domestic politics and it was in fact founded with the support of the police. But as so often happened in the history of terrorist movements, the sorcerer's apprentice developed an identity of his own. Soon demands for the redistribution of land and the shortening of the working day were voiced and the members of an organization established to defend the monarchy were complaining that it would be preferable to have no government rather than the existing one. It was said that a few resolute officers, like those in Serbia, would do a world of good — a reference to Serbian regicides.

In the years after World War I terrorist operations were mainly sponsored by right-wing and nationalist-separatist groups. Sometimes these groups were both right-wing and separatist, as in the case of the Croatian Ustacha, which received most of its support from Fascist Italy and Hungary. The Croatians wanted independence and they had no compunction about accepting support from any quarter; like the Irish they have continued their struggle to the present day. Systematic terrorism was found in the 1920s mainly on the fringes of the budding Fascist movements or among their precursors such as the *Freikorps* in Germany, certain French Fascist groups, in Hungary and, above all, among the Rumanian "Iron Guard." But by and large there was comparatively little terror, for this was the age of mass parties both on the right and left; anarchism had long outgrown its terrorist phase. There were a few spectacular political assassinations like those of Liebknecht and Luxemburg in 1919, of Rathenau in 1922 and of King Alexander of Yugoslavia and Barthou in Marseilles in April 1934. As this latter was clearly a case of international terrorism in which at least four governments were involved, the League of Nations intervened; resolutions were passed and committees were established with a view to combatting terrorism on an international basis.[19] All these exercises were quite futile for the obvious reason that, although some governments were opposed to terror, others favored it as long as it served their purposes. Three decades later the United Nations faced a similar situation.

Outside Europe too, terrorist operations were as yet infrequent. The murder of the Egyptian prime minister, Boutros Pasha, in 1910 was the action of an individual. So was the assassination in 1924 of Sir Lee Stack, commander in chief of the Egyptian army. But in the 1930s and especially in the 1940s the Muslim Brotherhood and other extreme right-wing groups such as Young Egypt were converted to systematic terrorism and killed two prime ministers and a few other leading officials. In Mandatory Palestine, the *Irgun Zvai Leumi* and LEHI (Fighters for the Freedom of Israel) opted for individual terrorism. Irgun ceased its anti-British activities in 1939 but the more extreme LEHI continued its struggle; the murder of Lord Moyne was its most spectacular operation. Even in India, the country of nonviolence, the terrorist Bhagat Singh had, in Nehru's words, a sudden and amazing popularity in the 1920s. Nehru was inclined to belittle terrorism: it represented the infancy of a revolutionary urge (he wrote); India had passed that stage and terrorism was about to die out.[20] Yet Nehru's prediction was premature; ten years later he again toured Bengal to denounce terrorism. Terrorism, he said, was the glamour of secret work and risk-taking attracting adventurous young men and women: "It is the call of the detective story."[21] But detective stories, for better or worse, have always found more readers than high literature. In Japan during the 1930s a group of junior army officers engaged in terror; their actions had a certain impact on the conduct of Japanese foreign policy.

Individual terrorism played a subordinate role in the European resistance movement during the Second World War. Heydrich, the governor of the Czech protectorate, was killed; so was Wilhelm Kube, the Nazi governor of White Russia, and some minor French collaborators. A few bombs were placed in Parisian cinemas. Overall there is no evidence that the German war effort or the morale of the soldiers was affected by terrorist activity. For many years after the war urban terror was overshadowed by large-scale guerrilla wars such as in China. It was only in predominantly urban regions such as Mandatory Palestine and, later, Cyprus and Aden that the terrorist strategy prevailed. This is not to say that rural guerrillas would not on occasion ambush and kill enemy leaders; the assassination of Sir Henry Gurney, the British governor-general in Malaya, may have been an accident. The killing of thousands of South Vietnamese village headmen in the late 1950s and early 1960s, on the other hand, was certainly a systematic operation of the North Vietnamese and part of their general strategy.

The urban terrorist, in contrast to the rural guerrilla, could not transform small assault groups into regiments or even divisions, and the establishment of liberated zones was ruled out — except in very rare conditions when government no longer functioned. The struggles for Tel Aviv (1945–1947), Nicosia (1955–1958) and Aden (1964–1967) lasted for three years. The attacks of Jewish and Greek Cypriot terrorists were directed against the British, but the presence of Arab and Turkish communities caused major complications. With the outbreak of the civil war in Palestine in late 1947 and the subsequent invasion of Arab armies, the terrorist groups were absorbed into the Israeli army. EOKA activities had led to communal riots as early as 1957 and there is little doubt that their terrorism contributed to the subsequent tragic events in Cyprus. Viewed in retrospect the number of victims and the damage caused by terrorist activities in Palestine and Cyprus was very small indeed. But weakened as the result of the Second World War, Britain was about to dismantle its empire in any case and not much violence was needed to hasten the process. Aden was one of Britain's last outposts but, after India had been lost, the Crown Colony was no longer of strategic importance. The struggle for Aden began on a small scale in 1964 and culminated in the occupation of the Crater area, the oldest part of the town, in 1967. The British forces reoccupied it without much difficulty two weeks later, but the rebels had nevertheless scored a political victory which led to the British exodus in November of that year.[22]

A decade earlier the Algerian FLN had tried to seize and hold an urban area in a far bloodier battle. By mid-1956 the slums of Algiers (the Casbah section) were securely in their hands, but the moment antiterrorist actions were begun by the French army (January 1957) the fate of the insurgents was sealed. The FLN did not regain its position in the capital up to the very end of the war. But the tough methods used by General Massu's Paras in combatting systematic terror with systematic torture provoked a worldwide outcry. The guerrilla war continued in the Algerian countryside; politically and economically it became too costly for France to combat and eventually the French forces had to withdraw.

These, then, were the major cases of urban terrorism during the two decades after the end of World War II. A great many guerrilla wars were going on at the time all over the world, but the main scene of action was in the countryside, as all the theoreticians from Mao to Castro and Guevara agreed it should be. Urban terrorism was regarded at best as a supplementary form of warfare, at worst as a dangerous aberration. Castro and Guevara were firmly convinced that the city was the "graveyard" of the revolutionary freedom fighter.[23] It was only in the middle 1960s that urban terrorism came into its own — mainly as the result of the defeat of the rural guerrillas in Latin America but also following the emergence (or in some cases the reactivation) of urban terrorist groups in Europe, North America and Japan. Thus, it was only a little more than a decade ago that urban terror began to attract general attention. Seen in historical perspective it was no more than a revival of certain forms of political violence that had been used previously in many parts of the world. These methods had been widely described, analyzed and debated at the time from every possible angle. But given the frailty of human memory it was perhaps not surprising that the reemergence of terrorism should have been regarded in recent years as an altogether novel phenomenon and that its causes and the ways to cope with it should have been discussed as if nothing of the kind had ever happened before.

2

The Philosophy of the Bomb

The doctrinal origins of the philosophy of the bomb emerged in the nineteenth century but its antecedents predate the invention of modern explosives. Terrorism has always been justified as a means of resisting despotism and as such its origins are of course to be found in antiquity. Plato and Aristotle regarded tyranny as a deviation, a perversion, the worst form of government. Tyrannicides in ancient Greece were elevated to the rank of national heroes. Cicero noted in his *De Officiis* that tyrants had always found a violent end and that the Romans had usually acclaimed those who killed them. The saying was attributed to Seneca that no victim was more agreeable to god than the blood of a tyrant. The civic virtues of a Brutus were praised by his fellow Romans.

The early Church fathers did not see eye to eye about regicide but there was an influential school of thought which maintained that tyranny might be resisted as it violated divine and natural law alike. As St. Isidore put it, it was the task of the ruler to maintain justice and the tyrant consequently had no claim to obedience. Thomas Aquinas drew a distinction between the *tyrannus ex defectu tituli*, the usurper, who could be killed by any individual, and the *tyrannus ex parte exercitii*, who could be punished only by *publica auctoritas*. John of Salisbury in the twelfth century was the first medieval author to provide an explicit defense of tyrannicide. Referring to the legends of Jael and Sisara, of Judith and Holofernes and a great many other examples, he argued that there was a basic difference between a good king, who, in observing the law, was the guardian of the well-being of his people, and the oppressor whose rule was merely based on force: he who usurps the sword was worthy to die of the sword.[1]

Dante had banished the murderers of Caesar to the depths of his Inferno but the Renaissance rectified their place in history. The Council of Constance (1414–1418) had banned tyrannicide but the concept was widely accepted in the sixteenth century by Catholic and Protestant thinkers alike: the people had an inherent right to resist the command of the prince if it was contrary to the law of God. According to Mariana (1536–1623), the power of the king was based on a contract with the people; if the king violated his part of the contract he could and should be removed, and any private citizen was entitled to kill him, if necessary by poison. Even earlier George Buchanan (1506–1582) in his *De Jure Regnis apud Scotos* had argued that it was "most just" to wage a war against a tyrant who was an enemy of all mankind; all good men should engage in perpetual warfare with such a public enemy. The author of *De droit des magistrats* (1574) noted with disdain that among the Jews, killers of tyrants had to be specially commissioned by God (implying that the Jews should have been less fainthearted and taken the initiative without divine prodding).[2] The Monarchomachs of the sixteenth and seventeenth centuries discussed at great length the circumstances in which a king might become a tyrant. They developed a theory of popular sovereignty and this, in turn, led them into accepting the right of resistance.

The writings of these ancient and medieval authors are of more than academic interest in the context of modern terrorism for the ancient concept of justified tyrannicide provided inspiration for nineteenth-century terrorist thought. The program of the Narodnaya Volya as drafted at their first convention (Lipetsk, June 1879) stated explicitly that "we will fight with the means employed by Wilhelm Tell." Very few of these young Russians knew of Buchanan, but all of them had read Schiller, so dear to successive generations of Russian progressives, and they knew the "In Tyrannos" literature, often by heart. Nikolai Morozov, one of the first theoreticians of Russian terrorism, chose as a motto to his pamphlet quotations from Saint-Just and Robespierre to the effect that it was perfectly justifiable to execute a tyrant without any legal niceties.[3] But tyrants were usually not alone, they could not function without assistants, and the death of a tyrant was not necessarily the end of tyranny. Hence the necessity to attack the system on a broader front, first discussed in the secret societies of the late eighteenth and early nineteenth centuries. Secret societies, with their magical and religious preoccupations (but often also with very tangible social functions) and their *rites de passage,* have existed since time immemorial in many civilizations; as a very result of their secrecy, the scope and importance of their activities has frequently been overrated. The eighteenth-century secret societies might debate the inequities of the world but they did not, as a rule, engage in conspiracies aimed at the violent overthrow of the existing political and social order. Alfieri, the poet of Italian liberty, discussed in the 1770s the most effective ways of doing away with tyranny *in un instante e con tutta certezza.*[4] But it was only after the Thermidor that the idea took firm root. When asked at his trial about the means he counted upon employing, Baboeuf proudly declared: "All means are legitimate against tyrants." And later on, Buonarroti echoed him: "No means are criminal which are employed to obtain a sacred end." Baboeuvisme was a movement without the people, and aimed at a dictatorship; the absence of anything specifically popular was precisely what made it into terrorism.[5] Buonarroti's *History of Baboeuf's Conspiracy* remained the bible of two generations of young revolutionaries all over Europe. Seen in historical perspective, it was the precursor of Blanquism, of armed insurrection rather than of individual terror. But it also influenced latter-day terrorist thought through its advocacy of violence, its scant regard for human life, and its belief that a few determined people could make a revolution; what did the fate of a few individuals matter if the future of twenty-five millions was at stake? In the French Revolution the practice of intimidating the enemy by means of terror had gained ground, instinctive and spontaneous at first, later on bureaucratic and doctrinaire. Until in the end the *sans culottes* lost faith in terror and its leading advocates were swept from the scene by the reaction triggered off by their excesses. But *terreur* was not quite synonymous with terrorism, and its proponents did not yet have a clear concept as to how it should be utilized in the long term. A Jacobin tradition whose aims were vague and ill-defined failed to make any notable inroads against a government which had both public support and a fairly effective police force.[6]

Elsewhere, in Spain, Piedmont and Sicily the Carbonari, their successors, and similar such groups succeeded in overturning governments, much to the consternation of the Holy Alliance, but this was the result of insurrections rather than systematic campaigns of terror. The critics of the Carbonari attributed to them the most terrible and sanguinary plans for revolt; the "good cousins" through their *venditi* (branches, literally shops) were said to have fomented terror, setting fire to their enemies' houses, and helping prisoners to escape; "several individuals, who were adverse to their maxims were destined to the poignard," and when this was too risky, poison was used as a fitter method of liquidation.[7] The Carbonari were said to be pitiless professional revolutionaries, ready to kill anyone. Once having joined the conspiracy, their members lost all individuality, without family or fatherland, and belonged totally to their masters. At a signal they had to obey them blindly, knife in hand.[8] It is true that the language used by the Carbonari was bloodthirsty. The following passage conveys something of its flavor:

> The cross should serve to crucify the tyrant who persecutes us and troubles our sacred operations. The crown of thorns should serve to pierce his head. The thread denotes the cord to lead him to the gibbet; the ladder will aid him to mount. The leaves are nails to pierce his hands and feet. The pick-axe will penetrate his breast, and shed the impure blood that flows in his veins. The axe will separate his head from his body, as the wolf who disturbs our pacific labors. The salt will prevent the corruption of his head, that it may last as a monument of the eternal infamy of despots [etc., etc.].[9]

Little is known to this day about the origins of the Carboneria other than the mere fact that the movement appeared first in Naples in 1807. Whether it drew its inspiration from earlier anti-Austrian secret societies in northern Italy or whether French republicans and freemasons had a hand in founding the movement is still a matter of contention.[10] It is certain however that the terrorist element in Carbonari activities was grossly exaggerated. Occasional terrorist acts were perpetrated but they did not amount to a systematic campaign.

Elsewhere, I have discussed the ideas of Carlo Bianco, Conte di

Saint Jorioz, who was first in Europe to outline a strategy of a national war of liberation by means of guerrilla tactics; he also wrote about the necessity of imposing a revolutionary dictatorship and of applying terrorist means against the enemies of the revolution.[11] But such suggestions remained unanswered. Three decades later Orsini tried to kill Napoleon III and Cavour denounced the "villainous doctrine of political assassination practised by the execrable sectarians." Mazzini in an open letter wrote a withering reply: you exhumed the theory of the dagger, a theory unknown in Italy. Do you take us for villains and madmen? For whom and to what end could the death of Victor Emmanuel serve?[12] In fact, Mazzini's attitude to assassination was not that unambiguous for in letters to friends he had written that holy was the sword in the hand of Judith, the dagger of Harmodios and Brutus, the poignard of the Sicilian who had initiated the Vespers and the arrow of Wilhelm Tell — was not the finger of God to be discerned in the individual who rose against the tyrant's despotism?

In some of the secret societies of Central Europe, such as the "League of the Just" (which later became the Communist League), the doctrine of terror was first discussed — only to be rejected. Wilhelm Weitling, a tailor and the first German Communist, suggested in letters to his friends in Paris various ways of "founding the kingdom of heaven by unleashing the furies of hell." They were shocked by his suggestions which also included community of women; they were positively horrified when he proposed to turn loose the "thieving proletariat" on society. Weitling thought he could mobilize some 20,000 "smart and courageous" murderers and thieves. His correspondents thought that a desirable end could not possibly be attained by "Jesuit tactics."[13] It would do the cause irreparable harm if murderers and thieves were proudly to style themselves Communists. Their moral standards would not be improved by the example set by Weitling: they would not surrender their ill-gotten gains for a political movement to use; any such suggestion would be vastly amusing to them, and very likely they would kill Weitling. This exchange of letters took place in 1843, unknown to Marx and Engels who, in any event, had misgivings about Weitling's capacity as a systematic thinker. They argued that it was fraudulent to arouse the people without a sound and considered basis for action. But Weitling was not deterred by the arguments of his friends in Paris and the idea of the noble robber continued to figure in his writings in later years. In a new edition of his main opus, *Garantien der Harmonie und Freiheit,* published after the failure of the revolution of 1848, he wrote that public opinion ought to be persuaded that a robber who found his death in the fight was a martyr in a holy cause. Anyone who informed on such a man should not rest secure for a single moment from the people's vengeance, and those who sought to take revenge upon him should be given protection and cover.[14] The year of the revolution, 1848, also gave fresh impetus to the concept of terrorism, expressed most succinctly perhaps in an essay entitled "Murder" *(Der Mord)* written by the German radical democrat Karl Heinzen (1809–1880). He argued that while murder was forbidden in principle this prohibition did not apply to politics. The physical liquidation of hundreds or thousands of people could still be in the higher interests of humanity. Heinzen took tyrannicide as his starting point; he pointed out that such acts of liberation had been undertaken at all times and in all places. But it soon emerged that he was willing to justify terrorist tactics on a much more massive scale: "If you have to blow up half a continent and pour out a sea of blood in order to destroy the party of the barbarians, have no scruples of conscience. He is no true republican who would not gladly pay with his life for the satisfaction of exterminating a million barbarians." There could be no social and political progress unless kings and generals, the foes of liberty, were removed.

Seen in retrospect, Karl Heinzen was the first to provide a full-fledged doctrine of modern terrorism; most elements of latter-day terrorist thought can be found in the writings of this forgotten German radical democrat. It was a confused doctrine, to be sure; on one hand he argued that killing was always a crime, but on the other hand he claimed that murder might well be a "physical necessity," that the atmosphere or the soil of the earth needed a certain quantity of blood. *(Die Evolution,* January 26, 1849). He maintained that it was absolutely certain that the forces of progress would prevail over the reactionaries in any case but doubted whether the spirit of freedom and the "good cause" would win without using dagger, poison and explosives: "We have to become more energetic, more desperate." This led him into speculations about the use of arms of mass destruction. For the greater strength, training and discipline of the forces of repression could be counterbalanced only by weapons that could be employed by a few people and that would cause great havoc. These weapons, Heinzen thought, could not be used by armies against a few individual fighters. Hence the great hopes attached to the potential of poison gas, to ballistic missiles (known at the time as Congreve rockets) and mines which one day "could destroy whole cities with 100,000 inhabitants" (*Die Evolution,* February 16, 1849). Heinzen blamed the revolutionaries of 1848 for not having shown sufficient ruthlessness; the party of freedom would be defeated unless it gave the highest priority to the development of the art of murder. Heinzen, like Most after him, came to see the key to revolution in modern technology: new explosives would have to be invented, bombs planted under pavements, new means of poisoning food explored. To expedite progress he advocated prizes for research in these fields.[15] Heinzen's subsequent career was not, however, in the field of professional terrorism; he did not blow up half a continent but migrated to the United States and became an editor of various short-lived German-language newspapers, first in Louisville, Kentucky, and eventually in Boston — "the most civilized city in America."

The idea of the alliance between the revolutionary avant-garde and the criminal underworld was to reappear from time to time in the history of nineteenth-century terrorist movements (pace the Narodnaya Volya) and again among the American and West German New Left militants of the 1960s. Pavel Akselrod, one of the fathers of Russian socialism, relates in his autobiography how in 1874 he and Breshkovskaya, the future "grandmother of the Russian revolution," went searching the forests of southern Russia, without evident success, for a famous robber who had the reputation of plundering rich landowners and Jews and distributing his booty among poor peasants.[16] Weitling's theory had been forgotten by that time but like all revolutionaries of his generation Akselrod had read Bakunin; Bakunin, in turn, had met Weitling in Zürich and had been deeply influenced by him. This meeting was one of the formative events of Bakunin's life, "completing his transformation from a speculative philosopher into a practical revolutionary."[17]

In his never-ending search for the main catalysts of the forthcoming Russian revolution, Bakunin placed high hopes on the religious sectarians. But he was even more sanguine about the rebel-robbers in the tradition of Stenka Rasin and Pugachov and had nothing but contempt for the Marxists and "Liberals" who preferred not to appeal to the so-called evil passions of the people. The robber (Bakunin wrote) was the only sincere revolutionary in Russia, a revolutionary without phraseology, without bookish rhetoric, irreconcilable and indefatigable, a revolutionary of the deed. The robber was traditionally a hero, a savior of the people, the enemy *par excellence* of the state and its entire social order. Without an understanding of the robber one could not understand the history of the Russian people; whosoever wanted a real, popular revolution had to go to this world. It was a cruel, merciless world, but this was only the outcome of government oppression. An end to this underworld would spell either the death of the people or their final liberation. Hence Bakunin's conclusion that a truly popular revolution would emerge only if a peasants' revolt merged with a rebellion of the robbers. And the season was at hand to accomplish this task.[18] Bakunin, however, placed no emphasis on individual terror or even on guerrilla warfare. In 1848, he envisaged the emergence of a regular revolutionary army, trained with the help of former Polish officers and, perhaps, by some junior Austrian officers.[19] It was only after Bakunin's death that his Anarchist followers committed themselves to "propaganda of the deed."

Though Bakunin was second to none in his revolutionary enthusiasm ever since he first appeared on the European scene in the 1840s, it was only two decades later, once he had met Nechaev (that "magnificent young fanatic, that believer without God, hero without rhetoric"), that Bakunin developed a theory of destruction. In the *Principles of Revolution,* published in 1869, he wrote that "we recognize no other action save destruction though we admit that the forms in which such action will show itself will be exceedingly varied — poison, the knife, the rope etc." Those intended for liquidation had already been singled out. Weeping and wailing would follow: "society" would experience fear and remorse. The revolutionaries, however, should show indifference toward the lamentations of the doomed, and were not to enter into any compromise. Their approach might be called terroristic but this ought not to deter them. The final aim was to achieve revolution, the cause of eradicating evil was holy, Russian soil would be cleansed by sword and fire.

The demand that the revolutionary should have but one thought day and night, that is, merciless destruction, recurs in the most famous document of the period, the "Revolutionary Catechism."[20] The Catechism has frequently been quoted and a short summary will suffice for our purposes. It opens with a general list of rules for organization and then characterizes the attitude of the revolutionary toward himself and others. He is a lost man, without interests, belongings, personal ties of his own — not even a name. (The idea of the nameless soldier of the revolution was later to recur in many terrorist organizations as far afield as Ireland and Serbia where members were known by number rather than by name.) He must be absorbed by a single interest, thought and passion — the revolution. He has broken with society and its laws and conventions; he must eschew doctrinairism and despise public opinion, be prepared for torture and death at any time. Hard toward himself, he must be hard toward others, leaving no place for love, friendship, gratitude or even honor — room was to be spared only for the cold passion of the revolutionary cause whose success was to give him his pleasure, gratification and reward.

Tactical advice follows: in order to effect merciless destruction, the revolutionary has to pretend to be what he is not, to infiltrate the Church, the world of business, the bureaucracy and army, the secret police and even the royal palace. Bakunin divided "society" into six categories: intelligent and energetic individuals, particularly dangerous to the revolutionary organization, were to be killed first, for their sudden and violent death would inspire fear among the government; secondly there were those, albeit no less guilty, whose lives should be temporarily spared, for their monstrous crimes objectively fomented revolution. The third category consisted of the high-ranking, the rich and powerful; they were mere "animals," neither particularly intelligent nor dynamic, who should be duped and blackmailed. Use should be made of ambitious politicians, including the liberals among them. The revolutionaries should conspire with them, pretending to follow them blindly, but at the same time ferreting out their secrets, thereby compromising them to such a degree as would cut off their retreat from the struggle against the authorities. The fifth category, the loudmouths, those platonic advocates of revolution, should be engineered into making dangerous declarations; most would perish in the struggle but a few might become authentic revolutionaries. Finally, the women: some were useless and stupid and were to be treated like categories three and four; others were capable, passionate and devoted even though they might not yet have acquired full revolutionary consciousness. The sixth category comprised those who had completely thrown in their lot with the revolutionaries; they were the most precious possession of the revolutionary party, and their aid was absolutely essential. In its final section, the Catechism emphasizes the need for total revolution: institutions, social structures, civilization and morality were to be destroyed, root and branch. A closing reference is made to the world of brigands, the only real revolutionaries who, once united, would bring into being a terrible and invincible power.

Bakunin's Catechism was written for the benefit of a nonexistent terrorist group — Nechaev's *Narodnaya Rasprava;* like Bakunin's "World Revolutionary Union," it was a mere figment of imagination. The only victim of Nechaev's terrorism was a fellow conspirator, a student, Ivan Ivanovich Ivanov, who was killed in 1869 by his comrades for reasons which have remained obscure. With all his extremist rhetoric Bakunin would have lacked the ruthlessness (even if he had had the following) to practice his philosophy of pan-destructionism.

Young revolutionaries had pronounced similar ideas even before Bakunin, no doubt also without the capacity to put them into practice. Zaichnevski, the son of a landowner in the Orel district, was twenty-one years of age when he published a leaflet on behalf of "Young Russia." His group felt that the revolutionaries ought to be prepared for any operation, however dangerous. They ought to storm the Winter Palace, the residence of the tsar, and destroy all those who lived there. Perhaps it might be sufficient to kill only the tsar and his family? Should, however, the whole "Tsarist party" — the landowners, rich merchants, etc. — rise like one man in defense of the emperor, no pardon ought to be given them, just as they had given no pardon to the revolutionaries. Those who were not with the revolutionaries were against them and were enemies to be destroyed by every possible means.[21] Zaichnevski was openly contemptuous of the liberal critics of the regime, including those who lived abroad, and his critics reciprocated by dismissing his appeals as immature and un-Russian, a mixture of undigested Schiller *(Karl Moor)*, Baboeuf, Blanqui and Feuerbach. At the time even Bakunin attacked him for his unabashed elitism and doctrinaire scorn of the people. Zaichnevski and his few comrades were arrested soon after his appeal was published. It had had no political significance but did reflect a certain mood among the students and, as such, was a precursor of the terrorism of the 1870s.

Ishutin's "organization" came into being two years later. It was called "Hell" and purported to be the Russian branch of a (needless to say, nonexistent) international organization of terrorists, the "European Revolutionary Committee." Some of its members spoke of assassinating the tsar, and their basic ideas bore a striking resemblance to concepts developed a few years later by Bakunin and Nechaev. Their aim was to kill members of the government and big landowners. Lots were to be cast among the revolutionaries to establish who was to carry out the assassinations. The terrorist should live under an assumed name, break all ties with his family, give up his friends, and forgo marriage. He should cut himself off from his own comrades and find his friends in the underworld. On the day appointed for the assassination, he was to disfigure his face with chemicals to avoid being recognized. In his pocket he would carry a manifesto explaining his motives, and once he had carried out his attempt, he was to poison himself.[22] Not all the members of Ishutin's circle agreed with his prescriptions for revolutionary action; they preferred propaganda and the establishment of schools and cooperatives. They even thought of locking up the extremists in their ranks in lunatic asylums, and when Karakozov, a member of the group (and Ishutin's cousin) prepared for his attempt on the life of the tsar, Ishutin himself seems to have had second thoughts and tried to dissuade his cousin. Karakozov made his attempt, was apprehended, and hanged. Ishutin died in prison and a period of repression followed in which organized opposition within Russia was virtually stamped out.

Only in 1878, after Vera Zasulich's shooting of General Trepov, the governor of the Russian capital, did terrorism as a doctrine, the Russian version of Propaganda by Deed, finally emerge. The Tsarist authorities explained this sudden upsurge of terrorism as a result of the Narodniks' failure to "go to the people"; the peasants had been unresponsive, the workers had informed on the "apostles of future happiness." After their lack of success in mobilizing the masses, the authorities maintained, the revolutionaries had come to regard terror as the only effective means of discrediting the government and proving to society at large that a revolutionary party not only existed but was growing stronger.[23] This interpretation was not far from the truth. Plekhanov took virtually the same view when he wrote that terror was the product of the revolutionary party's weakness and followed on its realization that it could not stage a peasant uprising.[24]

Russian terrorism developed in several stages. It began with sporadic acts of armed defense in resisting arrest and as a reaction against individual police officers who had maltreated arrested revolutionaries. On a few occasions, spies who had infiltrated the revolutionary cells were executed. The very first manifesto announcing that a new era in revolutionary action had dawned was Serge Kravchinski's "A death for a death" in which he explained his reasons for having taken part in the assassination of General Mezentsev, the head of the "third section" (the Tsarist political police).[25] His manifesto was full of contradictions: on the one hand, he argued that "you, the representatives of power are our enemies and there can be no peace between us. You should and will be destroyed." Mezentsev, he claimed, had been sentenced to death by a revolutionary tribunal, in revenge for those who had been cruelly treated in prison. As long as the cruelty of the system continued, the revolutionary tribunal would hang over the rulers of the state like the sword of Damocles. At the moment, the movement was only of limited strength but it was growing hourly. Kravchinski, however, seemed to have had some doubts about the identity of his enemy, for in the same manifesto he contended that his real foes were the bourgeoisie and capitalists. He even suggested that the government should stay neutral in this struggle. But how was a line to be drawn between capitalism and the state? The program of the Narodnaya Volya specifically stated that the Russian government was a monster, that unlike Western European states, it was also the greatest capitalist exploiter, owning half of Russia's land. Revolutionaries were permitted to confiscate state property; private property was to be inviolate as long as it was not used in the fight against the revolutionary movement.[26]

Kravchinski's manifesto appeared in August 1878. In November that year the first issue of the journal *Zemlya i Volya* was circulated and Kravchinski wrote its editorial in which he announced that the working masses could not be liberated as a result of terrorist operations. Only the popular masses could bring about a revolution and destroy the system — against a class, only a class could rebel. The terrorists were no more than the military vanguard of the revolutionary movement. If all their forces were channeled into terrorist activities this would be tantamount to abandonment of their chief goal. Even if they succeeded in destroying the system, it would be a Pyrrhic victory because power would then pass into the hands of the bourgeoisie.

These reservations about the use of terror reassured some members of the revolutionary movement (such as Plekhanov) who all along had argued against the concentration on terrorist acts at the expense of all other activities. Dissension on the subject of terror could not be contained for long; in 1879, when terrorist attacks multiplied, debate became more and more heated, and ultimately led to a split. Morozov, amongst others, was in favor of "pure terror"; Zhelyabov and others aimed at a Jacobin-style coup and felt that terror should be used only as punishment meted out to the tsar and his hirelings for their policy of repression.[27] Aptekman, who aligned himself with Plekhanov, wrote that political terror was recognized at the time to be an extreme and exclusive instrument only to be employed in special circumstances.[28]

But the general mood gradually swung toward "armed struggle." An overwhelming desire to act took over and when the Central Committee voted in March 1879 on whether or not to assassinate Drenteln, the new head of the third section, Plekhanov found himself in a minority of one. To some extent this swing toward terrorism was engendered by the mass arrests, the savage sentences and the executions which continued all the time. But perhaps even more important a factor was the belief that terrorist operations were far more effective in promoting the revolution, if only because of the tremendous publicity they received — very much in contrast to illegal propaganda and organizational work which had no visible effect. By autumn 1879 the split was an accomplished fact. Earlier (in March 1879) the ideological justification for terrorism had already been outlined in some detail in the *Listok Narodnoi Voli*, the organ of the radical, activist trend edited by Morozov and Tikhomirov.

Political assassination was above all an act of revenge, but at the same time it was one of the best weapons of agitation. One had to strike at the center to shake the whole system. The future belonged to mass movements but terrorism had to show the masses the way. The program of the Narodnaya Volya Central Committee listed the liquidation of the most dangerous members of the government, the defense of the party against spies, and the punishment of those who had committed the most glaring oppression as the main tasks of the terrorist struggle. If ten to fifteen pillars of the establishment were killed at one and the same time, the government would panic and would lose its freedom of action. At the same time the masses would wake up.[29] But it was never made quite clear in what way such terror would lead to the actual conquest of power. Was the government simply to disintegrate or would there be a popular rising? If so, the party needed an organizational network to lead the masses and a few terrorist fighting groups would not suffice. Such an organization, however, did not exist. Tikhomirov thought that two or three years of systematic terror would bring about the collapse of the government; others, Sofia Perovskaya among them, were equally optimistic. At the very least, the government would have to make far reaching concessions and grant the basic freedoms of organization and speech. In that event the revolutionaries would cease their terrorist activities. It has been argued that not all *Narodovoltsy* were terrorists (and that not all terrorists were *Narodovoltsy*), that out of the 500-odd members who belonged to the party only a tenth actively took part in attacks and assassinations.[30]

As already noted, the mood was overwhelmingly pro-terrorist, reaching far beyond the ranks of the organization to students, the intelligentsia, and other sections of society. Even the Liberals were willing to give money for bombs (though not for socialist propaganda); grand old men of the Russian emigration, such as Lavrov and Mikhailovski, gave terrorism their blessing; even Marx and Engels believed that Russia was on the eve of a revolution as a result of the actions of the Narodnaya Volya. Plekhanov, who had warned time and again against terrorism, felt he could no longer speak out against it; it would have been futile, he later wrote, the intelligentsia believed in terror "like in God."[31]

The most outspoken protagonists of the terrorist approach, Morozov and Romanenko, outlined their views in two pamphlets published in England and Switzerland respectively.[32] These were not official "party documents" but they are of interest because they expressed a widespread mood and, after some initial hesitation, the party more or less accepted the reasoning on which they were based. True, the authors were as yet a little reluctant to call a spade by its real name just as Narodnaya Volya frequently referred to "disorganization" where terror would have been the more appropriate term. Tikhomirov wrote about "partisan warfare," and Morozov later confessed that he did not like the term "terror" either. Initially he had wanted to call his pamphlet "Neo-Partisan Warfare."[33]

Morozov described how the revolutionaries had advanced from self-defense to attack. The government with its guns, prisons, spies and millions of soldiers could easily defeat any frontal assault, but it was powerless against terrorist attacks. The only thing that the terrorists had to fear was lack of caution on the part of their own members.[34] Terrorism, according to Morozov, was an altogether new fighting method, far more "cost-effective" than an old-fashioned revolutionary mass struggle. Despite insignificant forces, it would still be possible to concentrate every effort upon the overthrow of tyranny. Since there was no limit to human inventiveness, it was virtually impossible for the tyrants to provide safeguards against attacks. Never before were conditions so auspicious from the point of view of the revolutionary party, and once a whole series of terrorist groups came into being, they would spell the final days of the monarchy. Terrorist attempts in the past had been acts of despair and frequently of suicide. This tragic element no longer existed: the terrorists simply carried out a death sentence which had been imposed by their tribunals and there was every reason to assume that the executioners would not be apprehended and would disappear without trace. Victory was inevitable sooner or later. In order to blunt the terrorist struggle and win over the bourgeoisie, the government was quite likely to grant a constitution. But the terrorist struggle could be conducted not only against tyranny but also against a constitutional oppression such as in Germany. Dictators like Napoleon or Bismarck should be liquidated at the very beginning of their rise to power *"pour décourager les autres"* and it was immaterial whether they were backed by an army or a plebiscite. In this way terror would remain a guarantee of freedom, a constant deterrent against would-be despots. In Morozov's view the principal assignments currently facing the revolutionaries were first to provide a theoretical foundation for terrorism "which so far every one understood in his own way"; second, to apply terrorism systematically so as to achieve the demoralization, weakening and final disorganization of the government.

Romanenko's views were on similar lines: terrorism was not only effective, it was humanitarian. It cost infinitely fewer victims than a mass struggle; in a popular revolution the best were killed while the real villains looked on from the sidelines. The blows of terrorism were directed against the main culprits; a few innocent people might suffer, but this was inevitable in warfare. Terrorism, then, was the application of modern science to the revolutionary struggle. He interpreted Russian history since the days of the Decembrists as a duel between the intelligentsia and the regime. It was pointless asking the people to rise against their oppressors for the masses were insufficiently strong. It was wrong to regard systematic terror as immoral, since everything that contributed to the liberating revolution was *a priori* moral.[35] The same idea of cost-effectiveness and, in particular, the humanitarian character of terrorism was also voiced by Zhelyabov, the central figure of the Narodnaya Volya and, most outspokenly, in a pamphlet by Lev Sternberg (1861–1927), *Politicheski Terror v Rossii.*[36] Terrorism, in Sternberg's view, was a safety valve; if there was no terror there would be a terrible explosion from below. It was the historical mission of the intelligentsia to prevent — or, to be precise, to preempt — this uncontrolled explosion.

Romanenko's pamphlet was written in answer to the critique of M. P. Dragomanov (1841–1895), the leading Ukrainian writer who, on the whole, was in sympathy with the Russian revolutionary movement. But Dragomanov denounced the "Machiavellianism" of the terrorists as well as attacks against banks and post offices in which mere guards had been killed. It was one thing, Dragomanov wrote, to accept terrorism in Russia as a natural response to the terror exerted by the government. It was another to make terrorism into a system, the cardinal principle of the revolutionary struggle. For terrorism, in the final analysis, was a pathological phenomenon, and if the aim of the revolutionaries was to be unsullied it could be achieved only by purity of method. Attacks in the open, attempts to liberate revolutionaries from prison and even attacks against the secret police were all justifiable, but individual terror as a system could not be morally justified.[37]

The subsequent fate of the main protagonists of the doctrine of terrorism is of some interest: Morozov spent more than twenty years in Tsarist prisons but was released in 1905; he published poems as well as papers on chemistry, cosmogony, history and Christianity. His chemistry, according to all accounts, was sounder than his history. He became a sympathizer of the Kadets (the liberal constitutionalists) but decided to remain in Russia after 1917 and was made an honorary member of the Academy of Sciences. He died in 1946. Gerasim Romanenko (1858–1927), on the other hand, gravitated toward the extreme right, the "Black Hundred"; some of his critics had argued from the beginning that he was a terrorist without being a socialist. Tikhomirov also solemnly renounced terrorism in later years, and became a conservative publicist. Sternberg made good use of his years in Siberian exile and became an ethnographer of world renown.

There was a striking discrepancy between the extreme means used by the Narodovoltsy and their relatively moderate political demands. In this respect they certainly did not agree with Bakunin's pan-destructionism. A letter which the Narodnaya Volya Executive Committee wrote to Alexander III, published in March 1881, ten days after the assassination of his predecessor, stated that terror was a sad necessity, that the terrorists only wanted a general amnesty and a constitution which provided elementary civil freedoms. If these demands were met, terrorist activity would cease, and a peaceful struggle of ideas would replace violence.[38] It has been said, and not without cause, that at least some of the Narodovoltsy were simply "liberals with a bomb." Kibalchich, the scientific genius, who produced dynamite for the Narodovoltsy, was the mildest of men in his private life as well as in his political views. If a peace-loving man like him agreed to cooperate with the terrorists, Lev Deitch later wrote, it only proved that people with a conscience saw no other way out in the given circumstances.[39] It is equally true that Nechaev (unlike Bakunin) was not a socialist but a Jacobin in the style of Robespierre, and that some of the main advocates and practitioners of Russian terrorism in the first decade of the twentieth century, such as Burt-sev, Savinkov and Schweitzer, were also radical liberals rather than socialists.

The terrorist campaign conducted by Narodnaya Volya was essentially different from anarchist activities elsewhere in Europe, which were carried out (as F. Venturi has noted) by isolated individuals inspired by obscure ideals. Russian terrorism was both one aspect of the formation of a revolutionary socialist party and a symptom of a general crisis in Russian society.[40] Vera Zasulich, who had opened the terrorist campaign, was later to write that terror had been like a major storm in an enclosed space: the waves rose high but the unrest did not spread. It exhausted the moral force of the intelligentsia.[41] Kravchinski, who wrote a most moving account of the heroism of the revolutionaries, concluded that terrorism as a system had outlived its era and that it could no longer be revived. The one side no longer had its previous faith and the other side no longer feared it.[42] Kravchinski's prophecy proved premature; terror was revived, but only two decades later by a new generation of revolutionaries.

The tradition of the Narodnaya Volya lingered on and attempts were made to reestablish the party. From time to time its program (in slightly modified form) and other literature was published.[43] In Russian emigré circles it had its strong defenders who disputed the strategy of the orthodox Marxists. Alexander Ulianov, Lenin's older brother, was the head of a small terrorist group of students, whose leading members were arrested and hanged in 1887. He, too, advocated "systematic terrorism" and believed that the initiative had to come from the intelligentsia since the common people had no rights and were altogether unprepared to act.[44] The first to reemphasize the importance of terrorist action after a long period of silence was Burtsev, a radical-democratic opponent of the regime, in a new journal, *Narodovolets* (1897), published in London.[45] In the very first number he stated unequivocally that terrorism in the tradition of the Narodnaya Volya was the only policy that held out any promise. Burtsev was arrested after intervention by the Russian government, but subsequently was released. He issued a new pamphlet in which he stressed that support for terrorism was growing fast, that all those who approved of terrorism were of one family and that they should bury, at least for the time being, all differences of opinion between them.[46] Support for terrorism came from unexpected quarters such as from the moderate socialist Krichevski, who regarded the new terrorist wave after the turn of the century as a turning point of historical significance. Others who came out in its support were Grigorovich (i.e., Zhitlovski), as well as writers in various Russian and Polish language periodicals which began to appear at the time, such as *Nakanune, Przedswit, Revoliutsionnaya Rossiia* and *Vestnik Russkoi Revoliutsii.*

In 1900 the Social Revolutionary party was eventually founded in Kharkov and it was this movement that became the main agent of the second wave of terror, beginning with the assassination of Sipyagin the Minister of the Interior in 1902. The leaders of the new party, which included some survivors of the old Narodnaya Volya such as Gots and Rusanov, maintained that terrorism was necessary and unavoidable. It was not intended to replace the mass struggle; on the contrary it would strengthen and supplement the revolutionization of the masses. Systematic terrorism, the party stated, in conjunction with other forms of open mass struggle such as industrial riots, agrarian risings and demonstrations, would lead to the disorganization of the enemy. "Terrorist activity will cease only with victory over autocracy and the complete attainment of political liberty."[47] A terrorist "Fighting Organization" (*Boevaya Organisatsia* — BO) was set up and given autonomy within the party. The political purpose of terror was defined by the party leadership in a polemic against the Social Democrats.[48] The old quarrel as to the use of terrorist tactics had been resolved in the light of historical experience. There were always ideological reasons against terrorism, but revolutionaries were driven to it, unable to choose the means they were forced to employ. Self-defense was necessary against the attacks of Tsarist autocracy which engaged the Cossacks and their whips (*nagaikas)* to destroy the human dignity of their victims. Imprisoned revolutionaries were driven to suicide and despair. *Iskra,* the organ of the Social Democrats, had argued that the only effects of terrorism were to isolate the revolutionary vanguard from the masses and to hamper organizational work.[49] Yet at the same time *Iskra* demanded that the government should be made to behave with humanity toward striking workers and political prisoners. How could it be compelled to do so? Perhaps by speeches and articles! The whistle of bullets was the only sound that the rulers heeded. More and more people on the left were learning the propagandistic effect of the terrorist act. (It should be noted in passing that many, perhaps most, leading members of the "Fighting Organization" such as Kalyayev, Balmashev, Savinkov and Karpovich had initially belonged to Social Democratic, anti-terrorist organizations.) Terror, claimed the Social Revolutionaries, caused chaos within the establishment. Again, the statement was not exaggerated as subsequent events were to show: Gerassimov, head of the political police at the time, later wrote that the terrorist operations had indeed disoriented the regime: "All ministers are human and they want to live. . . ."[50] Durnovo, minister of the interior, used almost identical words when, in later years, Tikhomirov spoke to him of the folly of terror — "stupid it may be, but it is a very poisonous idea, a very terrible one, creating power out of impotence."[51]

The Social Revolutionaries argued that even the actions of the Narodnaya Volya twenty-five years earlier, despite comparatively little public support, had had a tremendous effect, and for a while the authorities had contemplated constitutional reforms. How much greater was the impact likely to be now that the revolutionary movement had reached more sections of the population? Although the Social Revolutionaries regarded terror as a psychological necessity, it was only one weapon among several; it should not be self-perpetuating. No illusions, no exaggerated optimism as to its consequences should be entertained, and it was clear that terror was a temporary phenomenon — the result of specific Russian conditions. It simply strengthened other forms of the struggle. Again the Social Revolutionaries criticized the Social Democrat *Iskra* which had objected to planned, organized, systematic terror, but accepted accidental *("stychic")* terror. Unplanned terror would by necessity be indiscriminate and was bound to entail unnecessary victims. The party, the organization, would have to decide whom to attack and when. These views about the strictly rational character of terror endorsed by party ideologists abroad were not necessarily shared by the terrorists within Russia. The very language the terrorists used pointed to their irrationality: the revolutionary was a hero driven by hate, inspired by honor and willingness to sacrifice himself — bomb-throwing was "holy."[52]

The impact of terrorist operations on Russian public opinion during the early years of the century was startling. During 1878–1881, there had been some support among the intelligentsia, whereas two decades later "society" in its majority was sympathetic. After the assassination of Plehwe, the minister of the interior, in 1903, even Plekhanov, a lifelong opponent of terrorism, was prepared to justify such operations under certain circumstances and suggested cooperating with the Social Revolutionaries. It was only after leading Social Democrats such as Akselrod and Martov threatened to leave the party that he withdrew his suggestion of cooperation.

In October 1905, when the csar published his famous manifesto announcing the creation of a legislative assembly, the Socialist Revolutionaries suspended terrorist activities. They were resumed in January 1906, suspended again when the First Duma opened, and renewed when the Duma was dissolved in July 1906.[53] Meanwhile a more radical faction, the "Maximalists" had split away and established its own fighting organization. By that time the debate about terrorism had virtually ended for during the revolution political violence had become a daily occurrence. The Bolsheviks engaged in it on occasion, the Black Hundred organized pogroms and assassinated political opponents. The only discussions concerned terrorist tactics. The Maximalists criticized the Fighting Organization of the Social Revolutionaries for its strictly centralist, hierarchical structure: its leadership was appointed from above, and its members had no right to criticize operational plans. Such centralism had its advantages, argued the Maximalists, provided a man of genius like Gershuni was at its head, but it was bound to create dissatisfaction and frustration in the ranks, who would lose their capacity for inventiveness and improvisation. When the supreme commander was a police agent (as had been the case) it naturally led to total disaster.[54] The Maximalists were aware that far-reaching decentralization also had its disadvantages: it was likely to cost more victims, and result in operations that were badly timed from a political point of view. Decentralized terror groups could not be guaranteed against penetration by police agents either. Thus, the ideal solution was to combine the advantages of centralized and decentralized terror, granting a greater measure of autonomy to local groups while retaining a strong central leadership.

It was easier, however, to discuss ideal tactics in the abstract than to carry them out in practice, and these debates, in any case, belonged to a period when terrorism had virtually petered out. There was no Maximalist fighting organization after 1907 and a similar fate had befallen the Social Revolutionaries even before Azev had been unmasked as a spy in 1909. At the Socialist Revolutionary party conference of May 1909 Rubanovich had sharply denounced terrorism, which, he claimed, had become a "business enterprise." Everyone agreed that terrorism ought to be temporarily suspended, but what was its role in the more distant future? Chernov argued that the Azev affair had compromised the terrorists but not the system as such, whereas the critics insisted on the dissolution of the "Fighting Organization." Recent events had shown that the revolutionary party in Russia no longer faced just the Tsarist regime; social classes had emerged in the revolution and individual terror was of no avail in the class struggle. This in turn was rejected as a quasi-Marxist argument and the debate continued for some three more years; but while there were some more sporadic terrorist actions there was no longer any "systematic terrorism."[55]

During and after the revolution of 1905 there was much freewheeling terrorism in the Caucasus. Anarchist groups preached "ruthless and total people's vengeance." One of their sections, the *Bezmotivniki* (the motiveless ones), declaring "death to the bourgeois," contemplated and occasionally committed acts of indiscriminate terror, such as throwing bombs in cafés, restaurants and theaters. Attacks took place at the Hotel Bristol in Warsaw and Café Libman in Odessa, which, it was subsequently pointed out, was not at all a café of the rich.[56] But anarchism in Russia itself was ineffectual and its operations were on a much lesser scale than the far-reaching campaign of the Social Revolutionaries. It made no theoretical contribution to the cause of the armed struggle, except for some appeals in the style of the Futurist manifesto of 1909 which complained of the "poisonous breath of civilization: Take the picks and hammers! Undermine the foundations of venerable towns! Everything is ours, outside us is only death. . . . All to the street! Forward! Destroy! Kill!"[57] The proper place of appeals of this kind is in the annals of expressionist literature, not in the history of terrorism.

TURKEY, INDIA AND THE RUSSIAN EXAMPLE

The example set by the Russians had a considerable influence on terrorist movements, contemporaneous and subsequent, throughout the world. Its impact was felt all over Europe, and its methods were studied even in Ireland and America. Polish socialists came under its particular sway and also engaged in attacks on government offices, in individual assassinations, and, in particular, in "expropriations," i.e., armed robbery of banks and trains. Strong repercussions were felt in the Balkans where terrorism in various forms had been endemic for a long time. The attraction was not one-sided: Kravchinski had gone to fight in Herzegovina in the 1870s and Kalyayev once told a comrade that while there were only a few Russian terrorists as yet, he hoped he would live to see the existence of a really popular terrorist movement as existed in Macedonia.[58] But the Balkan terrorists were first and foremost (and usually exclusively) nationalists; if some of the southern Slavs were familiar with the writings of Bakunin and Kropotkin, the ideological inspiration of the Young Bosnians, for instance, owed much more to Mazzini than to the Narodnaya Volya. They did resemble the Narodniki in their asceticism, the chastity they observed and in their belief that only persons of nobility of character were capable of political assassination.[59]

There is evidence to the effect that the methods of the Armenian revolutionaries of the late 1880s and 1890s were largely borrowed from the Narodnaya Volya. Their first leader in Turkey was Avetis Nazarbeck, who was converted to socialism by his fiancée. She reportedly spoke only Russian and had taken part in the Russian revolutionary movement.[60] The program of the Dashnak party (1892) stated that the revolutionary bands intended "to terrorize government officials, informers, traitors, usurers and every kind of exploiter." Organizational links with Armenians living in Russia were close: weapons were produced in a plant by workers who had gained experience in the Tula arms factory or were bought (albeit not through official channels) from the Russian government armory in Tiflis.[61]

The political problems facing the Armenian terrorist movement were, of couse, sui generis: they were a minority, facing both a tyrannical government and a hostile population. Some of them advocated an immediate struggle, others warned against frittering away their forces and suggested waiting until the Ottoman government was embroiled in Arabia, Crete or with some European powers in order to strike.[62] The proponents of immediate action prevailed, and since they could not possibly hope to overthrow the government, their strategy had to be based on provocation. They assumed, in all probability, that their attacks on the Turks would provoke savage retaliation, and that as a result the Armenian population would be radicalized; more decisive yet, the Western powers, appalled by the massacres, would intervene on their behalf as they did for the Bulgarians two decades earlier. Lastly, they seem to have hoped that their example would lead to risings among other nationalities in the Ottoman empire, as well as perhaps inspiring disaffected Turks.[63] Their most spectacular action was the seizure of the Ottoman Bank in Constantinople in August 1896. But the results were disastrous: a three-day massacre followed in which thousands of Armenians were killed. Europe showed "murderous indifference" and a friend of the Armenian cause, criticizing the revolutionaries, wrote that "if our Henchakists and Drojakists continue their crazy enterprises, very few Armenians will be left in Turkey to profit one day from the application of reforms."[64]

The Armenian example clearly showed the difficulties facing a national minority that resorted to terrorist methods. When Karakozov fired at the tsar in 1866 he was apprehended by passersby and his shouts, "Fools, I have done this for you," were to no avail, for the "masses," far from assisting him, were loyal to the tsar. (The tsar asked: Are you a Pole?) In the eyes of the Turkish population the Armenian terrorists were just foreign agents, traitors, and not much encouragement by the authorities was needed to instigate massacres against the enemies of Islam and the Turkish nation.

The Russian example gave some impetus to the revolutionary movement in India. "Protests are of no avail," Tilak wrote in 1906, "days of prayer have gone. . . . Look to the examples of Ireland, Japan and Russia and follow their methods."[65] There was advice of a more practical nature, too. A Russian chemical engineer gave Senapati Bapat a Russian manual for the manufacture of bombs in 1908, and a Russian student translated it for the benefit of the revolutionaries of the "Free India Society" in North London.[66] The manual was cyclostyled and sent to India.

But the doctrine of the Narodniki contained elements quite indigestible to India; the burning idealist patriotism of Mazzini appealed much more than the polemics between various socialist factions. Savarkar, the most fiery apostle of early Indian terrorism, wrote a life of Mazzini in Marathi, a book which became the first victim of the Indian Press Act.

Indian terrorism was relatively infrequent and on the whole quite ineffective: more often than not the Indian terrorists managed to kill some innocent bystanders rather than their intended victims. Yet the ideology of Indian terrorism is of some interest for it contained a strange mixture of Indian traditions and Western influences. In 1897 Tilak wrote that the Hindu rebel leader Shivaji had been entitled two centuries earlier to kill Afzal Khan, a Muslim general, at a peace parley: Shivaji had now become a national hero with his own festivals.[67] Gandhi, it should be added in parenthesis, regarded Shivaji as a misguided patriot. Marathi newspapers quite openly justified murder when inspired by a higher purpose. The young patriots, fired by these teachings, were orthodox Hindus and they despised the reformist politicians of the Congress parties who, they claimed, violated religious principle by partaking of biscuits, loaves, meat and spirits. In their manifestoes they announced that "we shall assuredly shed upon the earth the life-blood of the enemies who destroy religion."[68] When ten years later the most successful of the vernacular dailies, *Yugantar,* began to appear, the same message was preached with even greater emphasis and detail. Theft and dacoity were normally regarded as crimes, but destruction for the highest good was justified; it was work of religious merit. The murder of foreigners was no sin but *jagna,* a ceremonial sacrifice.[69] Bombs should be manufactured in secret and guns imported from abroad, for "the people of the West will sell their own motherland for money." Tilak, who invoked the goddess Kali in his patriotic speeches ("We are all Hindus and idolators and I am not ashamed of it"), likened the bomb to a sacred formula, to "magic" and an "amulet." Savarkar and his pupils not surprisingly turned against pacifism and the universalist element (the "mumbo jumbo") of Hindu religion; nonviolence would crush "the faculty of resisting sin" and destroy the power of national resistance. In his book on the Indian War of Independence of 1857, which became something of a classic among the extremists, Savarkar wrote that the sword of Brutus was holy and the arrow of Wilhelm Tell divine, and he cited some incidents in Indian history too — every Hiranyakashipu had his Narasimha, every Dushshasana had his Bheema, every evildoer his avenger.[70] The *Indian Sociologist* published by Krishna Varma in London also justified political assassination. The British authorities took a dim view. Like other periodicals such as *Bande Mataram* and *Talvar* it had to transfer its activities from Highgate, N.6, to the continent.

There was an upsurge of terrorist activities in 1909 when Sir William Curzon Wyllie, Lord Morley's political secretary, was killed in London by one of Krishna Varma's students. But this spurt was short-lived and it was only in the 1920s that a new wave of terrorist actions took place. Indian terrorism, as preached by Savarkar and others, was directed not only against the British but also against Muslims, and, by implication, against political enemies within their own ranks. In later years Savarkar became the leader of the Hindu Mahasabha and its military-terrorist arm the RSSS *(Rashtriya Swayam Sewak Sangh).* They preached that India was one and indivisible, and everyone who did not accept this precept was a traitor. The leadership of the RSSS consisted of Brahmins, mainly from Poona, Savarkar's home town and political base. One of them, Nathuram Godse, shot Gandhi in 1948. He had been Savarkar's chief aide for several years, but Savarkar's complicity could not be proven in court. He was released and died at the ripe old age of eighty-three in 1966.[71]

The inspiration of the next generation of Indian terrorists at first sight seemed altogether different. Most of them had been members of Gandhi's nonviolent noncooperation movement during its early phase, and it was only after the hopes accompanying it had ebbed away that they began to turn to revolutionary ideas. The Hindustan Socialist Republican Association *(HSRA)* was founded in 1928. Some of its leaders, such as Bhagat Singh, had allegedly read *Das Kapital* and they were great admirers of the Soviet Union.[72] Their doctrine, as summarized in a work entitled *The Philosophy of the Bomb,* stated that they did not ask for mercy and gave no quarter: "Ours is a war to the end — to Victory or Death." Yet at the same time they disclaimed that their revolution was to be identified with violence, or, more specifically, with the cult of the pistol and the bomb. In their writings they emphasized the leading role of the working class. Unfortunately, workers and peasants were as yet "passive, dumb and voiceless" and the radical nationalist youth, idealist and restless, would have to act as the vanguard of the revolution.[73] This then was their historical mission: the youth of India, being the salt of the earth, was to conduct not just "propaganda by deed" but propaganda by death. These glaring contradictions between doctrine and practice are not too difficult to explain. The young revolutionaries were both impatient and isolated. A Russian-style "going to the people" was ruled out; in India — as in Latin America and Africa — manual labor has never been held in high esteem among members of the upper classes, including the revolutionaries among them. A sympathetic historian notes that the HSRA failed to do any political work among the common people, and hardly had any link or contact with them. In theory they had become totally committed to revolutionary socialism, yet the "revolutionary consciousness" which they invoked so frequently was purely nationalist, and the young militants could be used therefore almost exclusively for nationalist action.[74]

The origins of *The Philosophy of the Bomb*, the HSRA manifesto, should be mentioned at least in passing.[75] Following the attempt of Indian terrorists to blow up the vice-regal special train in 1929, Gandhi made a speech to an Indian Congress meeting (later published as an article in *Young India* under the title "The Cult of Violence") and drafted a resolution rejecting terrorism. The terrorists were denounced as "cowards," their actions described as "dastardly." Gandhi wrote that he would despair of nonviolence if he was not certain that bomb-throwing was nothing but "froth coming to the surface in an agitated liquid." Gandhi also warned against terrorism in view of the likely internal consequences: from violence done to the foreign ruler there was only an "easy, natural step to violence to our own people whom we may consider to be obstructing the country's progress."[76] Prophetic words in the light of the tragic death of the Mahatma.

Gandhi had denounced terrorism, of course, on many previous occasions. History had proved, he told Calcutta students in 1915, that assassinations ("a Western institution") had done no good: "What have they done to the Western World? We would not hesitate to rise against those who wanted to terrorize the country."[77] The philosophers of the bomb argued on the other hand that while terrorism was not a complete revolution, revolution was not complete without terrorism. Nor was terrorism a European product; it was homegrown. "Terrorism instills fear in the hearts of the oppressors, it brings hope of revenge and redemption to the oppressed masses. It gives courage and self confidence to the wavering, it shatters the spell of the subject race in the eyes of the world, because it is the most convincing proof of a nation's hunger for freedom."[78] The average Indian, the terrorists claimed, understood little about fine theological necessities of love for one's enemy. Gandhi's gospel of love would not sway the British viceroys and generals. Violence did not impede the march toward social progress and political freedom: "Take the case of Russia and Turkey for example."[79] Gandhi, they claimed, did not understand revolutionary psychology. A terrorist did not sacrifice his life because the crowd might shout "bravo" in appreciation; he engaged in terrorism because reason forced him into that course and because conscience dictated it. "It is to reason and reason alone that he bows." There was no crime that Britain had not committed in India: "As a race and as a people we stand dishonoured and outraged. Do people still expect us to forget and to forgive? We shall have our revenge, a people's righteous revenge on the tyrant."[80]

The terrorists distributed *The Philosophy of the Bomb* and some other manifestoes but their impact on the masses was insignificant compared with Gandhism. There were a few demonstrations of "propaganda by deed." A police officer was shot in Lahore in November 1928. In April 1929 Bhagat Singh and Batukeswar Datta threw two small bombs from the public gallery into the Delhi Legislative Assembly. They made no attempt to escape. Both were executed: in their statement in court they said that their sole purpose had been "to make the deaf hear," to register a protest on behalf of those who had no other means left to give expression to their heartrending agony. They said they had been inspired by the ideals which guided Guru Govnd Singh and Shivaji, Kemal Pasha and Reza Khan, Washington and Garibaldi, Lafayette and Lenin.[81]

There were some other examples of "propaganda by deed" such as the Chittagong raid in 1930. The same year the Yugantar party in Calcutta drew up a terrorist manifesto calling for the assassination of

Europeans in hotels, clubs and cinemas, the burning of the aero-
drome in Dum-Dum, the destruction of gas and electricity works.[82]
But these few manifestoes and actions apart, a marked decline in
terrorist activities took place after 1932, coinciding with the collapse
of the Civil Disobedience movement. The emergency regulations
adopted by the government were quite effective, and the constitutional reforms of 1935 (in the words of one historian) blunted the edge
of both the violent and nonviolent methods of Indian politics.[83] Terrorism had a short-lived revival only during the Second World War.
With Partition, revolutionary violence became transformed from individual to mass terror and civil war.

PROPAGANDA BY DEED

The concept of "propaganda by deed" has been traced back by a
historian of anarchism to Carlo Pisacane, the hero of the Risor-
gimento who lost his life in a tragically futile expedition to Calabria
in 1857. Pisacane had written that the propaganda of the idea was a
chimera and that ideas result from deeds.[84] Similar thoughts, in fact,
were expressed well before, but the era of "propaganda by deed"
was heralded in a statement by the Italian Anarchists Malatesta and
Cafiero, in 1876. They made it known that their Federation believed
that "the insurrectional fact destined to affirm socialist principles by
deeds is the most effective means of propaganda and the only one
which, without tricking and corrupting the masses, can penetrate the
deepest social layers and draw the living forces of humanity into the
struggle sustained by the International."[85] Soon after, writing in
the same journal, Paul Brousse, a young French physician, coined the
phrase "propaganda by deed."[86] Theoretical propaganda — whether
mass meetings, newspapers, or pamphlets — was of limited efficacy;
moreover, the venal bourgeois press could always calumniate and
disguise ("manipulate" in latter-day jargon) the true message and
bourgeois orators could wheedle popular assemblies. Furthermore,
workers who returned home, after an exhausting working day of
eleven or twelve hours, had little desire to read socialist literature.
Proudhon had written brilliant studies, but who had read them ex-

cept a handful of people? Practical demonstrations, such as the Paris Commune, had presented the issues at stake in so dramatic a way that they could no longer be shirked. Propaganda by deed, in short, was a powerful weapon to awaken the consciousness of the people.[87] Yet Brousse did not preach political assassination in so many words; on the contrary, he expressed doubt whether political assassination could possibly change a political system. It was only two years later that Kropotkin provided the classic formulation, defining Anarchist action as permanent incitement through the spoken and written word, the knife, the rifle, dynamite — everything, provided it was not legal. One single deed created more propaganda in a few days than a thousand leaflets. The government would endeavor to defend itself by intensifying its oppression, but further deeds would then be committed by one or more persons, thus driving the revolutionaries to ever more heroic acts. One deed would bring forth another, more and more people would join in the struggle and the government would lose its unity and self-confidence. Any concessions it might make would come too late, and eventually a general revolution would take place.[88]

Prince Kropotkin, the son of a high-ranking Russian officer, had served in the Corps of Pages; he joined a group of revolutionaries, was arrested in 1874, but succeeded in escaping two years later. His political career belongs to the history of the Anarchist movement of which he became a leading ideologist; all that need be noted in this context is that, very much in contrast to the Nechaevs of this world, he was an almost saintly figure who, in later years, came out strongly against "mindless terror." But it cannot be denied that when he took over the leadership of the Anarchist movement in the late 1870s he was one of the main protagonists of individual terror as a means to arouse the spirit of revolt among the masses.[88] Even in later years he was able to justify the assassination of Alexander II and attempts on the lives of leading political figures in the West in the 1880s and 1890s as acts committed by desperate men in response to unbearable conditions. The individuals responsible were not to be blamed. Society was answerable for it had taught them contempt for human life. He fully endorsed Kravchinski's view that while terror was profoundly distasteful, to submit to violence was even worse.[90]

The concept of "propaganda by deed" figured prominently in the deliberations of the International Anarchist Congress which took place in London in July 1881. One of the delegates, Ganz, suggested that greater attention be given to the study of chemistry and technology in order to supply dreadful weapons for the struggle against the oppressors. Kropotkin thought that these were praiseworthy sentiments but noted that it was an illusion to assume that one could become a chemist or electrician in a few hours; a handful of experts could deal with these problems more competently.[91] Nor were chemistry and pyrotechnics a panacea: it was more important to understand how to mobilize the masses. The Congress nevertheless passed a resolution that as technical and chemical sciences had already rendered service to the revolutionary cause and were bound to render still greater services in the future, affiliated organizations and individuals should devote themselves to the study of these sciences.[92] These suggestions were based on the assumption — again to quote the resolution — that a general conflagration was not far distant; "propaganda by deed" had to reinforce oral and written propaganda and arouse the spirit of the masses insofar as illusions still existed about the effectiveness of legal methods. But the conflagration did not take place, and more than a decade was to pass before certain French, Italian and Spanish Anarchists engaged in "propaganda by deed." There were only a few bombings and assassinations throughout Western Europe during the 1880s, and most of these, such as the attempt to kill the German Emperor Wilhelm I, were not undertaken by Anarchists. The original impulse for the new doctrine, of course, had been provided by the example of the Russian revolutionaries, but by the time the London resolutions were adopted the terrorist wave had abated even in Russia.

Thus the Anarchist appeals had no serious consequence other than alarming the general public. There is evidence that in their endeavor to penetrate the ranks of the Anarchists the police actually provided money for Anarchist publications and, in some cases, apparently also for terrorist operations. One of the most bloodcurdling appeals was published in a police-sponsored French-language periodical in London: it called for blows against the left, right and center, against religion and patriotism. Theft, murder and arson were legitimate means in the struggle and so, of course, was the great friend, the "thunder of dynamite."[93] In 1880 the French Anarchist journal *La*

Révolution Sociale began publishing instructions for the fabrication of bombs. At the time this paper was edited by Serreaux, a police spy, with money provided by Louis Andrieux, the prefect of the Paris police, who thoughtfully left us with detailed memoirs. On the other hand, the bomb, "the last weapon of revolt," was also praised in bona fide Anarchist publications such as Most's *Freiheit, La Lutte Sociale,* and Swiss publications. Advice was given to place bombs or inflammable materials near storehouses where cotton or alcohol were kept. Chemical formulae for making *produits anti-bourgeoises* were published. Of course, one could not be too specific: *"L'action ne se conseille, ni ne se parle, ni ne s'écrit — elle se fait."*[94] Marie Constant, a revolutionary Paris shoemaker, composed a popular song ending

> Maintenant la danse tragique
> vent une plus forte musique:
> Dynamitons, dynamitons.

After the execution of Ravachol, a new verb came into being, *ravacholiser;* the *Ravachole* was sung to the tune of the *Carmagnole, Vive le son d'l'explosion.* A Ravachol cult caused considerable accession of strength to Anarchism.[95] Among the more far-fetched suggestions was advice to domestic servants to poison their employers, to churchgoers to poison clerics, to soak rats in petrol, set them on fire and then let them loose in buildings marked for destruction.[96] Anarchist journals called on their followers to arm themselves with every weapon provided by science, to destroy the criminal institutions of a society based on the most extreme egoism: *"Pillons, brûlons, détrusions."* The new revolutionary strategy, it was announced, was no longer based on open, frontal battles, *"mais une guerre des partisans menés de façon occulte."*[97]

When the London Congress adopted its militant resolutions, the Italian Anarchists, who had wielded considerable influence in the 1870s, were already in rapid decline. After a few ineffectual insurrections the momentum petered out altogether. The murder of a Viennese shoemaker in 1882, the assassination of a police inspector the year after, of a police agent and of a money changer in 1884, also in Vienna, did nothing to bring the revolution any nearer. The fact that the small children of the money changer had also been killed in order to dispose of witnesses did not endear the terrorists to the masses either. A pharmacist was murdered in Strassburg and a banker in Mannheim. In both these cases robbery seems to have been the motive and not political principles. A few minor incidents took place in Switzerland. This was about the sum total of "propaganda by deed" in Central Europe. The change came only with a series of terrorist actions that took place in France between March 1892 and June 1894. After 1894 there were still a few spectacular political assassinations usually carried out by Italians. But these actions were undertaken by individuals, and as far as can be established no organization supported them. (The only possible exception was in the case of Bresci, the murderer of King Umberto of Italy in 1900, who had apparently been chosen and assisted by a group of Italian Anarchists in Paterson, New Jersey.)[98] The "great international Anarchist conspiracy" existed only in the imagination of police chiefs and the press; its main importance in retrospect was to have inspired novels by Henry James, Joseph Conrad, Emile Zola, and some others, just as the Russian Anarchists had inspired Dostoevsky. But there was no "Anarchist party." When Emile Henry, who had thrown the bomb at the Café Terminus, declared at his trial that "we ask no pity in this pitiless war which we have declared on the bourgeoisie," he was speaking for no one but himself.[99] Anarchist periodicals had virtually ceased to recommend "propaganda by deed" several years before, noting that it was utopian to believe that individual terror could possibly be the basis of rational, active and sustained propaganda.[100] Kropotkin, once one of the most outspoken advocates of terrorism, admitted in 1891 that a mistake had been made: the revolution would not come as the result of some heroic actions. Inspired by the Russian revolutionaries in 1881, European Anarchists had erroneously believed that a handful of dedicated revolutionaries armed with a few bombs could bring about a social revolution, as though a building rooted in centuries could be destroyed by a few kilograms of explosives.[101] But if the appeal of 1881 for "propaganda by deed" had been ignored for ten years, so was the call for retreat in 1891. There was no global conspiracy, no high command, no "party discipline"; each individual Anarchist, each group, felt free to register his protest in the form and at the time he saw fit.

ARMS AND THE CLASS STRUGGLE

In Spain terrorist operations were to continue for longer than else-where. It began with the mysterious *Maño Negra* movement, a peas-ant revolt in Andalusia in the 1880s, continued mainly in Catalonia in the 1890s, and reaching a climax in Barcelona, in 1904–1909 and again between 1917 and 1922. Two pronounced features of Spanish terrorism were the *atentados sociales,* i.e., violence accompanying labor disputes (and conflicts between unions) and the subsequent widespread participation of criminal elements *(pistoleros),* "thieves and gunmen who certainly would not have been accepted by any other working-class party together with idealists of the purest and most selfless kind."[102] Behind the "strategic terrorism" of 1905, cul-minating in the attempted assassination of King Alfonso, there might have been a design to trigger off a revolutionary movement. But the terror during and after the First World War, rooted according to Angel Pestaña in a "mystical and apocalyptic idealism," soon became commercialized with the *pistoleros* acting as dues collectors for the unions, terrorizing workers as well as overseers and employers.[103] Terrorism in Spain ought to be viewed in the light of Spain's long tradition of political violence, and the country's particular social con-ditions. The role of ideology was insignificant, nor indeed was any such doctrine needed.

Terrorist acts in the United States resembled those in Spain insofar as there was a tradition of violence and a long history of stormy, often bloody, labor disputes. This was particularly true among the miners, and continued from the days of the Molly Maguires to the Western Federation of Miners under Bill Haywood and the IWW. Following the arrival of German and later of East European proponents of "propaganda by deed," an ideological element was infused which did not exist in southern Europe. The antiparliamentarian International Working People's Association, founded in Pittsburgh in 1883, was syndicalist in character and advocated violence in the form of mass strikes and sabotage rather than acts of terror. Chicago was the cen-ter of these activities.

But as the industrial conflicts worsened and tempers rose, the *Alarm* and the *Chicagoer Arbeiterzeitung* became advocates of individual as well as mass terror. Dynamite was the great social solvent, the emancipator, and instruction was freely offered to workers on how to handle arms: "The Weapons of the Social Revolutionist Placed within the Reach of All." Dynamite, a reader wrote, "of all good stuff, this is *the* stuff. . . . It is something not very ornamental but exceedingly useful. It can be used against persons and things, it is better to use it against the former than against bricks and masonry."[104] C. S. Griffin argued that no government can exist without a head, and "by assassinating the head just as fast as a government head appeared, the government could be destroyed, and, generally speaking all governments be kept out of existence. Those least offensive to the people should be destroyed last."[105] Albert Parsons, one of the accused in the Haymarket affair, editor of *Alarm* and former chief deputy collector of Internal Revenue in Austin, Texas, defended the use of dynamite even in court: it was democratic, it made everybody equal. It was a peacemaker, man's best friend. As force was the law of the universe, dynamite made all men equal and therefore free. But Parsons denied that he had anything to do with throwing the bomb.[106] Those allegedly involved in the Haymarket affair were the contemporaries and pupils of Johann Most, for many years the high priest of terrorism in America.

In the 1890s, younger and even more radical activists such as Emma Goldman and Alexander Berkman came to the fore. In July 1892, Berkman tried to shoot Henry C. Frick of the Carnegie Company, whom he regarded responsible for the outrages committed during the Homestead strike earlier that year. Aged twenty-one at the time, Berkman had arrived in the United States five years previously. He was an enthusiast; Bazarov, Hegel, "Liberty" and Chernishevski (apparently in this order) were his idols.[107] As he saw it, only the toilers, the producers, counted; the rest were parasites who had no right to exist. All means were justifiable, nay advisable in the fight against them: the more radical the treatment, the quicker the cure. Society was a patient, sick constitutionally and functionally; in the circumstances surgical treatment was imperative. The removal of a tyrant was an act of liberation, the highest duty of any revolutionary. As an enemy of the people, his assassination was in no way to be considered as the taking of human life.[108] Berkman's action was not only rejected by most Americans, it also caused a deep split in Anarchist ranks: Most, in *Freiheit*, denounced him, while Emma Goldman in the *Anarchist* came to his defense. The fact that Most, the "incarnation of defiance and revolt," repudiated Berkman had come to her and her circle as a bombshell.[109] It was almost as if Marx in his old age had been converted to capitalism.

MOST

Johann Most, born in Germany in 1846, had had an unhappy childhood in his native country. After an apprenticeship as a bookbinder and some *Wanderjahre*, as was customary among artisans at the time, he was arrested as a radical agitator in Austria. Later he became one of the leading figures of the German Social Democrats. He was an indefatigable organizer, an effective speaker and a fluent, if erratic, strident writer. Although a member of the *Reichstag*, he had to flee Germany when Bismarck enacted his antisocialist emergency laws. Most founded and edited *Freiheit*, a Social Democratic weekly, in London. In 1879 he was still a Marxist: "As old Socialists we preach revolution not a *putsch*," he wrote. But by temperament he was always more radical than the party leadership. At first he still covered himself by invoking the authority of others when preaching more extreme doctrines; for example, he approvingly quoted Wilhelm Liebknecht who had said that in certain circumstances, such as in a barbaric country like Russia, it might be possible to destroy the system by means of the dagger and the revolver.[110]

But why only in Russia? Most was dissatisfied with Marxist explanations, and by September 1880 he reached the conclusion that Anarchist principles should be discussed in his paper. After all, they were being received with much more enthusiasm (as events in Russia showed) than social democratic gradualism. He published Bakunin's Revolutionary Catechism for the benefit of revolutionaries who (he predicted) were about to copy the Russian Anarchists' tactics in Germany.[111] He hailed the Irish dynamiters: no honest social revolutionary could blame them, even if their acts of vengeance proved cruel: "Once we shall be stronger, we shall act like them; a party waging war cannot tolerate traitors in its ranks. The devil take the false, weak-hearted humanitarian approach. Long live hate! Long live vengeance!" Or on another occasion: "Let us all do our duty. Let us all work for the day when attacks will multiply against all those who bear responsibility for the servitude, exploitation and misery of the people." After an enthusiastic editorial ("Victory, Victory"), hailing the assassination of Alexander II, Most was sent to prison by a London court.[112] In the meantime he had also been expelled from the ranks of the German Social Democrats.

Freiheit was transferred to the United States and during the next few years it became the world's most uninhibited Anarchist mouthpiece, preaching propaganda by deed. It was also the most influential; some issues had a circulation of 25,000, and Most's pamphlets such as *The Beast of Property* and *The Revolutionary Science of War* were widely read.

Most rejected the European socialist parties' approach. He did not believe, as they did, in patient organizational and propagandistic work; he rejected their assumption that sooner or later strong left-wing parties would emerge and that the system would collapse as a result of its own contradictions. He was convinced that the people, at all times and in every country, were mature for revolution (and the state of freedom that would follow it) but that they lacked the courage to undertake a determined effort. Thus a small minority was called upon to show the way: the mass of people had always borne a certain resemblance to something monkey- and parrot-like, and it was quite ludicrous to wait for an initiative from the unenlightened, volatile and hesitant masses.[113] Few of those born into servitude could get rid of their chains by their own efforts, but nonetheless they should not be required to bow to the majority. Even in a future, free society there should be no tyranny by the majority. A revolutionary who really meant business had to engage in conspiracy. Once he sought his goal he could not possibly reject the means that were to lead to a realization of his aim.[114] The means were bound to be barbaric — not because the revolutionaries chose them but because the present system was essentially barbaric and could be overthrown only by its own weapons. The murderers themselves had to be killed. The road to *Humanitaet* led through barbarism.[115] The law of the jungle had forever prevailed in history; the victor had always been right. No Russian revolutionary of the 1880s would have accepted any such doctrine but, unlike them, Most and some of his Anarchist comrades were influenced by various contemporary Social Darwinist philosophers who glorified the elite and even the superman. One of the forgotten prophets of this subculture was Ragnar Redbeard, whose writings appealed both to the extreme left and the far right, and thus should be mentioned — at least in passing.

Blessed are the strong, Redbeard wrote, for they shall possess the earth; cursed are the weak, for they shall inherit the yoke. Blessed are the unmerciful, their posterity shall own the world. Human rights and wrongs are not determined by Justice but by Might. The naked sword is still kingmaker and kingbreaker as of yore — all other theories are lies and lures. Each molecule, each animal fights for its life, the workers have to fight for theirs or surrender. The survival of the strongest is the iron law of history; personal cowardice is the greatest vice of a demoralized age. Courage that delights in danger is needed, and must not know despair.[116] Parts of Redbeard's books read in sections like a precursor of *Mein Kampf* or Alfred Rosenberg, with tirades against the non-Aryans and appeals that "we must either abandon our reason or abandon Christ." Jesus, Peter, Paul and James were crude socialist reformers with misshapen souls, demagogues, politicians-of-the-slum. Nothing that is noble can ever emerge from the slums. Socialism, Christianity, Democracy, Equality are all the whining yelpings of base-bred mongrel-multitudes.[117]

Such reasoning was not uncommon toward the end of the nineteenth century. One of Redbeard's idols was Cecil Rhodes ("there is no cant and hypocrisy about him"). Teddy Roosevelt apparently liked the book. It was an all-purpose philosophy: the left could draw encouragement from Redbeard's thesis that not once in the whole course of human history had a subjugated people ever regained their liberty without first butchering their oppressors and then confiscating the property of their former masters. Redbeard was certainly sure of his case: he offered 50,000 ounces of pure gold to anyone who could show him one authentic example to the contrary.[118]

Traces of Redbeard's message can be detected in Most's writings. In order for the masses to be free, the rulers must be killed. Powder and lead, poison, dynamite, fire and knives were more telling than a thousand revolutionary speeches. Most did not rule out propaganda, but only propaganda by deed could be regarded as effective in sowing confusion among the rulers and mobilizing the masses. He was one of the first to recognize the importance of the media: with modern means of communication, terrorist actions would immediately be known all over the globe; wherever people met they would discuss its causes. Most apprehended what became known much later as the "echo effect": the deed would be imitated every day, even every hour.[119] He had no patience with those who argued that revolutionaries fought against a system not against individuals. There were no social systems which were not represented and, indeed, made to work, by persons. The system was defended by the forces of "law and order"; to kill them was not murder, for policemen and spies were not human.[120] The enemies were pigs, dogs, bestial monsters, devils in human shape, reptiles, parasites, scum, the dregs of society, canaille, hellhounds. How could one exterminate them all in the most effective way? *Freiheit,* like some of the French Anarchist periodicals, freely offered advice, and like them and the Russian journals saw in dynamite the tool for the destruction of society. The "New Messiah" was hailed in editorials and even poems:

> *Zuletzt ein Hoch der Wissenschaft.*
> *Dem Dynamit, das heisst der Kraft*
> *Der Kraft in uns'ren Haenden*
> *Die Welt wird besser Tag fuer Tag.*[121]
> [At last a toast to Science
> To dynamite that is the force
> The force in our own hands;
> The world gets better day by day.]

At one time Most took a job in an explosives factory in Jersey City Heights receiving on-the-job training in the production of explosives. He stole a little dynamite and found that it was more reliable than the homemade variety.[122] He pioneered various innovations such as the letter (incendiary) bomb and in a remarkable flight of fantasy even envisaged bombing the enemy from the air. With the help of dirigible airships it would be possible one day to drop dynamite on military parades attended by tsars and emperors; neither infantry, cavalry nor artillery would be able to prevent such attacks.[123] Dynamite, in short, was an invincible weapon. Some "innocents" (Most's quotation marks) were bound to get hurt but this did not bother him unduly: it was not their business to be in places where a bomb was likely to explode. British women and children had been injured by Irish bombs, but the British in their "wars of extermination" had committed worse outrages in many parts of the world. (Most was not, however, an uncritical admirer of the Irish and frequently dissociated himself from the "sectarian" character of their struggle.) The revolutionary should not be guided by considerations of chivalry; bombs should be placed quite indiscriminately wherever the upper ten thousand were likely to meet — for example, in churches and dance halls. Furthermore, a revolutionary about to commit a terrorist act was duty-bound to kill any witness likely to betray him.[124]

The question whether assassination of individual monarchs, ministers, and generals would have any decisive political impact (and the arguments of his socialist opponents to the contrary) preoccupied Most throughout his life. In later years he admitted that it was illusory to believe that the removal of individual generals would lead to the defeat of an enemy army as long as the proletariat itself was not up in arms. At the same time, however, he stressed that the repressive system was highly centralized, and that a blow at the heart of tyranny would remove a not easily replaceable dangerous foe[125] (akin to the reasoning of the Russian revolutionaries about "hitting at the center"). Again, defending himself against charges about the inhuman character of the kind of war he preached, Most argued that governments were using the very same weapons he advocated — only theirs were a hundred times stronger and more destructive. He made it known that a pamphlet of his about the revolutionary science of war had largely been copied from a book issued under the auspices of the Austrian general staff. The revolutionary party was not a state and could not play such games as breaking off diplomatic relations. In reply to a charge that he had been ill advised to discuss the use of poison, Most replied that arsenic and strychnine had first been recommended by American newspapers to eliminate useless elements in society.[126]

Most maintained that in money — even more than in dynamite — was the key to success to be found. Money could buy more reliable and effective explosives than those made at home. A revolutionary who could somehow put his hands on a hundred million dollars would do mankind a greater service than by killing ten monarchs; this kind of money could turn the world upside down. The few cents collected among workers were quite insufficient for any meaningful conspiratorial work. Gold would open a great many doors normally closed to the terrorist, corrupting and disarming enemy agents, and enabling the revolutionary to infiltrate "society." In short, funds were needed to carry out the "deed" and these had to be "confiscated."[127]

It has been said that by mid-1885 Most had mellowed, and had begun to doubt the efficacy of "propaganda by deed."[128] In 1890, however, he still argued that it was necessary to engage in deeds, even of a bestial kind, and he continued to justify political assassinations wherever they occurred.[129] But it is quite true that there was a gradual shift in emphasis, and that in later years he put greater stress on propaganda. Most praised the Russian revolutionaries not only for throwing bombs but also for risking their lives by establishing secret printing presses. He argued that terrorist acts per se had little, if any, impact unless they took place at the right time and place, and that "propaganda by deed" was no children's game.[130] Most was in favor of a dual strategy: legal or semilegal organizations with meetings and publications, on one hand, and on the other operations of small conspiratorial groups. The fewer people who knew about terrorist actions, the more assured would be their success. Militants usually had families and it was irresponsible to jeopardize their livelihood; intellectuals would immediately lose their jobs if it became known that they belonged to the Anarchist movement.[131] There was yet another consideration which made a division of labor imperative: some revolutionaries were capable speakers and writers and might also prove good fighters in the heat of battle, but they were temperamentally incapable of planning cold-blooded assassination. This was not cowardice — such men and women were simply too goodhearted, too idealistic. Though it was desirable that every "theoretical revolutionary" ought also to be a man of action, it was clearly unrealistic to expect this from every one of them. Out of a false sense of shame many a theoretician could not admit even to himself that he was not born to commit murder. The revolutionary movement had to accept this fact of political life which regrettably meant fewer assassinations, thereby prolonging the "transition period," but nothing could be done about it. These then were Most's views in his later years, and it was not surprising therefore that he condemned Berkman's attack — a condemnation which made Emma Goldman so angry that she horsewhipped her former guru.

The American atmosphere was corrosive. Most's New York group with its beer evenings, excursions and amateur theatrical performances gradually came to resemble a German *Verein* rather than a Russian terrorist organization. Much of his activity was absorbed by internal dissension. His influence, by and large, was restricted to German-speaking workers; some Italians and East European Jews also came to his meetings and, on occasion, a few native Americans, but they were the exceptions. Despite all his inexhaustible energy, Most came to realize toward the end of his life that America was not to be the center of a world revolution and that his was a voice calling in the desert. At long last he also understood that the wall dividing Anarchists and the trade union movement had to be pulled down and even though he continued to oppose the American unions, he favored the principle of worker organization.

At a distance of almost a century Most's hyper-radicalism seems both absurd and self-defeating. But in fairness his views have to be examined against the general background of time and place. It was a violent age, when public opinion freely held that workers who went on strike for higher wages and shorter working hours should be shot. A great deal of brutality accompanied labor disputes and Anarchists were submitted to constant harassment by the police. On the other hand it was only in America that a newspaper such as *Freiheit* could appear for any length of time. Though the employers had the right to exploit their employees, the workers, too, could freely organize themselves and take counteraction. America, after all, was neither Tsarist Russia nor Ireland. There were effective forms of political struggle other than violence. Most failed to make a convincing case as to why terrorism was necessary or likely to succeed in the United States and for this reason his influence remained restricted to a small group of newly arrived immigrants.

MARX, ENGELS AND THE PROBLEM OF TERRORISM

Marx and Engels regarded Most and his supporters as semieducated, muddleheaded men — or, alternatively, as dangerous charlatans. Nonetheless the issue of individual terror was to occupy orthodox Marxism for a long time. Engels's common-law wife, Lizzy Burns, was a Fenian, and their house in Manchester provided a shelter for Irish militants. In a letter to Kugelmann, Engels welcomed the Fenian raid in Manchester (September 1867) in which a prison van transporting Fenians was attacked. Three months later the three main accused were hanged. Engels wrote that the only thing the Fenians had lacked were a few martyrs; he admired the violent anti-English character of their movement and thought that agrarian terror was the only effective means of protecting the Irish against extermination by the landlords. Despite their approval in principle of the Fenian approach, Marx and Engels condemned the "foolishness which is to be found in every conspiracy." They denounced the purposeless "propaganda by deed" for which their party ought not to be made responsible and dissociated themselves from individual actions such as the Fenian bombing of Clerkenwell Prison. It was one thing to call for an overthrow of Irish landlordism and to denounce Britain's truly "Prussian behaviour" in Ireland; it was another to give unconditional support to the strictly nationalist, religious-sectarian approach of the Irish radicals who had no sympathies for Marxism and the policies of the First International.[132]

The issue of individual terror also played a certain role in the campaign of Marx and Engels against Bakunin, their main rival in the First International. In these attacks they made use of the revelations of the Nechaev trial and the brochures which Bakunin had written in 1869, in part inspired by Nechaev. Engels wrote that only a police agent could have glorified the bandit as the authentic revolutionary and identified revolution with individual and collective murder.[133] They might have taken a more tolerant view had it not been for Bakunin's Panslavism and, above all, his influence in certain sections of the International. For the Marxist attitude toward the terror of the Narodnaya Volya was by no means consistent and unambiguous. Plekhanov had correctly predicted in 1879 that a terrorist campaign would end in catastrophe and setback for socialism in Russia. But Plekhanov was not yet a full-fledged Marxist at the time and his conversion certainly did not become easier when he realized that Marx and Engels who had so bitterly denounced Bakunin had encouraging words for the neo-Bakuninists in Russia and refrained from criticizing their clearly nonsensical theoretical program. When Plekhanov published his *Nashe Raznoglasiya* (Our Differences) in 1884 Engels dryly noted that the Narodniki were after all the only people in Russia who were doing something. And Marx's comment on the assassins of Alexander II is worth recalling: in his eyes they were sterling people through and through, simple, businesslike and heroic; they endeavored to show Europe that their *modi operandi* were specifically Russian and historically inevitable. One could no more moralize about their action (for or against) Marx wrote, than about the earthquake of Chios.[134]

Marx and Engels exaggerated the strength of the Narodnaya Volya and overestimated the weakness of Tsarist despotism. "Russia is France of this century," Engels told Lopatin, a Russian emigrant. And, in a letter to Vera Zasulich he wrote that the revolution might break out any day in Russia, just a push was needed. Perhaps Blanqui and his fantasies had been right after all — with regard to Russia only, of course. Perhaps a small conspiracy could overthrow a whole society? Perhaps this was one of the few cases in which a handful of people could "make" a revolution? Such comments were anathema to Plekhanov and he must have welcomed the fact that Engels later revised his views. In retrospect (in 1894) Engels noted that there had been an acute revolutionary situation in Russia and for this reason Marx had told the Russian revolutionaries in the late 1870s not to be in too much of a hurry to "jump" into capitalism. There had been, in fact, two governments: on the one hand the tsar, and on the other, the Executive Committee of the conspirators and the terrorists, whose power grew by the day. The overthrow of Tsarism seemed at hand.[135] Fifteen years later these illusions had faded away and the Marxist attitude to terrorism changed. With regard to Western Europe, Marx and Engels had not been willing to make allowances for terrorism in any event: revolutions were made by classes not by a few conspirators. Hence Marx's scathing comment on Most's theoretical attempts to ascribe to the assassination of the tsar a panacea

— this was just "childish" (Marx in a letter dated April 1881 to his daughter Jenny). In January 1885 Engels took an even dimmer view of the activities of the Irish dynamiters and others in Western Europe who wanted to copy the terrorist struggle. This, he said, was revolution à la *Schinderhannes* (a famous German eighteenth-century robber), for it directed one's weapons not against one's real enemies but against the public at large. Such terrorists were not the friends of Russian revolutionaries but their worst enemies. Only the Russian government was interested in actions of this kind. One could possibly understand the motives of the Irish who had been driven to despair, but their effect was to stir up blind rage among British public opinion. Marx and Engels, as already noted, were highly critical of the Fenian leaders who were "mostly asses and partly exploiters." The Clerkenwell explosion, Marx wrote to Engels, was a very stupid act; one could not really expect the London proletarians to be blown up in honor of the Fenian emissaries: "There is always a kind of fatality about such a secret, melodramatic conspiracy."[136] Engels reacted even more strongly; "cannibals," "cowards," "stupid fanatics" were some of the epithets used. After the Phoenix Park murders Engels wrote that such bragging purposeless *propaganda par le fait* should be left to the Bakuninists, Mostians, and those who threatened an Irish revolution which never materialized. True, on another occasion Marx wrote to his daughter that his whole family supported the Fenians. But he offered an interesting explanation: his motives were not simply humanitarian — "To accelerate social development in Europe, you must push on the catastrophe of official England. To do so you must attack it in Ireland."[137]

Yet with all these reservations the influence of Blanquism (which always implied an element of terrorism) on Marx and Engels, and *a fortiori* on Lenin, was stronger than they were generally prepared to admit. They rejected, of course, primitive Blanquism, the conspiracy of a handful of people who aimed at insurrection. Such attempts were invariably doomed to failure because they lacked mass support. But Marx and Engels knew, or instinctively felt, that the masses could not seize power unaided, that they needed a leadership and that in the final analysis "Blanquism on a higher level" was essential. A conspiracy was needed that could mobilize the masses. Whether a conspiracy such as this aimed at insurrection, civil war, sabotage, a terrorist campaign, or a combination of these and other elements were secondary questions. While the Marxists rejected terrorism as unsuitable for advanced Western countries, they could not possibly reject it *tout court*.

The German Social Democratic leaders were certainly more emphatic about terrorism than their teachers in London. Wilhelm Liebknecht thought Most clinically mad, Bebel took a somewhat more charitable view: Most was a gifted man but was in need of someone to discipline and guide him. The terrorist organizations, Bebel said, were deeply penetrated by police spies and agents provocateurs. Furthermore, the Anarchists assisted the police in creating a public climate in which all left-wing opposition could be branded as "terrorist." In fact, the police considered the Anarchists harmless; it was the Social Democrats they feared, and they were grateful for any pretext given to suppress them.

The debate on terrorism was resumed among the Russian Marxists when the Social Revolutionaries took up terrorist operations around the turn of the century. Lenin's attitude to individual terror was ambivalent: while paying tribute to their heroism, he rejected terrorism as practiced by the *Narodovoltsy*. Then, it had been restricted to a group of intellectuals who were cut off from the working class and the peasants; quoting his late brother who had believed in terrorism and, at the same time, dissociating himself from him, Lenin wrote that Russian terror "was and remains a specific kind of struggle practised by the intelligentsia."[138] He was all the more opposed to the Social Revolutionaries practicing "old-style terror" at a time when a revolutionary mass movement had emerged. At best, it made organizational and political work among the people more complicated. According to Lenin, experience had shown Anarchist terror, in the form of individual assassination, as harmful and counterproductive. He juxtaposed assassinations carried out in the name of the people (by the Socialist Revolutionaries) to revolutionary activities undertaken by the Bolsheviks "together with the people" (whatever that may have meant in practice).[139] The long and arduous work of organization and political propaganda was preferable to a repetition of "easy" tactics which had never proved their worth. In the final analysis Lenin's rejection of terror was tactical, not, as in Plekhanov's case, a matter of principle. He thought Plekhanov's total rejection of

terror philistine and wrote in *Iskra* that he had never rejected terror
in principle for the simple reason that it was a form of military
operation that might be usefully applied or even be essential in
certain moments of battle.[140] When Friedrich Adler shot Stuergkh,
the Austrian prime minister, in October 1916, Lenin wrote that he
was not opposed to political murder per se. In 1901, fifteen years
previously, different conditions had prevailed and he thought that at
that time terror was inadvisable as likely to disrupt the revolutionary
forces and not the government. By contrast, in October 1905, at the
height of the first Russian revolution, he expressed real anguish that
his party had merely been talking about bombs but that not a single
one had been made. Terrorism was to be recommended provided
that the mood of the masses and the working-class movement on the
spot was taken into account.

Rosa Luxemburg and Martov thought it harmful (not only aesthetically) that ordinary bandits should collaborate with revolutionary
workers. Lenin had no such scruples. In fact, several prominent
Bolsheviks cooperated in terrorist enterprises: Krassin, who was an
engineer, supervised the manufacture of bombs for the Maximalists;
"Kamo" (Ter Petrosian) organized some daring and successful armed
robberies in the Caucasus; Litvinov and Semashko (the future minister of health) were arrested in Germany when they tried to change
the money that they had "expropriated." The Mensheviks denounced the Bolshevik tactics, but Lenin did not even bother to
reply.[141] After the suppression of the first revolution, Lenin (and also
Trotsky) again argued that terror was ineffectual: the assassination of
a minister would not bring the overthrow of capitalism nearer.
Trotsky in 1911 wrote in the Austrian Social Democratic organ *Der
Kampf* that he had grave doubts as to the efficacy of terror. Even
successful terrorist operations only temporarily introduced confusion
into the ranks of the establishment; the capitalist state did
not rest upon ministers alone and could not be destroyed with
them:

> The classes whom the state serves will always find new men — the
> mechanism remains intact and continues to function. Far deeper is the
> confusion that terrorist attempts introduce into the ranks of the work-
> ing masses. If it suffices to arm oneself with a revolver in order to reach

our goal, then to what end are the goals of the class struggle? If a pinch of powder and a slug of lead are enough to destroy the enemy, what need is there of a class organization? If there is rhyme or reason in scaring titled personages with the noise of an explosion, what need is there for a party?[142]

These observations of Trotsky have frequently been quoted by subsequent generations of Trotskyites in their disputations with comrades who advocate a more militant line. But it is also true that Trotsky's attitude, like Lenin's, was in fact more ambiguous than would appear. He derided the "eunuchs and pharisees" who opposed terrorism as a matter of principle. However, the account with capitalism was too great to be settled by the assassination of individual ministers — only collective action would repay the debt. On another occasion he noted that while terrorism in Russia was a thing of the past, it might have a future in what would now be called the "Third World"; there were auspicious conditions in Bengal and Punjab; it was part of the political awakening in these countries.[143] In 1934, after the murder of Kirov, Trotsky defined individual terrorism as "bureaucratism turned inside out" — not one of his most brilliant formulations and not even relevant to the Kirov case — indicative of his views on individual as distinct from collective terrorism, which he defended in a famous polemic with Kautsky when he was still in power.

Communist attitudes toward individual terror have shown the same ambiguity ever since. Terrorism might be rejected in principle; nonetheless on certain occasions terrorism in practice has not been ruled out (Spain after the First World War, Bulgaria in 1923, Germany in 1929–1931, or Venezuela in the early 1960s). In November 1931 when the Central Committee of the German Communist party came out against individual terror, many militants opposed this turn in the party line.[144] The official textbooks condemned individual terror in the sharpest possible terms but this did not deter the GPU, its predecessors and successors, from "liquidating" political enemies such as Trotsky, who were considered particularly dangerous. More recently, individual terror has been practiced on a fairly wide scale by Communist-led movements of national liberation such as in Vietnam — less so in China. Terror is regarded, however, to quote Lenin again, as merely one form of military operation — usually not a decisive one. Communist parties have bitterly attacked rival left-wing movements for concentrating on terrorism to the detriment of other forms of political and military struggle: the history of Communism in Latin America during the last two decades offers many such examples.

TERRORISM AND NATIONALISM

The belief has gained ground in recent years that terrorism has been, and is, the monopoly of the extreme left wing. But this is true only to the extent that theoretical problems of terrorism are always much more widely discussed by the left. At least as frequently, terrorism has been employed by right-wing groups and nationalist movements. Terrorism in India in the 1890s had a distinct religious infusion (the worship of Kali and Durga and the anti–cow killing campaign) and was frequently practiced by high-caste Brahmins. Nineteenth- and early twentieth-century Irish terrorism is a good example of empirical terrorism. While the American Clan na-Gael stood for "bloodless terrorism" directed against buildings and similar targets, O'Donovan Rossa favored indiscriminate attacks. The Invincibles of the 1880s practiced individual terror such as the Phoenix Park murders. The Irish proponents of terrorism were very much interested in gimmicks, whereas doctrinal issues hardly bothered them. They spent sixty thousand dollars on building three submarines in the United States which were never used; Rossa wanted to spray the House of Commons with osmic gas; and money was collected for the purchase of poison stilettoes, lucifer matches and other unlikely weapons.[145] They saw no need for elaborate theoretical justification: had Britain not behaved much worse all over the world, killing women and children in Africa, shooting into unarmed crowds, blowing Indian sepoys from cannon? The purpose of the dynamite campaign in the 1880s was to cause maximum dislocation and annoyance, to harm the tourist industry, to make travel in underground railways risky, to cause widespread "moral panic" and the paralysis of business.[146] The Invincibles predicted that the new "mysterious and overshadowing war of destruction" would eventually result in Britain having to adopt fiercer coercion laws at home than Ireland had known. But if the Irish leaders were not ideologists they were not ignorant men and, given the occasion, they could be quite eloquent on the subject of terrorism: "Despotism violates the moral frontier as invasion violates the geographical frontier," one of them wrote. "To drive out the tyrant or to drive out the English is in either case to retake your territory. There comes an hour when protest no longer suffices. After philosophy there must be action. The strong hand finishes what the idea has planned. Prometheus Bound begins, Aristogeiton completes; the Encyclopaedics enlighten souls, the 6th of May electrifies them."

Or on mass psychology: "The multitude has a tendency to accept a master. Their mass deposits apathy. A mob easily totalizes itself into obedience. Men must be aroused, pushed, shocked by the very benefits of their deliverance, their eyes wounded with the truth, light thrown in terrible handfuls."[147]

Heated debates took place among the Irish leaders, but these were on tactics rather than issues of principle. John Devoy thought Rossa's dynamiters "fools, imbeciles, insane designers," the whole show was a burlesque "which makes us appear fools and ignoramuses."[148] But this did not prevent Devoy from threatening in 1881 to take a British minister's life in reprisal for every Irishman killed. Thus, he repeated Rossa's threat, five years earlier, that if a skirmisher was hanged, the minister who ordered the execution would be killed and the city in which the patriot was hanged would be burned down.[149] And even Parnell, who never expressed sympathy for terrorism in public, frequently conveyed in private the impression that he sympathized with the militants. His, too, was a dual strategy: constitutional means reinforced by the actions of secret organizations. No one knows to what extent he was involved in the terrorist campaign.[150] The reasons for the opposition of Devoy and most other Irish leaders to individual assassination up to the First World War was that Britain was too powerful, that Irish resources were insufficient, and that there were other, more effective means of struggle for the time being.

THE PHILOSOPHY OF THE BOMB — THE RIGHT-WING VERSION

Assassinations of political opponents carried out by the Black Hundred in prewar Russia are examples of terrorism as carried out by the extreme right. There were many more cases of assassination after the end of the First World War in other parts of Europe. Hitler had said more than once that "heads would roll, ours, or the others" — and the Nazis would ensure that it would be those of the others. Giving evidence in the trial of four National Socialists in Berlin in 1931, he argued that this had just been a parable, a synonym for ideological confrontation, and that he had always demanded strict observance of legality. If his veto on illegality was violated, those responsible were brought to account. Acts of violence had never been contemplated by his party.[151] But if Hitler had to stick to certain legal niceties, his aides were under no such constraints. Thus Joseph Goebbels: whoever defended his own *Weltanschauung* with terror and brutality would one day gain power. The "street," as Goebbels saw it, was the decisive place in which policy was made. Conquest of the street meant the gain of the masses: he who had the masses would conquer the state.[152] The basic Nazi strategy was to mobilize the masses in order to conquer the street, disrupt meetings of other parties, and attack their opponents' demonstrations. Occasionally they would engage in terrorism, and in defense they quoted the authority of Mussolini. "Terror? Never. It simply is social hygiene, taking those individuals out of circulation like a doctor would take out a bacillus."[153] Mussolini, a radical socialist in his younger years, had welcomed terrorist actions in various parts of the world: *"il proletario deve essere psicologicamente preparato all'uso della violenza liberatice,"* he once wrote.[154] His orientation toward the proletariat changed, but Mussolini's belief in "liberating violence" remained. There was progressive, liberating violence, he said on one occasion, and stupid, reactionary violence — that used by his political enemies. The Socialists ask what is our program? he once wrote in *Popolo d'Italia*. Our program is to smash the heads of the Socialists.

This, too, was terror, but of a different kind — mass violence intended to intimidate opponents rather than eliminate individual enemy leaders. The Nazis always stressed that they were never the first to engage in terror. True, they were not "bourgeois aesthetes" but only engaged in "terror against terror" in self-defense.[155] On the other hand, no German political party appreciated better than the Nazis the tremendous uses to which political violence could be put so as to maximize publicity in the mass media. Any clash was bound to be reported on the front page of the newspapers, and a small and uninfluential group soon became nationally known. This was Goebbels' strategy in the "conquest of Berlin" and his example was copied elsewhere.[156]

Neither the Nazis nor the Italian Fascists needed ideological justification for political violence. Theirs was the generation that had fought in the First World War, and to them it was perfectly obvious that in the struggle for power, all forms of violence were permissible. The friend-foe dichotomy was at the bottom of their politics, taking it for granted that the enemy would not be defeated by persuasion alone. The enemy was the democratic-liberal system, and radical, pseudo-socialist undertones were by no means absent in the onslaught on the "system." This emerged from Mussolini's early program, also appearing in Nazi slogans during the *Kampfzeit*. The Nazis quite frankly admitted that they would cause maximum disruption, for as long as "business was good" they would not be feared.[157] At a Berlin trial against Nazi storm troopers, Count Helldorf, their leader, argued that it was quite absurd to accuse them of having attacked Jews, for they were fighting against the capitalist system, which was represented, after all, not only by Jews. . . .[158]

On the whole, however, individual terror was comparatively rare in Germany and Italy; it was more frequently used by the smaller Fascist and proto-Fascist groups — precisely because they were small. These groups are usually labeled "right-wing extremist," but such labels are only of limited help in understanding their motives and strategy. Certain German Free Corps such as the *Organization Consul*, engaged in systematic terror in 1921–1922.[159] But they were radicals, not conservatives, and the last thing they wanted was to prop up a "doomed bourgeois society." Some of them were pure Nihilists; Ernst von Salomon later wrote about himself and his comrades that they "killed whoever fell into our hands, we burned whatever could be burned. . . . The march into an uncertain future was for us sufficiently meaningful and suited the demands of our blood."[160] This was gibberish, of course, but it described fairly accurately the mood prevailing in these circles. When the terrorists decided to kill Rathenau, the German foreign minister, it was not because they hated him or thought him particularly wicked; on the contrary they admired him. He had to be removed because he was more significant than mere mediocrities. They saw the struggle as a "duel between giants" (an image that had frequently been invoked by the terrorist faction of the Narodnaya Volya). At one stage the *Freikorps* terrorists planned to kill von Seeckt, head of the *Reichswehr,* and the Hungarian Fascists planned the assassination of the right-wing minister of the interior. The Rumanian Iron Guard assassinated two prime ministers — Duca in 1933 and Calinescu in 1939. None of these victims, or intended victims, was a man of the left, or a liberal.

The composition of "right-wing" terrorist groups varied greatly from country to country. Many criminal elements were found among the members of the Hungarian "Arrow Cross"; the Macedonian IMRO, once a patriotic movement, developed into a Mafia-type organization, accepting "contracts" from the highest bidders and engaging, *inter alia,* in the traffic of narcotics.[161] The Rumanian Iron Guard on the other hand consisted largely of young idealists of sorts (the "legionnaires") who stood for a religious revival, spiritual regeneration, sacrifice and martyrdom: "You want programs?" the "Manual of the Legionnaires" asked. "They are on everybody's lips. Better look for men. Anyone can turn out a programme in one night: that is not what the country needs."[162] The legionnaires were in a moral quandary: as good Christians they believed in forgiveness, but as patriots they felt that the nation could be saved only by un-Christian acts. Murder had to be committed but had also to be expiated, either by surrender after the deed or at least by suffering for their sins in their hearts. Similar to certain Anarchist groups that preceded them, the legionnaires came to believe that there was only one ideology, the Deed *(Vasile Marin).* Like Sorel before, and a great many minor thinkers after, they believed in "the ethical value of force."[163] Their terrorism comprised a mystique of death. "Legionnaires are born to die," it was said in their songs, and "Death is a gladsome wedding for us." Lombroso had first noted a suicidal impulse among Anarchist groups in Western Europe and this impulse could be found among them, too. Although the Rumanian authorities claimed that the legionnaires had plans to seize power it is not certain if they ever seriously intended to do so.

A common denominator marked terrorist movements of the "left" and the "right" in Europe, indicating a protest against modern society, against corrupt political parties and "plutocracy." Patriotic and religious motivations were called in as reinforcements. This reaction was not limited to Europe. Japanese terrorism drew its inspiration from the knightly spirit of the Samurai; more surprising is the fact that some of its prominent practitioners had once been Anarchists or belonged to the Tolstoyan "School of Love for the Native Soil."[164] Capitalism and Western civilization had to be destroyed; the members of the "Terrorist League of Blood" were called upon to sacrifice themselves for the principle of the love for the soil, to abandon their families (shades of Ishutin and Nechaev) and renounce their personal existences forever. The Japanese terrorists of the 1920s were manipulated by military leaders and right-wing adventurers, who wanted to frighten the emperor, the court and the government into accepting a more aggressive policy: peace at home, expansion abroad.[165] But the threat of assassination alone would not have sufficed in a country with traditions like those of Japan. Terrorism was also a moral force, inducing an uneasy conscience among those it threatened and intimidating the politicians who did not wish to appear disloyal to the terrorists' concept of the historical mission of the Japanese people.

Right-wing terror in Europe between the two world wars took many different forms. In France the activists of the extreme right limited their activities to the universities and the theaters, intimidating unpopular professors and playwrights. This was terror of incitement — of speech, of the written word which drove Roger Salengro to suicide. There was also more tangible terrorism such as that of the CSAR, a small Fascist group, on which more below, leading to assassination. If the French right used journalism for its purposes, the early Austrian Nazis (and the Japanese extremists) regarded the press as one of its main enemies. "One kills these dogs by shooting or poisoning them, every means is right," one of the early advocates of Austrian terrorism wrote. His comrades planned to send letter bombs to leading journalists and to destroy the printing presses.[166] The Finnish

Lapua movement did not kill their opponents but kidnaped them, beat them up, and dropped them over the Russian border. The Italian Fascists forcibly fed castor oil to their opponents adding insult (and ridicule) to injury.

But individual terror, to repeat once again, was relatively infrequent among the Fascist mass parties; Rathenau and Erzberger were killed by small groups who had no clear political program. Dollfuss, the Austrian chancellor, was assassinated in the course of an armed insurrection and Matteoti was murdered when the Fascists were already in power. Terrorism in Fascist, as in Communist, strategy was accredited only a minor place for reasons of effectiveness; there was nothing in Fascist doctrine which would have ruled out terrorism in principle. The thoughts of right-wing activism on the subject were expressed most succinctly by Carl Schmitt in his writings on the "political soldier": the ethics of the Sermon on the Mount applied to the private enemy, the *inimicus*, not to the *hostis*, the public foe. Political conflicts were settled not by discussion, persuasion or barter, as the liberals mistakenly believed, but by struggle, both in foreign as well as domestic policy.[167] In the final analysis, Nazis, Fascists and other extreme right-wing groups did not need a philosopher to teach them that "love your enemies" did not apply to politics. They knew this instinctively.

The similarities between the inspiration underlying terrorism of "Right" and "Left" have been noted: the assumption that the deed was more important than words; the belief that any change would be for the better; a contempt for liberalism and bourgeois democracy; a sense of the historical mission of the chosen few. It was no mere coincidence that Carl Schmitt, who provided the most sophisticated justification for political violence as practiced by the right, should develop a "theory of the partisan" after the Second World War in which he expressed admiration for Mao and left-wing revolutionaries — his philosophy of violence is truly value-free. On both extremes of the political spectrum terrorism was regarded as a useful weapon to discredit the "system." The SS too held to a perverse idealism, a belief that only they took values seriously, that they were chosen for the same quasi-religious moment of sacrifice. The *Narodovoltsy* killed with a bad conscience, whereas the Fascists had no such qualms of conscience. The Anarchists of "propaganda by deed" did not weep for their victims either. When Emile Henry, who had thrown a bomb at the Café Terminus appeared in court, he declared "there are no innocent bourgeois"; some of his comrades went further, expressing the view that there were no innocent human beings in general. There were, of course, differences between the terror of the left and the right in other respects: the *Narodovoltsy* practiced terror because they saw no other way to make their demands heard in a regime which had outlawed all opposition. They denounced acts of terror committed in countries in which normal political activity was possible (as in their message after the assassination of President Garfield). They genuinely believed in a free and nonviolent society. The terrorists of the right did not share this belief in the essential goodness of human nature. Their ideal society was of a very different kind.

Terrorist doctrine is of considerable importance for the understanding of the terrorist phenomenon but it is only one of the motivating forces, and not always the decisive one. The Macedonian IMRO and the Croatian Ustacha began as genuine patriotic movements. By the 1930s they had become play-balls of foreign interests: the Macedonians must have known that they could not possibly attain national independence, and the Croatian separatists were aware that they would have to pay a heavy price, such as the surrender of Dalmatia to their Italian protectors. The Croatians launched indiscriminate attacks inside Yugoslavia; the Macedonian terrorists killed each other and were also used by the Bulgarian government for the liquidation of political opponents. Croats and Macedonians probably still believed that operations directed against their oppressors coupled with foreign help might one day result in a favorable international constellation in which they could attain their aims. But it is impossible to say with any degree of certainty whether they (and other groups) still predominantly comprised a political movement, or whether the key to their activities must be found in other levels of social behavior. There was, furthermore, "instinctive terrorism" among movements with national or social grievances that fitted into no known ideological category. It can be taken for granted that the Ukrainians in eastern Poland and the peasants of Schleswig-Holstein at the time of the Great Depression had never read terrorist tracts.[168] But they knew, even if they had not read it in books, that publicity was needed to make their protest known; it was far more likely that they would be listened to if political pressure was reinforced by terrorist action. Sometimes there was a simple division of labor: the more militant wing of a movement, dissatisfied with the lack of progress, would opt for "direct action," whereas the more moderate would continue their nonviolent activities. In short, if it has been possible since time immemorial to make love or to cook without the help of textbooks, the same applies to terrorism. In some cases the decision to adopt a terrorist strategy was taken on the basis of a detailed political analysis. But usually the mood came first, and ideological rationalization only after. On occasion this led to the emergence of a systematic strategy of terrorism and to bitter debates between proponents and opponents. But terrorism also took place without precise doctrine and systematic strategy, with only hazy notions about the direction of the struggle and its aim. Like Faust, the terrorists could truly claim *Im Anfang war die Tat* — in the beginning there was the deed.

3

The Sociology of Terrorism

Terrorism, interpreted here as the use of covert violence by a group for political ends, is usually directed against a government, less frequently against another group, class or party. The ends may vary from the redress of specific "grievances" to the overthrow of a government and the taking over of power, or to the liberation of a country from foreign rule. Terrorists seek to cause political, social and economic disruption, and for this purpose frequently engage in planned or indiscriminate murder.* It may appear in conjunction with a political campaign or with guerrilla war, but also in a "pure" form. It has been waged by national or religious groups, by the left or by the right, by nationalist as well as internationalist movements and on some rare occasions even by liberals and conservatives. Terrorist movements have mainly consisted of members of the educated middle classes, but there has also been agrarian terrorism, terror by the uprooted and the rejected, and trade union and working-class

*Any definition of political terrorism venturing beyond noting the systematic use of murder, injury and destruction or the threats of such acts toward achieving political ends is bound to lead to endless controversies. Some terrorist groups have been indiscriminate and their victims are "symbolic," others have acted differently. Some merely wanted to create a climate of fear, others aimed at the physical destruction of their opponents *tout court*. Purists will argue that one is not even entitled to stress the systematic character of terrorism because in some cases the execution of a single act did have the desired effect (Sarajevo in 1914). It can be predicted with confidence that the disputes about a comprehensive, detailed definition of terrorism will continue for a long time, that they will not result in a consensus and that they will make no notable contribution toward the understanding of terrorism.

terror (United States 1880–1910; Spain 1890–1936). Terror has been directed against autocratic regimes as well as democracies; sometimes there has been an obvious link with social dislocation and economic crisis, at other times there has been no such connection. Movements of national liberation and social revolution (or reaction) have turned to terrorism after political action failed. But elsewhere and at other times terrorism has not been the consequence of political failure but has been chosen by militant groups even before other options were tried. Terrorism has never occurred in modern totalitarian regimes; individual attempts at assassinations have taken place but the means of control and repression at the disposal of a totalitarian state rule out any organized terrorism. It has been infrequent in modern societies where violence has not been part of the political culture, but outside totalitarian rule few parts of the world have been altogether free from it.

National oppression and social inequities are frequently mentioned as the main factors responsible for the spread of terrorism, and it is of course true that happy, contented people seldom, if ever, throw bombs. But this does not explain why the struggle for political freedom, for national liberation or for secession, or for other aims, sometimes has led to terrorism but at other times has not. Furthermore, any analysis of terrorism is incomplete unless it considers those against whom terror is directed: terrorist groups have made their appearance in our time in Britain and in France, in Spain and in Ethiopia; they have not been seen in Russia or China or the countries of Eastern Europe. Generalizations about terrorism are exceedingly difficult for yet another reason: terrorist movements are usually small; some are very small indeed, and while historians and sociologists can sometimes account for mass movements, the movements of small particles in politics as in physics often defy any explanation.

Some of the most startling assassinations of the last hundred years were carried out by individuals without the help or knowledge of any organized body — the murders of Stolypin and President McKinley; the killing of President Carnot, of Gandhi and President Kennedy. Such individual actions apart, there have been groups which killed and bombed in order to express protest rather than in the hope of defeating their enemies. The anarchist propagandists of the deed clearly belong to this category. Some of them registered their protest in their novels, some in their pictures and others threw bombs. Frequently there has been a general concept, sometimes vague, sometimes quite precise, underlying acts of terror. The advocates of "pure terror" in Russia assumed that the assassination of a handful of leading officials and other pillars of the establishment would lead to the downfall of the regime. They were not, as a rule, concerned with what would happen beyond this point; their historical mission, as they saw it, ended with the destruction of the system (or of foreign oppression). Yet almost inevitably, as the terrorist campaign continued, the terrorists became concerned with the seizure of power and more distant perspectives. This happened for instance to Narodnaya Volya, who eventually came to envisage a general insurrection even though they must have been aware that they were far too few to organize and direct a popular movement. Right-wing terrorists such as the German Organization Consul or the Japanese officers of the 1930s had more modest aims — they wanted to change the policy of the government so as to prevent "national betrayal." It is doubtful whether the Rumanian Iron Guard ever seriously intended to conquer power even though at one time it constituted a serious danger to the government. The extreme wing of the Fenians announced in 1885 that "this dynamite work will go on till Ireland is free, or till London is laid in ashes."[1] Again, it is very unlikely that they thought this to be a realistic alternative. What they actually expected was a more complicated sequence of action and counteraction: as Captain Lomasney explained to Jim Devoy, the Irish bombings would provoke British countermeasures but these would not succeed, for the Irish were a fighting race and their fighting spirit would be aroused by the struggle, the sympathy of the world would be won for Ireland, the English would have to make concessions and these could be used to wring further concessions and eventually Ireland would win full freedom.[2] Similarly, in 1918 the Russian Social Revolutionaries assumed that the murder of the German ambassador in Moscow and the German governor general of the occupied part of Ukraine would lead to the renewal of hostilities between Russia and Germany.

This, in a nutshell, is the strategy of provocation. The Armenians hoped that their actions would bring about the intervention of the European powers; a similar strategy, based on outside help, underlay the campaigns of Irgun, LEHI, the Palestinian Arab organizations and other such groups. The Serbian Black Hand decided to kill Archduke Franz Ferdinand not because they regarded him as particularly wicked but, on the contrary, because they were afraid that he would make political concessions, thus weakening the spirit of the nationalist movement in Bosnia.[3] For similar reasons the Freikorps terrorists killed Rathenau, the foreign minister of the Weimar Republic. The drawback to this strategy was that it worked only if the international constellation was auspicious. If it wasn't, terrorist acts made no difference, or even led to disaster, as the Armenians discovered to their cost. Orsini's attempt on the life of Napoleon III was a political success despite the fact that it failed. Orsini was executed but he became a hero with Napoleon's approval: his letter to the emperor ("Set my country free") was reproduced in full in the *Moniteur.* It was a success because Napoleon was already inclined to pursue an anti-Austrian policy.[4] A few years later a Pole tried to kill Napoleon III. The political effect was nil, for Poland was far away and the French emperor had no intention of antagonizing the Russians. Where terrorism has been successful its aims have usually been limited and clearly defined. The daily wage of the American iron workers (AFL) went up from $2.00 to $4.30 (for shor.er hours) between 1905 and 1910 as the result of the bombing of some one hundred buildings and bridges.[5] Spanish workers, using similar methods, improved their wages during the First World War.[6] Alternatively, terrorist actions succeeded because they were used within the framework of a wider strategy. An obvious example was the systematic killing by the Vietcong of some 10,000 village elders during the late 1950s and early 1960s, thus preparing the ground for a takeover from within.[7] They used the same tactics against opponents of the left, such as the Saigon Trotskyites, as did the Algerian FLN vis-à-vis their nationalist rivals, the Messalists. But the use of "urban guerrilla" tactics against the French was much less successful and in any case neither the Vietcong nor the FLN was predominantly a terrorist movement.

It is widely believed that with the growing vulnerability of modern technological society the prospects for urban terror are now greater than ever before. But "pure terrorism" has so far only succeeded in very specific circumstances which will be discussed later. Urban terrorists have, on the whole, been aware of the difficulties facing them and, in theory, urban terrorism should be linked with rural guerrilla warfare or with attempts to win over sections of the army or with the vision of a general insurrection or a people's war. But in practice the emphasis is usually on urban terror, either because the countries concerned are predominantly urbanized or because the masses do not respond or because the army is not inclined to cooperate with the terrorists. It should be noted in passing that while terrorist movements, including the right-wing terrorists of Central Europe, of Hungary and Rumania, attacked the police without hesitation, they were unwilling to take on the army and not only because they were afraid of the outcome of an unequal contest. Thus neither the Narodnaya Volya nor the Polish terrorists in 1905–1906 attacked army installations and personnel, in the hope that restraint would win over some officers; these hopes were by no means unjustified and eventually the Russians had a "military organization" consisting entirely of officers or ex-officers. The Palestinian Arab terrorists and the IMRO preferred to direct their operations against the civilian population, this, of course, being less risky. The IRA on the other hand had no such inhibitions; but then it knew that, given the political restrictions facing the army, the danger of retaliation was insubstantial. Latin American terrorists have tried with varying success to draw army officers into their ranks; as a rule they suffered badly whenever they clashed with soldiers.

There has always been a certain discrepancy between terrorist doctrine and practice. But even on the purely theoretical level, there was a great deal of inconsistency and some of the key questions were left unanswered. Was the terrorist struggle the prologue to the revolution (or to national liberation) or was it already the revolution? Were the terrorists the avant-garde of the revolutionary (or nationalist) movement — or were they the movement? Few terrorist groups have ever claimed that radical change could be effected without the active participation of the masses, but most of them have acted as if it could be done. But for how long could they continue to act (and to speak) on behalf of the masses without losing their credibility if the population was unenthusiastic or even hostile? The position of terrorist groups acting within the framework of political movements has been less complicated; they had to carry out a mission and no one expected them to worry about long-term perspectives. This applies, for instance, to the Social Revolutionaries, the Irish terrorists, *Irgun* and other such groups. But the division of labor has worked more easily in theory than in practice, for the "fighting organizations" always needed some autonomy and their political ideas usually diverged to some extent. There was always resentment against the "politicians" who risked so little and had therefore no moral right to dictate a course of action to the terrorists — unless it coincided with the wishes and the convictions of the "fighters." In short, there was almost always dissension and competition between the political and the terrorist wing of the movement, and a tendency toward full autonomy among the terrorists.

TERRORIST ORGANIZATION

Systematic terrorist operations involve careful planning, resembling the staff work of a minor military campaign. The intended victim has to be watched for a certain time, his habits and movements studied to establish the most promising place and time for the action. The terrorists need transport to and from the scene of the operation; they have to have false identity papers, effective arms and, above all, money. To make the most of their operation they need a publicity department. All major terrorist movements have had a central command, sometimes highly professional and efficient, at other times rudimentary and amateurish. Important decisions among the Narodnaya Volya were taken at committee meetings, but this system has usually proved ineffective in an emergency, and since terrorist groups face emergencies much of the time, the general tendency has been toward centralization and the leadership principle. But strong leadership tends to produce rivalry and opposition and the inevitable centralization also creates certain practical problems. Terrorism always involves an element of improvisation; even the most careful planning cannot possibly make provision for all eventualities. Elaborate planning that sacrifices the element of improvisation could redound to the disadvantage of the terrorists. A small local group, on the other hand, will usually lack the resources and the know-how for carrying out a major operation. The ideal pattern is strong central leadership concerned with broad strategy, but with the details left to the local branches. Mao had a great deal to say about this in his writings on guerrilla warfare but, again, it is a principle easier to adhere to in theory than to observe in practice.

The central command of the terrorist movement has sometimes been located abroad; Switzerland, the United States, Lebanon have been centers for movements operating elsewhere. The advantages are obvious; the terrorist leaders can move about freely without fear of arrest. But so are the drawbacks, for the more remote the head-quarters from the scene of action, the less complete its knowledge of current events, the more tenuous its contacts with its own men. While the Narodnaya Volya would never have envisaged operations outside Russia, some modern terrorist groups specialize in "third country operations." In 1973, for instance, out of 221 major terrorist operations all over the globe, 47 were carried out in third countries.[8]

The larger a terrorist movement, the greater the danger of detection. The Narodnaya Volya, at the height of its activities, had 500 members; the Fighting Organization of the Social Revolutionaries (1903–1907) was considerably smaller, though there was a large periphery which it could draw on for support. Both IZL and LEHI had only a few hundred members who could be enlisted for terrorist operations. The nineteenth-century Irish terrorist groups consisted of a few dozen militants. The IRA and Palestinian Arab terrorist organizations had many more members but only a small number were trained for terrorist action. Terrorist groups in contrast to guerrilla units do not grow beyond a certain limit. The basic unit usually consists of three to ten people. Some of the recent terrorist "armies" such as the Japanese Red Army, the Baader-Meinhof group (Rote Armee Fraktion), the Angry Brigade, the Symbionese Liberation Army, etc., numbered a few dozen members at the height of their exploits. The Tupamaros started their operations with 50 members in late 1966; five years later they had about 3,000; yet their success was their undoing, for the very size of the movement made it easy for the security forces to track down the terrorists and eventually to arrest many of them and to destroy their organization. The Argentinian ERP was believed to have 5,000 members in 1975, but again, only a part were engaged in fighting operations.* The Montoneros

*The ERP repeated some of the mistakes committed earlier by the Tupamaros and in addition, against all the rules of urban terror, frontally attacked major army units. About 70 of them were killed in the attempt to storm the Monte Chingolo army camp in the spring of 1976.

were even more numerous but lacked cohesion and split into several factions.

Urban terrorist campaigns have seldom lasted longer than three to four years. Once the security forces have mastered counter techniques, terrorist losses usually become unacceptably high. Furthermore, the initial enthusiasm in the ranks of the terrorist groups has tended to wane, once it appears that even a series of successful operations fails to bring about the downfall of the system. In a few cases, terrorist campaigns have lasted longer — when launched from sanctuaries, as in the case of the Palestinian organizations — or when the terrorists have fairly strong mass support, usually of a nationalist-separatist or religious kind (IRA, Euzkadi). According to Z. Ivianski, terrorism frequently occurs in cyclical upsurges.[9] The *ère des attentats* in France came twenty years after the Paris Commune, and two decades later there was another, albeit minor, wave of terrorist operations. In Russia, too, twenty years were to pass before a new generation resumed the terrorist tradition of the Narodnaya Volya. In Ireland, on the other hand, the intervals between the terrorist upsurges were considerably longer. Once a terrorist organization has failed to attain its objectives, the fighting spirit of a new generation is needed to rekindle the flame. Seen in this light, terrorism is a concomitant of generational revolt; but there is no eternal law of generational revolt and even when it occurs it does not necessarily turn to terrorism. Furthermore, there are a great many factors that either hasten or delay the outbreak of a terrorist campaign even in countries in which violence is more or less endemic; the international political constellation, for instance. At other times the echo effect has obviously had a certain impact insofar as a terrorist campaign in one country has provided inspiration for others elsewhere.

TERRORIST FINANCES

Modern terrorists do not live by enthusiasm alone; they need a great deal of money. The preparations for major operations may be expensive and money is needed to bribe government and police officials.

Nineteenth-century terrorist movements could sometimes be run on a shoestring. The Narodnaya Volya got the little it needed from well-to-do members or sympathizers; the Social Revolutionaries relied mainly on "expropriations." The Anarchists were poor, and had no significant outside support, apart from occasional windfalls. Francisco Ferrer, the Spanish Anarchist, received a million francs from a French lady he had befriended. The Irish Revolutionary Brotherhood was founded in a Dublin timberyard on St. Patrick's Day 1858 with four hundred dollars received from the U.S.A.; more substantial sums were collected in later years (the "Special National Fund," Rossa's Skirmishing Fund). Some of the money was contributed by a sympathizer who was a billiards champion. Irgun and, to a lesser extent, LEHI received financial support from Jews in the United States and also engaged in "expropriations." Occasionally the political police would contribute indirectly to the budget of Anarchist and terrorist groups but these gifts were hardly ever of great importance. In 1906–1907, Indian terrorists tried to manufacture forged notes, counterfeit coins and even prepare "chemical gold." When these attempts to raise money failed they turned to robbery (dacoity). Some of them suggested that only government funds should be stolen but this was considered impractical and a resolution was passed that an accurate account should be kept of the amounts taken from private individuals with a view to returning them after independence was achieved. It was also suggested that only those who had amassed wealth by dishonest means should be victimized. But, as noted by a historian of the Indian freedom movement, "it is difficult to believe that this principle was always followed in practice." Nor could all terrorists, "human nature being what it is," live up to the ideals of high moral purpose and absence of greed; dacoities were committed for personal ends, and political objectives were used as a disguise.[10] The Ustasha forged Yugoslav 1,000 dinar notes, apparently with Italian help, and LEHI printed government bonds with the assistance of a specialist serving in the Polish army in exile.*

After the First World War it became the fashion among some

---

*The IRA in Ulster was reported to have derived some of its income from legitimate business ventures (such as running taxi services) but also from extorting protection money.

governments to finance terrorist groups; thus the Italians and the Hungarians gave money to the Croatians and IMRO (44 million lira in 1929–1933). IMRO also received funds from the Bulgarians, and the Poles allegedly paid the Rumanian Iron Guard, although this had not been proved. This fashion became even more popular after the Second World War. The Soviet Union either directly or through its East European satellites has supplied arms, technical instruction and possibly money to terrorist groups in various parts of the world; Libya, Algeria and other Arab countries have distributed money on a rather lavish scale — sometimes, as in Ulster, supporting both sides in a conflict. The IRA have continued to receive contributions from the U.S.A. and the Palestinian Arab terrorist groups have been given hundreds of millions of dollars from the oil-producing countries. Latin American groups such as the ERP and the Montoneros extorted millions of dollars from the firms and families of kidnaped businessmen. Nineteenth-century terrorist groups had been more or less uniformly poor, whereas more recently there has been a clear "class differentiation": a terrorist aristocracy with rich and powerful protectors has emerged on the one hand, and a terrorist proletariat on the other.

This development was first noted in the 1930s. Who are the assassins? asked a contemporary commentator after the murder of King Alexander of Yugoslavia in Marseilles in 1934.[11] Are they Croats, or Czech, or German or perhaps Hungarian? Everything about them is wrong — with the exception of their money and their arms. Where did the money come from, how have these poor, persecuted Croats been able to pay for expensive journeys through many countries? Who has armed and financed them, who has provided their false passports? In short, who has commissioned them?[12] No one had asked questions of this kind about the Narodovoltsy or the Anarchists, because they had been poor and there had been no secret about their funds. But in the 1930s and *a fortiori* after the Second World War, terrorism became, on occasion, big business with multinational ramifications and a great deal of effort was spent in keeping their sources of income obscure. The "proletarians," such as the South Moluccans, could not obtain outside help because their objectives did not coincide with the interests of foreign governments. The affluent groups could engage in expensive operations far beyond the reach of the poor terrorists; they could employ costly equipment, hire assistants, buy information without having to worry about where the money would come from. Sometimes this money was given in the form of an annual subsidy, sometimes as a reward for specific actions; Black September reportedly received seven million dollars for the Munich murder of Israeli athletes.[13] On the other hand, this new wealth created temptations that had not existed before. True, even among the Fenians in the 1880s and among the Russian Maximalists there had been occasional accusations about misappropriation of money, about squandering of funds and spending for personal use. But the sums involved were insignificant in comparison with the millions amassed by Arab and Latin American terrorists in the 1960s and 1970s.

In the affluent groups, officials were paid salaries far above what they could earn in any legitimate profession. Swiss bank accounts were opened; there were investments in real estate and other transactions more in line with major business enterprises than the traditional terrorist ethos of the Narodnaya Volya or the Fenians. Prolonged exposure to life in luxury hotels produced a new type of terrorist different from the lean and hungry fighters of a previous generation. A member of the Berlin urban terrorists relates that his group split on account of money: "When there is too much money, unnecessary things are bought, first a record player and a television set, then expensive suits and cars, and in the end you look like something straight out of *Playboy*. . . ."[14] In the history of Irish terrorism, there were many accusations of misuse of money and embezzlement; the most recent concerned a Provisional IRA man from County Tyrone who fled to the U.S. with about £100,000 seized in a bank raid in County Meath in 1975. A spokesman of his organization said, "A certain decision was taken in relation to Hughes and it did not include military honours at his funeral."[15]

Terrorist Budgets*

Year	Terrorist Group	Country	Income (in 1976 dollars)	Source
1880	Narodnaya Volya	Russia	insignificant	donations from well-wishers
1880	Irish dynamiters	Ireland	50,000	Irish sympathizers in U.S.
1896	Anarchists	France, Italy	insignificant	donations
1906	Social Revo-lutionaries and other groups	Russia	5–10 million	robberies, some voluntary donations
1932	IMRO	Bulgaria	2–3 million	extortion, Bulgaria, Italy
1933	Ustasha	Yugo-slavia	1–2 million	Italy, Hungary
1947	IZL—Stern Gang	Palestine	1–2 million	donations from well-wishers, robbery
1970	Tupamaros	Uruguay	5–10 million	abductions, robbery
1970	ALN	Brazil	5–10 million	abductions, bank robbery
1974	ERP—Mon-toneros†	Argentina	50–100 million	abductions, robbery
1975	Fatah‡	Middle East	150–200 million	mainly donations from Arab oil-producing countries
1975	PFLP, PDFLP, Saiqa	Middle East	20–30 million	donations from Libya, Iraq and Syria
1975	IRA, provisionals and regulars	Ireland, Ulster	1–3 million	donations and robberies, protection rackets and income from legitimate business
1975	UDA, UVF	Ulster	?	same

*The figures are based on estimates; terrorist movements have not as a rule kept accounts to be examined by outsiders or tax inspectors. However, enough facts and figures are known to give a general idea of their income. The estimates are calculated on the basis of 1976 dollars; the sums that were at the disposal of terrorist groups before the Second World War were, of course, in absolute terms much smaller. But prices were much lower too; the Irish paid 5 to 6 dollars for a rifle in 1914; the Russian AK-47 assault rifle is sold now for 110 dollars.

† 1974 and 1975 were exceptionally profitable years for the Argentinian terrorists.

‡ Estimates of the income of Palestinian terrorist organizations vary greatly. According to Israeli sources, Fatah has an income of $150–200 million; figures mentioned in the press of the "Rejection Front" and by Syrian spokesmen ($240 million) are higher. If expenses for political work and donations in kind rather than cash (arms, equipment, training camps, etc.) are included, the higher figures may well be close to the truth.

INTELLIGENCE

The success of terrorist operations depends on reliable information about the targets to be attacked and the movements of the victims to be killed or abducted. The Social Revolutionaries disguised themselves as coachmen and street traders in order to patrol unobtrusively in the neighborhood chosen for an attack.* Other terrorist groups used sympathizers, such as repair workers, postmen or street cleaners, for intelligence-gathering. Government employees were of great help and sources inside the police were invaluable since they could warn the terrorists about impending raids and help to unmask spies in their ranks. The Narodnaya Volya owed some of their successes to the information received from Nikolai Kletochnikov, who had found employment in the "third section," the Tsarist political police. From perusing police files, he established that there was a spy (Reinstein) among the Narodovoltsy — who was promptly killed. The Social Revolutionaries also had a sympathizer in the police who helped them on several occasions, and it is doubtful whether Azev would ever have been unmasked but for the information they received from leading police officials.[16] Michael Collins's attack against British intelligence headquarters in Dublin in November 1920 effectively paralyzed British operations during the critical period of the insurrection, since vital documents were destroyed and undercover agents were discovered and killed. The IRA regarded the "G" Division of the Dublin Metropolitan Police as its main target; the British could always send new soldiers to Ireland but the number of knowledgeable intelligence officers was limited and they could not easily be replaced.

Nationalist terror groups such as the Irgun had sources of information in the police who collaborated with them, either because they were sympathizers or because they were paid. Schulze and Tillesen, the murderers of Erzberger, the leading Catholic politician, were warned by the German police and succeeded in escaping abroad.

*When Bhagwati Charan and his friends of the Hindustan Socialist Revolutionary Army planned to blow up the viceroy's train near Delhi in 1929, one of the group disguised himself as a fakir so as to study the locality without arousing suspicion. (Yashpal, *Singhavalokan II* (Lucknow, 1951), 93, quoted in Vajpeyi, *The Extremist Movement in India* (Allahabad, 1974), 247.

The Nazis boasted on occasion that they received copies of the secret communications of the police and of the ministry of the interior almost as soon as they had been dispatched from headquarters.[17] Latin American terrorists had well-wishers in key positions, and the multinational terrorist groups of the 1960s and 1970s, with almost unlimited funds at their disposal, had no difficulty in getting information, including presumably Interpol bulletins.

TERRORIST ARMS

The dagger and the pistol were the traditional terrorist weapons up to the dawning of the age of dynamite. The invention of the first time bomb is attributed to a M. Chevalier, a resident of Paris; he produced a cask filled with powder and missiles to which a musket barrel with a trigger was attached. A similar machine was used by one St. Regent, a former naval officer who tried to blow up Napoleon when he was still First Consul. The barrel was placed on a cart at the corner of the Rue Nicaise, on the road from the Tuilleries to the Rue Richelieu. A time fuse was used, but either St. Regent had miscalculated or Napoleon's driver was in a hurry — the explosion took place a little too late.[18] Explosives such as gunpowder and fulminate of mercury had been used before Alfred Nobel made his invention, and occasionally with great effect: 12 persons were killed and 120 injured in the Fenian mining of Clerkenwell Prison in December 1867; 500 pounds of black powder were used on that occasion. A decade earlier, in Paris, Orsini's bombs left 8 dead and 156 wounded. The quantities of explosives needed were considerable; it was difficult to transport them without arousing suspicion and it was only with the invention of nitroglycerine and later of nitrocellulose (gelignite) in the 1860s and 1870s that bombing and mining became much easier. It was widely believed at the time that dynamite was the ultimate weapon; the American and the French Anarchists based their whole strategy on its use and Patrick Rallihan of Brooklyn published a paper with the title *Ireland's Liberator and Dynamite Monthly.*[19]

Narodnaya Volya was the first to use dynamite on a wide scale; one of their members, Serge Kibalchich, was an accomplished scientist who introduced important innovations such as mixing nitroglycerine with other materials, using fulminate of mercury as a detonator.[20] But if the new explosives were highly effective they were also extremely dangerous. Quite a few Russian revolutionaries were killed while producing or transporting dynamite. Grinevetski was blown up by the very bomb which killed the tsar in 1881; Rokotilov was fatally injured while preparing bombs; Dembov lost his life while experimenting with dynamite, as did Schweitzer, one of the leaders of the Social Revolutionaries and their main weapons expert. Similar mishaps were frequent in the history of Irish terrorism, from the time of Captain Lomasney to present-day operations in Ulster. Since the early exaggerated hopes connected with dynamite were not fulfilled, the revolver, the rifle and even the dagger remained often-used terrorist weapons — President Carnot was knifed, as was Empress Elizabeth of Austria in 1898.

Dynamite was far more destructive than all previous explosives, but the quantities needed were still substantial. The average mine prepared by the Narodnaya Volya weighed sixty pounds or more and even then it did not always have the desired effect. Khalturin, who had access to the Winter Palace and placed a bomb there, asked his comrades for a mine of about two hundred pounds. They gave him only seventy pounds of dynamite which, as it emerged, was not enough for his purpose. The mines used by the Irish dynamiters of the 1880s were smaller and on the whole not very effective. In his handbook, Most had solemnly predicted that a ten-pound bomb would totally destroy any warship; the terrorists were learning by trial and error that this was just not so.[21]

The great technical problem that faced the terrorist during the last third of the nineteenth century was the miniaturization of bombs, the production of a hand grenade no bigger than an apple which could easily be hidden and thrown a considerable distance, while having as much explosive power as an old-fashioned mine. The Austrian terrorists of the 1880s experimented with metal boxes containing some five pounds of dynamite. But workable grenades of this weight were produced only by the Social Revolutionaries and were used in the killing of Plehwe and the Grand Duke Alexei.

The bomb clearly was not the all-destroying weapon it had been thought to be, but it had become a symbol replacing the barricade, and it certainly made a great deal of noise. Ivan Dragomiroff, the head of the Assassination Bureau in Jack London's novel, while giving a cut rate to anarchists, regretted their enthusiasm for dynamite and other extremely hazardous machines to insure that their executions were sensational and spectacular ("our killings must be red. . . ."). Dragomiroff charged them ten thousand dollars for the killing of a police chief of a great city, half a million for a major king or emperor, seventy-five to a hundred thousand for second- or third-rate kings.[22]

The American Irish made many suggestions for improving terrorist technology. These included an early version of the Molotov cocktail — a zinc vessel filled with a pint and a half of benzine regulated by a clock connected to it to light and burn for a certain time.[23] Rossa's plan for using osmic gas in the British Houses of Parliament has been mentioned. The British government was worried, unnecessarily as it emerged, by the reports concerning submarines built in New York. Sixty thousand dollars were spent on building three such vessels but it appears that only one was actually constructed, by Messrs. Delamater & Co. of New York. This "Torpedo Boat" was said to have "most wonderful powers as a destructive machine; more so than any boat yet invented."[24] But the ship never saw action. Captain McCafferty pioneered the idea of using a railway train and a steamer in a terrorist operation in the 1860s but the raid did not materialize.

The idea of preparing letter bombs seems to have first occurred to the Russian terrorists of the 1880s. They discussed the dispatch of small quantities of explosives to the tsar in little parcels purporting to contain drugs against rheumatism and asthma.[25] But this plan was apparently not carried out. Johann Most, in his journal and in his other writings, recommended incendiary devices contained in letters and small parcels, but again the technical difficulties were apparently insurmountable at the time.* One of the first successful cases

*The first recorded actual use of a letter bomb (or, to be precise, a parcel bomb weighing some twenty-five pounds) was in June 1895 when a package that was leaking was opened in a Berlin post office. It had been prepared and dispatched by Paul Koschemann, a mechanic twenty-one years of age with anarchist leanings. It was addressed to a senior police officer. But the addressee was not at all connected with the political police, nor did Koschemann have the backing of any organized group; the motive for the action did not become clearer in court. The design was primitive;

of assassination by means of a letter bomb was the killing of the Hungarian (Uniate) vicar general in Transylvania by a group of Rumanian terrorists just before the First World War. In 1908, Indian terrorists first used (unsuccessfully) a primitive letter bomb, or, to be precise, a book bomb. The Irgun used the technique on a few occasions and it was widely used by Arab terrorists and others in the early 1970s. Azev, the head of the Social Revolutionaries Fighting Organization, acutely feeling the need for innovation, told his comrades that new methods were needed since the police were familiar with all the old tricks. He intended to buy an automobile, and when he heard in 1906 that Buchalo, an anarchist engineer, was constructing a new type of airplane in Munich he gave him 20,000 rubles in the hope of using the plane in a future operation.[26] It was however only some seventy years later, in January 1974, that a plane was used for the first time in a terrorist operation, when the IRA dropped two bombs from a stolen helicopter. Buchalo's plane was never completed and motorcars were first used for terrorist purposes by the Bonnot gang in Paris in 1913 to facilitate their escape following bank raids. The modern submachine guns were first used, so far as can be established, by the IRA shortly after the First World War; Irish sympathizers had just delivered a few specimens of Colonel Thompson's new gun.[27]

If the terrorists did not find the miracle weapon, they had no great difficulties in obtaining firearms and explosives; there was usually ample opportunity for buying or stealing them. Arms for the Irish terrorists were smuggled in ships from the United States; revolvers for the Indian terrorists came from Britain. The Armenians smuggled some of their weapons from Russia and the Balkan terrorists received theirs from their protectors abroad. Army arsenals were always a potential source of supply, either because individual officers or soldiers sympathized with the terrorists or because the terrorists found some venal official. Following major wars, weapons and explosives were in ample supply all over the world. The Western Federation of Mine Workers in the United States certainly had no difficulty in

---

Koschemann used gunpowder, bottles filled with ligroin and a little revolver activated by an alarm clock was to serve as the detonator (H. Friedlaender, *Interessante Kriminalprozesse* (Berlin, 1922), II, 156). A few years later more sophisticated parcel bombs were already used by criminals in the United States (Roy A. Giles in *Scientific American* (April 1923), 226).

getting explosives for their operations in the early years of the century, and in the 1960s, with the emergence of multinational terrorism, plastic bombs and even missile launchers were transported from country to country under the seal of diplomatic baggage. Since the Second World War, explosives have been made even more effective and the new developments taken up by the terrorists with only a few years' delay.* TNT and picric acid, which had been the main military explosives in the First World War, have recently been replaced by the more powerful and durable RDX and PETN. New types of delay caps have come into use, while mercury fulminate, which served several generations of terrorists as both primary and secondary explosive, has gone out of fashion and considerable progress has been made with various Electro-Explosive Devices (EED). Arab terrorist groups have used Soviet-made RPG-2 and RPG-7 (Orly airport, 1975) grenade launchers and SA-7 heat-seeking rockets (Rome airport, 1973). Reports that American terrorists were experimentally manufacturing nerve gas were later denied.[28] Some bombs were carried in shopping bags or suitcases; at other times cars were used to store the explosives. The fuses were fired electrically, by pressure, by chemical methods; most recently photoelectric and X-ray-sensitive fuses have been used.[29] But with all these technological advances the accident rate among terrorists has remained high. Few terrorists use homemade explosives these days, and the accidents usually occur not in laboratories but while transporting the explosives or preparing the charges. There are no foolproof explosives, and as the technology has become more complicated few terrorists have the technical know-how required to handle them competently.

---

*The first booby-trapped bombs appeared well before the First World War. The public was warned that it was dangerous to tear out a burning fuse and then freely handle the bomb for "many dynamiters are ingenious enough to attach the fuses to the more dangerous bombs of the liquid type in order to mislead the finder" ("Studying the Anarchists' bombs scientifically," *Scientific American* (July 1911), 100; the article had been published originally in a German periodical *Reclam's Universum*). The great technical difficulties involved in the construction of homemade bombs were amply described in the professional literature. (See, for instance, Jules Bebie, *Manual of Explosives* (New York, 1943), 156.) Some of these complications vanished with the appearance of plastic explosives such as Nexit which were apparently used for the first time in the assassination of Heydrich, the head of the Gestapo in Prague on May 29, 1942. The bomb which exploded in Hitler's bunker on July 20, 1944, consisted of a similar material, presumably cyclonite mixed with a plasticizing medium.

COUNTERTERRORISM

Police forces in democratic societies, applying traditional methods, have found it exceedingly difficult to cope with terrorist activities. There are not enough policemen to deal with an enemy likely to strike at any time against almost any target. Even in a totalitarian regime the police force cannot guarantee the life of the dictator against attempted assassination by one man acting entirely on his own. Terrorists do sometimes fail through sheer incompetence — because they do not adhere to their own timetable, such as happened so often with nineteenth-century Irish terrorists, or because too many people know about the plot. Sometimes their weapons are not in good working order and sometimes they are simply out of luck. But they have the great advantage that, unlike the security forces in a democratic society, they do not have to act within the law. The police must not use illegal methods to repress terrorism — in theory, if not always in practice. They cannot engage in indiscriminate arrests nor torture captured terrorists to extract information. The forces of law and order have not always been able to hold those already arrested and sentenced; one need only recall the mass escapes from prison and internment camps of Irish terrorists or of members of the Irgun and the Stern Gang. Russian revolutionaries (including Bakunin, Kropotkin, Deitch, Savinkov, Trotsky and many others) escaped from prison or from Siberia. Hence it became and becomes ever more necessary for the police to collect information via informers. The success of the British police in repressing Irish terrorism throughout the nineteenth century was largely due to the presence of a few agents in the ranks of the terrorists (Leonard MacNally, Nagle, Corydon, Richard Pigott, "Red" Jim MacDermott, "Nero," Massey. The "Prince of Spies" was Major Le Caron (1841–1894) who first informed his father in 1865 that he had been contacted by an Irish revolutionary organization: the father told the police, and Le Caron supplied important information for the next two decades. His cover in the United States was that of an agent for drug manufacturers and he was thus able to travel constantly. Le Caron later wrote that he had done his duty as a man who loved his country and saw it threatened by a deadly and unscrupulous foe. "I consider myself a military spy and my conduct justifiable under the same ethical considerations which justify all military spies."[30] The French police were served by Lucien de la Hodde, the master spy and provocateur of the 1830s and 1840s, who later published an interesting if somewhat subjective history of the secret societies.[31] Even earlier, Baboeuf's conspiracy had been betrayed by Grisel, who in the words of Buonarroti had pretended to be the "most outrageous patriot"; the Dekabrist plot was denounced by Sherwood. Andrieux, prefect of the Paris police, had his agents among the Anarchists; he provided money for Anarchist newspapers and later wrote that though he fought Anarchism he preferred the spread of their doctrine by the press rather than by other means and saw "no reason for depriving myself longer of their gratitude."[32] The German and Austrian Anarchist movements were riddled with police spies, who included some of Most's closest collaborators. When Most was in a British prison, *Freiheit* was published by Schroeder, a police agent in Schaffhausen.[33] But these police agents were inclined, as Bismarck once put it in a letter to his wife, to "lie and exaggerate in a most inexcusable manner." For want of material, when there was nothing to report, they and their superiors began to play politics and to instigate acts of violence. Some of the heads of the Okhrana were past masters in this game; they had had their agents among the revolutionaries since the late 1880s, with Harting-Landesen as the most prominent among them. By 1912 the Okhrana had some 26,000 paid agents, most of them part-time informers, and in addition a permanent staff of some 50,000. Informers were paid between twenty and fifty rubles a month but Azev had a monthly salary of five hundred by 1902 and in later years presumably got even more.[34] Azev, a young Jewish engineer, had offered his services to the political police while studying in Germany. With the approval and help of his bosses he worked his way up in the Fighting Organization of the Social Revolutionaries until he became its commander. But his was a complex personality, for he was neither a petty provocateur out for a few rubles nor an admirer of the Tsarist system. He played a very intricate double game and, while betraying many of his comrades, also misled the Okhrana by withholding from them essential information about forthcoming terrorist operations. He was involved in the assassination of Plehwe and the Grand Duke Serge Alexeievich and other leading personalities. He was eventually unmasked in 1908 and the Social Revolutionary Fighting Organization never recovered from the blow. While he was active, much of the time and energy of the Okhrana had to be invested in combatting acts of terror they had themselves instigated. Azev's protectors in the Okhrana were driven by personal ambitions and rivalries, but they were also convinced that they had to demonstrate to the government (and public opinion) that there was a major terrorist menace which had to be fought against. For this purpose they needed occasional demonstration effects such as the assassination of highly placed personalities.[35] Mention has been made of the fact that a considerable proportion of the terrorist journals of the 1880s and 1890s were in fact founded or maintained by secret police money. The tendency of the secret police was usually to discredit the terrorists by sheer exaggeration. One such Russian emigré paper called not only for the killing of all landowners but also for the destruction of all their cattle.[36] Terrorist journals would accuse each other of cooperating with the police — and on occasion both were right. There was enormous confusion; those who had provided the funds obviously got value for money. In Russia special units were established to combat terrorism. These units acted separately from and often in competition with and opposition to the general police forces. This approach prevailed in most countries. When Brackenbury was appointed under secretary for police by Gladstone after the Phoenix Park murders in 1881, he argued from the very beginning that the police were quite incapable of coping with secret societies and that for this purpose a (secret and separate) organization was needed with a budget of its own (£20,000 at the time) to infiltrate the terrorists and "break their nerve."[37] But the British officials, unlike the heads of the Okhrana, did not believe in a mammoth counterorganization — nor would they have obtained a sufficiently high budget to keep such an apparatus going. Unless the terrorist movement was very strong and/or highly decentralized, a few police agents strategically placed were quite sufficient to paralyze the whole movement. One single agent, James McParlan, acting on behalf of the Pinkerton Agency, caused the downfall of the Molly Maguires in the 1870s.

TEMPTATIONS AND DANGERS

The most dangerous threat to terrorists is the promise of a reward
for information leading to their capture. This weapon has, of course,
been widely used. After the Phoenix Park murders an almost unprecedented reward of £10,000 was promised. Gershuni, the head of
the Fighting Organization of the Social Revolutionaries, had a price
of 15,000 rubles on his head. The Weimar government promised a
reward of one million marks for information leading to the capture
of the Rathenau murderers. In this way Nazi security forces caught
Heydrich's assassins and effectively smashed most of the Allied underground in occupied France. A terrorist, unlike a guerrilla, cannot
hide in forests, jungles and desolate mountain ranges; he has to find
cover among people, many of whom will feel no sympathy for him.
He needs a roof over his head, food and other supplies. He is never
alone in the big city, some people will know of his whereabouts,
many more will have their suspicions. He is exceedingly vulnerable,
and the greed of an informer or the ill-will of an enemy can over-
come the fear of vengeance — especially if the reward is high
enough.[38] But police forces in democratic societies have never been
at liberty to use this weapon to full effect, since informing has never
been considered an occupation for gentlemen and there has almost
always been opposition to encouraging the practice. After the Irish
dynamiters' attempt to blow up London Bridge in the 1880s a reward
of £5,000 was first promised — and then withdrawn. Furthermore,
the size of rewards in the 1960s and 1970s has been proportionally
much smaller than in the nineteenth century, and with the bureau-
cratization of police work informing has become much riskier. A
nineteenth-century police chief in Britain, France or Russia could
dispose of relatively large sums with no questions asked. Sir Robert
Anderson, from whom Joseph Conrad drew some of his inspiration
for the *Secret Agent,* related with some pride that his idea of secrecy
was not to tell the secretary of state:

> The first Fenian who ever gave me information was murdered on his
> arrival in New York. I had given his name to no one but Lord Mayo;
> and he assured me that he had mentioned it only to the Lord Lieuten-

ant, when sitting alone with him after dinner at the vice-regal lodge. But there happened to be a servant behind the screen, and through him it was, as the Dublin police ascertained, that the information reached the Fenians. Never again would I give an informant's name to anyone and no man who afterwards gave me information was ever betrayed.[39]

Today the chain of command in the police is far more complicated; decisions are taken by committees, officials are responsible to their superiors, accountants have to be informed and it may be very difficult to keep the identity of the informer secret. But the reward remains the most effective weapon by far, and when in 1975 Mr. Ross McWhirter was killed by the IRA it was precisely because he had announced a substantial reward to be given for the collection of information.

Many captured terrorists have behaved with great dignity and even heroism. Leonid Andreyev (*The Seven that were Hanged* [1908]) described the whole gamut of emotions among a group of Russian revolutionaries sentenced to death: "Werner, totally sure of himself, young Tanya caring like a mother for her comrades, Vasily absorbed in a frightful struggle 'between the intolerable terror of death and the desperate desire to subdue his fear and conceal it from his judges.'"

But not all men and women are heroes (or have suicidal impulses), and quite a few terrorists have broken down during interrogation though they were neither tortured nor even threatened with violence. Some have not even been promised that their sentence would be reduced. Every case has been different: some realized that what they had done was wrong. Ivan Okladski proudly declared at his trial in October 1880 that he would be deeply offended if he did not receive a death sentence. Soon afterward he became a police agent on a monthly salary of 200 rubles. Merkulov also became a police official. Mirski, Goldenberg and Rysakov quite unnecessarily implicated their comrades in their depositions; they were young, inexperienced and confused. Rysakov was executed anyway and Goldenberg committed suicide in prison after he had realized the enormity of his betrayal. There were those who after their arrest became police agents, others who pretended to serve the police but had no intention of working for their new masters, and there were all possible variations in between. Some acted as double agents with the knowledge of their comrades. As the result of Degayev's betrayal in 1883, the whole existing apparatus of the Narodnaya Volya was destroyed. The police engineered his escape from prison but Degayev deeply regretted his betrayal; to expiate his crime, he killed Sudeykin, a high official of the "third section." Degayev later voluntarily submitted to a trial by a revolutionary tribunal in Paris which expelled him. He went to the United States, changed his name to "Dr. Pell," graduated in mathematics from Johns Hopkins University, became a professor at the Armour Institute of Technology, and died at Bryn Mawr in 1921.[40]

Solomon Ryss ("Mortimer"), one of the leaders of the Maximalists, also collaborated with the police after his arrest; he too was helped to escape but returned to terrorist work and was again captured and this time hanged. His case, like that of Bagrov, the police agent who killed Stolypin, has remained a mystery to this day.[41] Among the anarchists there were few such startling intrigues and double games simply because most of them had acted alone, without the knowledge and help of an organization.

In Ireland too, cooperation with the police was by no means infrequent; Carey, one of the chief accused in the Phoenix Park murder trial, turned Queen's evidence. He was acquitted and left Britain, but was killed, allegedly by an "avenger" in circumstances that have remained obscure, on board a ship sailing between Cape Town and Port Elizabeth.

Many terrorist groups have attracted criminal elements at one time or another. Some originally bona fide politicals later turned to crime, others, such as the Mafia, were predominantly criminal from the very beginning but also had political interests. The dividing line between politics and crime was by no means always obvious and clear-cut: criminals were quite often good patriots or instinctive revolutionaries (or reactionaries) and they certainly could teach the terrorists more than a few tricks of the trade. But they would not accept discipline and their presence caused friction, corruption and eventually demoralization. The temptation to use the loot for private gain or to settle personal accounts was overwhelming. The Bonnot gang, the *bande tragique,* operating in Paris in 1912, kept 90 percent of their booty for personal use and only the remainder was allocated to the cause. Sometimes former terrorists engaged in blackmail or entered the protection racket. There was the famous case of Juan Rull who prepared bombs which were deposited by his old mother in the streets of Barcelona. As long as he was paid a monthly retainer by the authorities there were no bombs. Of great psychological interest are the terrorist groups which gradually changed their character. The lofty ideals of IMRO were movingly described in the diary of a young member:

> We know that the revolutionary is something of an ascetic who has given up the idea of enjoyment and personal happiness. Not one of us will marry and settle down. No one will leave Macedonia or think of studying. Whoever marries or leaves Macedonia or enrolls in a university is a villain, a traitor. Macedonia cannot wait. . . . There can be no other lover. . . .[42]

This was written on January 1, 1902; three decades later IMRO still existed, but it had become a group of hired assassins.

Criminal elements joined the ranks of terrorist groups in times of general unrest when there were good chances for looting, as in the Russian revolution of 1905, and on many subsequent occasions. The "Symbionese Liberation Army," like some early terrorist sects but unlike the Narodniks, deliberately enlisted criminals; they did not go to the people but to the underworld. In the age of the highly specialized multinational terrorism of the 1970s with so many interested parties and paymasters involved, it is no longer possible to know with any degree of accuracy to what extent these terrorists are still motivated by revolutionary or nationalist fervor or by any "cause" at all. Some undoubtedly are; for others it has simply become a way of life — the only one they know.

External dangers apart, terrorist groups have always been threatened by internal dissension. Most terrorist groups came into being in the first place as the result of a split between the moderate and the more extreme wing of an already-existing organization, and almost all of them later underwent further fission. This is true of the Narodnaya Volya, the Social Revolutionaries, the Fenians, the Spanish, Italian and American Anarchists, Irgun, the Palestinian Arab terrorists and, of course, the terrorists of the 1960s and 1970s. Outwardly, these splits were ideologically based but underlying political differences there was usually a clash of personalities. Terrorists' fighting potential was not always reduced thereby; despite their disagreements they did not necessarily strike at one another. The Socialist Revolutionaries did not attack the Maximalists; Irgun and LEHI kept a truce, and there has been an understanding of sorts between the various Palestinian Arab terrorists, and between the ERP and the Montoneros. In some ways these splits made the task of the police even more difficult, for its resources had to be spread even more thinly. In other cases, rivalry between terrorist groups led to bloody clashes: the Irish troubles in the early 1920s, the killing of IRA regulars by Provisionals and vice versa, the feud between Mikhailovists and Protogerovists in Bulgaria (40 of the former and 220 of the latter were killed between 1924 and 1934). Besides interfactional strife there was always the tendency in an underground movement to liquidate those who challenged the authority of the leader, as happened among the Iron Guard in Rumania and in various Latin American terrorist movements. Sometimes a leading member would be shot because he was considered a liability to the whole group (the case of "Shaul" in LEHI). In other cases mere suspicion of treason (*Verräter verfallen der Fehme* — the Freikorps) would be sufficient cause for murder. Dr. Patrick Cronin, the American-Irish patriot, was killed in May 1889 simply because he had accused another leader of misappropriating funds. This case profoundly shocked the whole movement; 12,000 men and women walked past his bier. History, as Albert Camus has noted, offers few examples of fanatics suffering from scruples. The Russian terrorists of 1881 and of 1905 were an exception, but from that time on a general decline set in and there have been few of which it could be said, as Savinkov said about Dora Brilliant, that terror weighed on them like a cross. Killing without hesitation, often without thought and reason, has become the rule, not the exception.

VARIETIES OF TERRORIST TACTICS

The assassination of leading representatives of the "system" is the oldest method and has been the one most frequently adopted by terrorists.[43] Indiscriminate terror has become widespread only in recent times with the invention of more effective explosives on one hand and the emergence of the modern mass media on the other. The case for indiscriminate murder is, of course, well known: it dramatizes the demands of the terrorists; it spreads a climate of fear and discredits the government incapable of suppressing it; and, if frequently repeated, it disrupts the normal functioning of society. At the same time, from the terrorist point of view it is far less risky than attempts against the lives of leading personalities who may be well guarded.

The drawbacks of indiscriminate terror are equally obvious — "intimidation by deed" will not gain political support and it is therefore mostly used against foreigners or by very small terrorist groups lacking both a clear political aim and a consistent strategy.

If the "death penalty" is the rule, other punishment has occasionally been meted out by terrorist groups; the Tupamaros set up "people's prisons" but the inmates were usually hostages to be released upon receipt of money. Irish terrorists have occasionally inflicted injuries on suspected minor spies or "collaborationists" and this has also been the practice of the Ku Klux Klan and similar organizations — ranging from beating up the victim and tarring and feathering to permanently depriving him of the use of a limb.

The second most frequent kind of terrorist operation has been "expropriation," i.e., bank robbery, or, less frequently, robbery of mail trains or vans transferring large sums of money. The Russian terrorists first attacked a bank in 1879 and the practice spread rapidly during the first Russian revolution (1905–1906). In October 1906 alone there were some 362 "expropriations." The most notable was the robbery (by the Maximalists) of a bank in Fonarny Pereulok in Moscow when some twenty assailants seized nearly a million rubles. Polish terrorists were even more successful in 1908, attacking the St. Petersburg–Warsaw mail train and getting away with more than two million rubles. The Bolsheviks netted more than 300,000 rubles when "Kamo" and his comrades robbed a convoy in Tiflis in June 1907. Banks were occasionally robbed by the Irgun and the Stern Gang and also by the small European and North American terrorist groups. It became almost a daily occurrence in Latin America in the late 1960s; it was generally considered the easiest kind of operation, in which new recruits could be tested. Well-established terrorist groups collected contributions from supporters or extracted money by threats. This was the practice among the Macedonian IMRO and the Palestinian terrorists before they received regular major allocations from the oil states.

The liberation of captured comrades from prison has always been a top priority for terrorists. The Fenians equipped and dispatched a ship (the *Catalpa*) to Australia to help in the escape of six of their members who had been exiled there. Their attempts to liberate Fenian prisoners in Clerkenwell and Manchester failed, with tragic consequences. Narodnaya Volya had to shelve a project to liberate Nechaev, for Schlüsselburg was too well guarded. But there were individual and mass escapes, usually with some help from outside, in Tsarist Russia, Mandatory Palestine (Latrun and Acre), Ulster, West Germany, Uruguay and Argentina.

Kidnapping for political purposes and the extortion of ransoms has been practiced since time immemorial. In 1819, Guiglielmo Pepe, Neapolitan general and Italian patriot, planned to capture Emperor Franz I and Metternich. But this plot proved to be as unrealistic as the Fenians' scheme in the 1860s to abduct the Prince of Wales. In 1920, the IRA kidnapped a British general while he was fishing. In the United States, following the arrest of Socialist militants and their extradition across state lines in the early years of the century, Eugene Debs threatened retaliation in kind: if kidnapping was a legitimate practice "we all have a perfect right to engage in it. . . ."[44] And he proposed that for every working man kidnapped a capitalist should be seized and held for ransom; the kidnapping of the first capitalist would convulse the nation. Even earlier, in a pamphlet published in London in 1903, Vladimir Burtsev had recommended kidnapping as one of the tactics to be used in the terrorist struggle, but his advice was not heeded by the Social Revolutionaries. In 1947 the Irgun kidnapped (and later hanged) two British sergeants in a futile attempt to prevent the execution of two of their members under sentence of death.

Abduction became exceedingly fashionable in the late 1960s. Among those kidnapped, to mention but a few of the outstanding cases, were the United States ambassadors to Guatemala and Brazil, the West German ambassadors to Guatemala, Haiti and Brazil; Aramburu, the former president of Argentina (May 1970); Pierre

Laporte, Quebec labor minister (October 1970); the Swiss ambassador to Brazil; the British ambassador to Uruguay (kidnapped in January 1971, released in September); the leader of the West Berlin Christian Democrats, as well as the whole OPEC executive in Vienna (December 1975), and countless consuls, public figures, businessmen, officers and even racing drivers, football stars and men and women who could not be considered public figures by any stretch of the imagination.[45] In some cases, no ransom terms were demanded and the victims were killed after a few hours or days; more often the release was made conditional on the release of political prisoners and payment of ransom and, of course, safe passage. In some of these instances huge ransoms were paid: in Argentina, $1,000,000 for Mr. Aaron Beilinson (May 1973); $2,000,000 for Charles Lockwood, a British business executive (June 1973); $3,000,000 for Mr. John R. Thompson (representing Firestone Tires, June 1973); Exxon allegedly paid $14,200,000 for Mr. Victor Samuelson, and Bunge and Born $60,-000,000 for three of their executives. In yet other cases, such as the OPEC hijack, no clear demands were made by the kidnappers. After 1973 the number of kidnappings decreased, partly, no doubt, for technical reasons. For while guerrillas can always conduct their hostages to a "liberated area," terrorists have, of course, much greater difficulty in hiding their victims.

This list of the varieties of terrorist activities is far from complete; agrarian terror was practiced in Andalusia in the early 1880s by a mysterious organization called the *Maño Negra*.[46] Agrarian terrorism also took place in Ireland, in eastern Poland and in north Germany (in the 1920s) against big landowners, tax collectors or government representatives. Industrialists and trade union leaders have been threatened and occasionally killed in labor disputes and systematic intimidation has been used against judges and journalists. A Berlin chief justice, von Drenkman, was killed by terrorists in West Berlin in the autumn of 1974. A fairly typical incident which took place before 1933 was described by a Nazi publication after Hitler had come to power. It was directed against a "disgusting scribbler" called Paeschke who edited a left-wing newspaper in the city of Reichenbach. Every day the storm troopers were subjected to poisonous comment and as a result a "few courageous men" decided to give this villain the deserts he had so amply deserved. Paeschke was to be killed on the way home from his office; unfortunately the artillery shell which was to serve as a landmine exploded in the hands of the SA man who carried it.[47] Similar methods were used in various parts of the world by left-wing and right-wing terrorists against public figures, sometimes to intimidate, at other times to kill. In February 1971 the Tupamaros kidnapped Homero Farina, editor of *Acción*, because (in their own words) "we wanted to make clear the role played by the media at that time, namely, the role of being part of the repressive forces. . . . We do ask them not to tell too many lies; we understand we cannot ask them not to lie at all because the lie is essential to bourgeois journalism."[48] Farina was released after eighteen days, having been given a stern warning.

Perhaps the most dramatic new technique used by terrorists has been the hijacking of airplanes. One of the first recorded cases was that of a Peruvian plane in 1931 during a military coup in that country. Between 1945 and 1950, some 25 hijackings took place; in most cases refugees from Iron Curtain countries used aircraft to escape to the West. During the 1960s, a great many American planes were compelled to fly to Cuba, not always by political terrorists — there were twenty-two such cases in 1968 and forty the year after. But, following an agreement between the United States and Cuba in 1969, the number fell rapidly. In July 1968, Palestinian terrorist organizations first hijacked an El Al plane which was flown to Algeria; the last passengers were released only after some eighteen arrested Arab terrorists had been freed in Israel. Following the introduction of stringent security measures, no further Israeli planes were successfully seized after that date. But the hijacking of third country aircraft increased rapidly, culminating in the Zerka incident in 1970 when several jumbo jets were compelled to land in an airfield in Jordan and were subsequently destroyed. These operations attracted enormous attention at the time, and great apprehension was expressed with regard to the future of civil aviation. But these fears were exaggerated — after 1972 there was a steady decrease, partly due to more effective security measures at airports and partly because of the growing reluctance of governments, even among the Arabs, to provide shelter for hijackers. Moreover, it was a case of diminishing returns, for there were few tangible achievements and even the publicity value of hijacking decreased with repetition.[49]

TERRORISM AND THE MEDIA

If individual journalists have suffered at the hands of terrorists, terrorist attitudes toward the media as a whole have been friendly, and with good reason. The success of a terrorist operation depends almost entirely on the amount of publicity it receives. This was one of the main reasons for the shift from rural guerrilla to urban terror in the 1960s; for in the cities the terrorists could always count on the presence of journalists and TV cameras and consequently a large audience. In the words of a Latin American terrorist: "If we put even a small bomb in a building in town we could be certain of making the headlines in the press. But if the 'rural' guerilleros liquidated some thirty soldiers there was just a small news item on the last page. The city is exceedingly important both for the political struggle and for propaganda."[50] The lesson was quickly learned by North African and Arab terrorists. Thus an Algerian leader: "Is it better for our cause to kill ten of our enemies in a remote village where this will not cause comment, or to kill one man in Algiers where the American press will get hold of the story the next day?" Abdul Fatah Ismail, who headed the anti-British struggle in the Aden protectorate, reached similar conclusions; the struggle in the countryside was not worthwhile because no attention would be paid to it.[51]

Thus, in the final analysis, it is not the magnitude of the terrorist operation that counts but the publicity; and this rule applies not only to single operations but to whole campaigns. Throughout the year 1975 twenty-six Israeli civilians were killed as well as fourteen soldiers and seven tourists as a result of terrorist operations — a number of victims considerably less than those killed in Argentina or Ulster in one month, or in Beirut during one night.[52] But far more foreign journalists are stationed in Israel than in Ulster or Argentina and so the impression was created that internal security had broken down and that a major political explosion was about to take place. The media, with their inbuilt tendency toward sensationalism, have always magnified terrorist exploits quite irrespective of their intrinsic importance. Terrorist groups numbering perhaps a dozen members have been described as "armies," their "official communiqués" have been discussed in countless television shows, radio broadcasts, articles and editorials. In a few cases even nonexistent groups have been given a great deal of publicity. All modern terrorist groups need publicity; the smaller they are, the more they depend on it, and this has, to a large extent, affected the choice of their targets. Even an apparently illogical or senseless attack becomes more effective if given wide coverage in the media than an operation against a seemingly obvious target. Thus Orsini chose Napoleon III as his target rather than some Italian ruler or a high Austrian official. Terrorist operations in Paraguay, the Philippines or Bangladesh will hardly ever be newsworthy, but an attack by Paraguayan or Philippine terrorists directed against their embassies in Washington, London or Paris will receive extensive coverage, and if they should choose the president of the United States or the head of some West European country as their victim they will receive even more publicity. It need scarcely be pointed out that such strategies work only in societies which have no censorship.

POPULAR SUPPORT

Terrorist groups usually hope for a measure of public support. Extreme nationalists operating against foreigners can always count on some sympathy among their fellow countrymen. The misguided actions of a few hotheads will be condemned but at the same time extenuating circumstances will be found to explain, if not altogether to excuse, their behavior. This goes for Irish, Basque and Palestinian terrorists, whereas public support for Armenian, Indian and Jewish (Irgun and LEHI) terrorism was less wholehearted because their activities were considered politically harmful.

Nationalist terrorist movements can at the very least expect not to be betrayed by their compatriots. In Palestine, the cooperation between the Hagana and the British Mandatory government against the "dissidents" (i.e., terrorists) was a rare exception and took place while the Second World War was still in progress. The support mustered by terrorists fighting their own government depends very much on the plausibility of their cause. The operations of Narodnaya Volya had not the slightest impact on the peasantry and very little on the working class. But the intelligentsia was overwhelmingly in sympathy, and the same was true for the next generation of Russian revolutionaries. The two major Russian writers who, in their novels, depicted terrorists in a negative light, Leskov and Dostoyevski, were never forgiven by the Russian intelligentsia even though they made amends in their later works, for example Dostoyevski's Pushkin anniversary speech. In intellectual circles such criticism was anathema; there was the belief — as in Latin America today — that even if the terrorists tended to make mistakes, they were motivated by a deep humanism and the desire to build a better world, and for this reason even their outrages were forgiven. In Western Europe support was limited, by and large, to fairly small sections of the intelligentsia. Quite a few French writers and artists toyed with Anarchism in the 1880s and 1890s, among them Zola, Paul Adam, Octave Mirbeau, Mallarmé, Pissaro, Seurat, Signac and Steinlen. They could understand the motives of a Vaillant and Emile Henry, even a Ravachol; they would sign petitions on behalf of Vaillant since no one had been killed by the bomb he had thrown: "We were all anarchists without throwing bombs," Kees van Donghen wrote in later years, "we had those kinds of ideas."[53] Mallarmé appeared as a character witness on behalf of his Anarchist friend Fénéon. Clemenceau, watching the execution of Emile Henry, was deeply disturbed; he saw a man (he wrote) with the face of a tormented Christ, terribly pale, implacable in expression, "trying to impose his intellectual pride upon his child's body." There was some sympathy even from the extreme right which hated the Third Republic and everything it stood for, and on the part of aesthetes like Laurent Tailhade whose *petite phrase* became immortal: *"Qu'importe les victimes si le geste est beau."* Tailhade, who lost an eye in a subsequent terrorist attack, was not exactly a man of the left, looking forward (as he once wrote) to the happy days when the plebs would kiss the poets' footprints. . . . But this was purely platonic support; in the last resort even the French intellectuals of the left were horrified by the senseless violence perpetrated by the Anarchists. There was even less sympathy for terrorism in Britain, and in the United States. There was some support for the victims of the Haymarket trial, but chiefly because those executed were almost certainly innocent of the crime.

The working-class terrorism of later years, such as the McNamara brothers' bombing of the *Los Angeles Times* building, was attacked even by the left; such acts, it was argued, were commercial, not idealistic. Enthusiasm for the terrorism of the 1960s was limited in extent and, like most fashions in America, short-lived.

Right-wing terrorists in Weimar Germany could almost always count on lenient judges and on support, hidden or open, from the nationalist parties. The murderers of Erzberger and Rathenau became heroes in these circles, for, to paraphrase a famous slogan of the period, there were "no enemies on the right." The Baader-Meinhof Gang and the June 2 Movement had some sympathizers among left-wing intellectuals; there was no attempt to justify their actions but they were understood: society was mainly to blame, not the terrorists. Thus, after Ulrike Meinhof's suicide in May 1976, a group of French intellectuals (including Sartre, Simone de Beauvoir, Claude Bourdet, Claude Mauriac and others) published an appeal deploring Meinhof's "inhuman sufferings" and stated that the practices of the federal German government reminded them of Nazism.[53] This despite the fact that the members of the Baader-Meinhof group and the June 2 Movement had been kept in prison in conditions of almost unparalleled permissiveness, and that, while in prison, they had in fact continued to direct the terrorist operations of those members of their group who were still at liberty.

In Latin America as in pre-revolutionary Russia, there has traditionally been a reservoir of goodwill for what the terrorists stand for. True, the Tupamaros and the Brazilian ALN were bitterly criticized by the left for their misguided and counterproductive actions. But in an emergency they could always rely on the support of intellectuals, churchmen and sections of the middle class to defend them against the harsher forms of government repression.

INTERNATIONAL LINKS

There have been conspiratorial ties between revolutionary groups in Europe since the early part of the nineteenth century with Mazzini's Young Europe as the precursor. But these relations were largely abstract, limited to verbal or written expressions of sympathy and solidarity. There was a great deal of cross-fertilization: the example of the Russian terrorists of 1881 inspired the Fenians and above all the Anarchists; the Russian Social Revolutionaries, the Italian terrorists of the nineteenth century and the early IRA found imitators in many parts of the world. It was certainly not true (as alleged at the time) that "Russian gold and Russian craft" governed Armenian terrorism. But the leaders of the movement who came to Turkey in 1892 were certainly of Russian origin.[55] The Indian nationalist press, on the other hand, frequently stressed that the application of "Russian methods" by the British administration was bound to lead to Russian methods of agitation, and a British committee of investigation on terrorism in India noted that, together with the emphasis on religious motives, Bengali terrorist propaganda dwelt heavily upon the "Russian rules" of revolutionary violence.[56] There were a few cases of active collaboration: Orsini had British friends who helped to pay for his bombs. In later years there was a London group of British friends of the Russian revolution which contributed to pro-terrorist publications. The Fenians consulted the French General Cluseret when planning a rising in 1867; at a later date the Clan na-Gael played with the idea of enlisting Russian help against Britain, just as Pilsudski envisaged an anti-Russian alliance with the Japanese. Devoy suggested helping the Mahdi with 20,000 armed Irishmen; John Mac-Bride and Arthur Lynch fought in the Boer War against the British.[57] Italian Anarchists operated in France, Switzerland and Spain as well as in their own country; Indian terrorists received theoretical instruction from the Russian Social Revolutionaries. Sometimes active intervention by foreign powers was alleged; thus Miguel Angiolilo, who killed the Spanish prime minister, Canovas, in August 1897, was said to have been paid by the Cuban rebels against the Spanish, but this has not been proved. Russian involvement with the Serbian Black Hand is well known, but whether the Russians actually knew about the preparations for the murder at Sarajevo is not at all certain; the Black Hand had in fact voted on June 14, 1914, against the assassination precisely because it feared war would ensue. Whether "Apis," who organized the assassination, informed his Russian contacts of the vote is doubtful. But the aims of the Black Hand certainly transcended Serbia; in 1911 they had planned the assassination of the king of Greece.

Neighboring countries often provided a sanctuary for terrorists; the Social Revolutionaries escaped whenever they could to semi-autonomous Finland where the Okhrana could not operate with as much ease as in Russia proper. One of the Sarajevo conspirators of 1914, Mehmedbasic, escaped to Montenegro; when the Austrians demanded his extradition, the government went through an elaborate charade of searching for him but in fact let him escape arrest. In later years IMRO had such a base for its forays in Bulgaria, the Croatians in Italy and Hungary, the IRA in the Republic of Ireland, the Palestinians first in Jordan and later in Lebanon. But for the existence of these sanctuaries many groups would have had to cease operations.

Mention has been made of the fact that the massive systematic involvement of governments in terrorist movements in foreign countries dates back to the 1920s. The Italians were most active in this respect; Balbo, Ciano and other Fascist luminaries met the leaders of the Croat Ustasha, provided them with every possible help and after the murder at Marseilles, Kvaternik and Pavelic, the main wire-pullers, escaped to Italy. The Italians refused to extradite them and at the same time Mussolini bitterly attacked those charging Italy with abetting terrorism: "We do not give our hands to murderers. Those who want to implicate Italy are cowards and liars." Declarations of this kind on the part of the Libyan and Algerian governments became quite frequent in the 1960s and 1970s. Italy also gave money and supplied arms to the Macedonian IMRO. Previously IMRO had gravitated toward the Soviet Union but opposition within the organization (and on the part of official Bulgarian circles) prevented a rapprochement with Moscow. The Italians also supported the French CSAR *(Comité Secret d'Action Révolutionnaire),* a right-wing terrorist group founded by Eugène Deloncle in 1936. These were the *cagoulards,* the hooded men, who assassinated, among others, the brothers Rosselli, leaders of the Italian anti-Fascist group *Giustizia è Libertà,* in their French exile. For these and other services rendered, the Italians sent the CSAR 12,000 hand grenades, 170 machine guns and submachine guns, as well as hundreds of pounds of explosives.[58] Right-wing terrorist groups in Germany after the First World War seem to have received only minimal help from abroad and the Rumanian legionaries apparently obtained none at all.

Nationalist terrorist groups usually had no scruples in looking for, and accepting, aid from foreign powers. Thus LEHI sent emissaries to Beirut in 1940 to establish contact with Italian and German officials, and four years later sought a link with Soviet representatives. IRA leaders collaborated with Nazi Germany during the Second World War, which did not prevent them from accepting help from communist countries two decades later. Members of LEHI or the IRA were not necessarily either Fascist or Communist. Like the Croats, the IMRO, the Palestinian Arabs or the Indian terrorists, they acted according to the time-honored principle that the enemy of their enemy was their friend. Some foreign aid was given without strings attached but this was not always so. The fact that Lenin accepted German money in 1917 did not make him a German agent — but not all terrorists had the strength of character and the clarity of vision of Lenin. Prolonged and substantial subventions by foreign governments usually had a demoralizing effect on both the leadership and the rank and file of terrorist movements, who became increasingly dependent on their sponsors. Sometimes, when the payments were stopped, the terrorists would turn against the paymasters — more often the movement would simply collapse, as happened to the IMRO after the Bulgarians withdrew their support.

Multinational terrorism reached its climax in the early 1970s, involving close cooperation between small terrorist groups in many countries, with the Libyans, the Algerians, the North Koreans and the Cubans acting as paymasters, suppliers of weapons and other equipment as well as coordinators, a fascinating amalgam of Communism East European and Latin American style, North African "clerico-fascism," West European anarchism, unpolitical technicians of terror and probably also a few madmen and madwomen. The Soviet Union supported a number of terrorist movements such as some Palestinian and African groups and the exile Croats; mostly such assistance would be given through various intermediaries so that its origins would be difficult to prove and any charges of complicity could be indignantly denied. Even the Libyans, who provide support to terrorists all over the world, will not always admit it. Countries such as South Yemen, Somalia and Uganda cooperated with the terrorists for both political and financial reasons, but this was represented as a humanitarian act motivated by the desire to save human lives. In short, terrorism became almost respectable, and there was a substantial majority at the United Nations opposing any effective international action directed against it.[59] This new multinational terrorism was, however, for all practical purposes surrogate warfare between governments; it had little in common, except in name, with the movements of national and social protest that had engaged in terrorist activities in previous decades. Some terrorist groups, to be sure, retained a substantial measure of independence, but others became almost entirely subservient to outside interests. If the Syrians supported Saiqa, one of the factions of the Palestinian "resistance," the Iraqis, Libyans and other Arab states would back other groups and, as the Lebanese civil war was to show, would expect their protégés to represent their interests. In brief, a new species of terrorism emerged, an almost impenetrable maze of linkages, intrigues, common and conflicting interests, open and covert collaboration with foreign governments who preferred to stay in the shadows.

IS TERRORISM EFFECTIVE?

That the murder of political opponents has altered, or could have altered the course of history goes without saying. If Pichegru or Cadoudal had killed Napoleon, if Lenin had met with an accident on the road to the Finland Station, if Hitler had been shot in front of the Munich Feldherrenhalle in 1923, the map of Europe would look different today. But these are the exceptions; in democratic and many undemocratic societies, statesmen are usually expendable. It has been said that Orsini's attempt on the life of Napoleon III contributed to the unification of Italy. But then Napoleon was in any case inclined to intervene in Italy. The Sarajevo assassination triggered off the First World War but, given the tensions and military preparations in Europe at the time, a war would probably have broken out — if not in 1914, perhaps a year or two later. It has been maintained that as a result of the murder of Canovas in 1897 and of King Umberto I in 1900, the treatment of political prisoners in Spain and Italy improved somewhat. But even if this were true, these were hardly results of world-shaking importance.[60] In a similar way, it has been argued that Sazonov's bomb which killed Plehwe, the Russian minister of the interior, intimidated the Tsarist regime and inaugurated a more liberal course. Sazonov, to be sure, was not sentenced to death; he died soon afterwards in prison. But the short-lived era of liberality was overtaken by the first Russian revolution, which was caused not so much by the bombs of the Social Revolutionaries as by the Russian defeat in the war against Japan. These examples refer to individual assassinations, but the results of systematic terrorist campaigns have not been very different. If there was an impact at all, it was usually negative; unlike King Midas, everything that was touched by the propagandists of the deed turned to ashes. Their actions usually produced violent repression and a polarization which precluded political progress. Anarchist activities bedeviled political life in Spain for decades, culminating in the Civil War of 1936–1939 and its fateful consequences. The activities of the Portuguese terrorists of the early 1920s had similar results; the murder of the right-wing dictator Major Sidonio Pais in December led to the butchery of the liberal government headed by Antonio Granjo in 1921. Left-wing and right-wing terrorist groups, the Red Legion *(Legião Vermelha)*, the Scorpions *(Os Lacraus)*, The Thirteen *(O Grupo des Treze)*, so proliferated in Portugal that one left-wing historian (A. H. de Oliveira Marques) later wrote of them that it was difficult to draw a clear line dividing political aims from criminal purposes. These and other groups decisively contributed to the fatal weakening of the democratic republic and the emergence of the dictatorship which ruled Portugal for the next four decades. While it is unlikely that Tsarism would have been able to change from within, whatever small hope there was for compromise and peaceful development was destroyed by the terrorists. The prospects for democracy in Central and Southeastern Europe were not promising after the First World War, but again, right-wing and, to a lesser extent, left-wing terrorism further reduced these chances. Following the Second World War, the strategy of provocation practiced by the "urban guerrillas" has had similar results; the Uruguayan experience is a striking example. The Tupamaros were one of the more attractive Latin American terrorist groups, reminiscent in some ways of the early Russian terrorists. They did not, on the whole, engage in indiscriminate murder, they wept when they killed (but they killed). They were genuine idealists; some of the best of the young generation belonged to them. Their

activities were initially quite successful, proving that civilian government could easily be disrupted and providing striking headlines for
the world press. But, in the final analysis, the only result of their
campaign was the destruction of freedom in a country which, alone
in Latin America, had had an unbroken democratic tradition of many
decades and which had been the first Latin American welfare state.
True, the Uruguay of the 1960s was far from perfect and was faced
with serious economic and social problems, but it is in any case
doubtful whether the Tupamaros had a better answer to these problems than the government of the day. The Tupamaros' campaign
resulted in the emergence of a right-wing military dictatorship; in
destroying the democratic system, they also destroyed their own
movement. By the 1970s they and their sympathizers were reduced
to bitter protests in exile against the crimes of a repressive regime
which, but for their own action, would not have come into existence.
The gravediggers of liberal Uruguay, as Regis Debray later wrote,
also dug their own grave. There were many other such cases of
sorcerer's apprentices bewailing the cruelties of the demons they
themselves had released. Terrorism from below produced massive
and infinitely more effective terror from above.

Terrorist groups that were more successful in attaining their objectives can be divided, broadly speaking, into three groups. There were
some that had narrow, clearly defined aims, for instance in an industrial dispute. Second, there were those with powerful outside protectors. The Palestinian Arab groups succeeded in keeping the Palestinian problem alive; so did the Croat Ustasha, who, for a while, got
their own state. Left to their own resources they would have been
no more successful than the South Moluccans (or the Kurds or the
South Sudanese tribes). Last, there were the terrorist groups facing
imperial powers, no longer able or willing to hold on to their colonies
or protectorates. Thus Britain gave up Ireland after the First World
War and the Palestine Mandate and Cyprus after the Second World
War; the terrorism of the IRA, the Irgun and LEHI and EOKA
certainly played a part in these decisions. But terrorism was not the
decisive factor in any of these countries, where the British retreat
was, after all, part of a general historical process. Political resistance
in Ireland, as in Palestine, while less dramatic and less widely publicized, was, in the long run, more effective. Historical experience

shows that the nationalist-sectarians stand a better chance of success than other types of terrorism. But even their achievements are often problematical. By aggravating the crisis, they make the solution of the problem more difficult cr even impossible. For national and religious minorities are dispersed in such a way in today's world that resolving one grievance usually creates a new one. Given the complexity of the modern world, not every minority can have a state of its own. Seemingly successful terrorist operations (such as in Cyprus) have, in fact, ended in disaster insofar as they have poisoned the relations between the communities and made peaceful coexistence impossible. Recent events in Ulster and the Middle East may have the same results: the longer terrorism lasts, the stronger the belief that there will be no peace until the other group is annihilated. With the progress in terrorist technology from the dagger to the means of mass destruction, the consequences seem ominous.

Seen in historical perspective, terrorism has been effective only in very specific circumstances. It has not succeeded against effective dictatorships, let alone modern totalitarian regimes. In democratic societies or against ineffective authoritarian regimes it has on occasion been more successful, but it is doubtful whether the Tupamaros have felt altogether happy, in retrospect, about their victory over the liberal system. There have been exceptions, but these have usually occurred whenever terrorism appears as part of a wider political strategy — against Machado in Cuba in 1933,[61] the systematic assassinations of village headmen by the Vietcong in the early 1960s, etc. This is not to say that terrorism has been doomed always and everywhere, or that its impact has invariably been negative. However, past experience shows that terrorism frequently occurs where there are other, nonviolent, political alternatives; where terrorism might be justified as the *ultima ratio,* such as against totalitarian rule, it has no chance, and where it seemingly succeeds, the political results are in the long run often self-defeating. Terrorism always attracts great publicity but its political impact is very often in inverse ratio to the attention it gets in the media. But terrorists are frequently driven by thirst for action rather than rational consideration of consequences, and there is no reason to assume that past failures will in any way act as a deterrent in the future.

THE "TERRORIST PERSONALITY"

Generalizations about the "terrorist personality" are of only limited assistance: even if one assumes that the Russian terrorists of the 1880s shared many common features of character — an assumption that can by no means be taken for granted — they had little in common with the Irish, and the Irish are quite different again from the Armenian or the Macedonian terrorists. Given that men and women at certain times and in various places have engaged in political violence, throwing bombs and firing pistols does not necessarily prove that they had more in common with one another than have rose growers or stamp collectors. Generalizations are of little validity because so much depends on the political and social conditions in which terrorism has occurred, on the historical and cultural context, on the purpose and character of the terror, and, of course, its targets. Seen in this light no two terrorist movements were alike, and in fact, few were even similar.

That their members have been young is the only feature common to all terrorist movements, and that hardly requires explanation. The latest calls to action don't usually fire the middle-aged and elderly with enthusiasm, and daring attacks also necessitate speed of movement.

Zhelyabov and Kravchinski, both aged thirty, were considered almost elderly by the members of Narodnaya Volya. Sofia Perovskaya was twenty-seven when she was sentenced to death, as was Kibalchich; Mikhailov was twenty-one. The average age of the Social Revolutionary terrorists was even lower; quite a number of them had not even graduated from high school. Sazonov, who killed Plehwe, was twenty-five, Balmashev was five years younger. Emile Henry, the French Anarchist, was twenty-one when he was executed. Most Latin American terrorists were, or are, of the same age group; Carlo Marighella became the leader of the Brazilian "urban guerrilla" in his fifties but this was a rare exception; another was Captain Lomasney who blew himself up while trying to mine London Bridge. Todor Alexandrov, who revived IMRO in the early 1920s, was forty at the time, and his chief aide, Protogerov, was in his fifties. But Alexandrov had become a member of the Central Committee of IMRO at twenty-eight and his successor Ivan Mikhailov, who took over in 1924, was not yet thirty. Many German and Italian terrorists of the 1920s were boys aged sixteen to nineteen "envenomed by the bad luck which made the war finish too soon for them."[62] Daniel Curley, hanged for his part in the Phoenix Park murders, was twenty years of age; Artal, who attacked the Spanish prime minister in 1904, was nineteen, as were Emelianov and Rysakov who threw the bomb at Alexander II. Gabriel Princip was twenty when he shot Franz Ferdinand in Sarajevo; his fellow conspirators, Popovic and Cabrinovic, were eighteen and seventeen respectively. None of them was executed, because they were under age. Alexander Berkman was nineteen when he tried to shoot Frick; Alexander Ulyanov, Lenin's elder brother, yet another leading advocate of "systematic" terror, was twenty-one when he was executed in 1887.

Apart from the fact that they belonged to a certain age group, it is difficult to find other features common to all of them. Some had unhappy, others happy childhoods. Alexander Mikhailov wrote that from his earliest days a happy star had shone on him — "my childhood was one of the happiest that a man can have."[63] Among the Russians, relations with their families were close, as shown by the letters to the parents of the terrorists about to be executed. Bakunin and Nechaev may be promising material for students of the human psyche, but Kropotkin and Weitling are not; they were outgoing, uncomplicated people who enjoyed life, anything but sinister figures. The Russian terrorists of the 1870s were on the whole remarkably "normal," i.e., sane and balanced human beings. So were Gershuni, who headed the Fighting Organization of the Social Revolutionaries, and Michael Collins, who led the Irish terrorists in 1919.

Almost a quarter of the Russian terrorists were women, whose devotion and courage are described in the works of many contemporary authors. But only in Russia were women to play such an important role at the time; there were no Judiths or Charlotte Cordays among the Anarchists (Emma Goldman being a rare exception) nor in other terrorist groups of the left or right, nor in national resistance movements. Female terrorists in Ireland or Japan were quite unthinkable and there were only two or three in India. Bomb-throwing was clearly considered a man's job; the growing role played by women in Europe and America is a phenomenon of recent date.

Minorities were (and are) prominently represented in many terrorist movements. There were quite a few Jews among the Narodnaya Volya and even more among the Social Revolutionaries. These included Gershuni and Azev, the two commanders of the "Fighting Organization." Some of the leaders of the nineteenth-century Irish revolutionary movement were Protestants. The head of the Rumanian Iron Guard was not a Rumanian by origin, nor was Szalazi, the Führer of the Arrow Cross, a Hungarian. Dr. Habash, the leader of the PFLP, the most extreme Palestinian terrorist organization, was a Christian, like his deputy Wadi Hadad, and Naif Hawatme, head of the rival PDFLP. Among the *Irgun* and the Stern Gang there were many youngsters from the Oriental Jewish community, which was not widely represented in the non-terrorist Hagana.* In some cases these terrorists from minority groups perhaps perceived grievances even more acutely than the others; more often there may have been a psychological need to prove themselves, to show that they were as good, or better, patriots (or revolutionaries) than their comrades.

Lucien de la Hodde, writing in 1850, provides a most interesting analysis of the social composition of the secret societies in Paris in the first half of the last century, groups who from time to time engaged in terrorist actions. He listed nine categories of participants: first, and above all, the students. There was a rebellious tradition among students dating back to the Middle Ages. De la Hodde made it clear, however, that he did not have in mind the students who studied but those who thought all bourgeois ideas ridiculous and who had a weakness for *le bruit, les coups, les évènements.* The author admired the British for their political wisdom in having set up their universities outside the capital. Secondly, de la Hodde lists *les impuissants* — advocates without clients, physicians without patients, writers without readers, merchants without buyers, and all unsophisticated souls who saw themselves as statesmen, having studied politics in the newspapers. In short: the educated, or semieducated, *déclassés,* who have always constituted the backbone of such groups. De la Hodde further lists *les bohêmes, une classe de fantaisistes ayant horreur de*

*George Schoeters, the founder of the Canadian FLQ, was a Belgian who had arrived in Canada only in 1951.

la vie ordinaire, mainly to be found in the capital, hardly ever outside it. Furthermore, *le peuple souverain,* i.e., the working class; *les gobe-mouche* — the simpletons, well-meaning but naïve and credulous people (and true believers); the permanently discontented; political refugees; and lastly the bandits, the criminal elements.[64] De la Hodde was the master spy of the French police in the ranks of the revolutionary movements; while detestation made him an astute observer, his description contains no mention of idealistic motives. But even had he noted evidence of idealism, his comments on France would still be of little help for an understanding of the social background of the secret societies that were to develop soon afterward in Ireland. Some members of Narodnaya Volya were of humble origin: Zhelyabov's father, for instance, had been a house serf. But the sons and daughters of the aristocracy and the landed gentry were far more numerous among them. Bakunin and Kropotkin, it should be noted in passing, came from upper-class families; Sofia Perovskaya's father had been governor general of Petersburg. A partial list of 365 revolutionaries arrested in the 1880s shows that 180 belonged to the gentry (including 32 officers), 104 were of middle-class or lower-middle-class origin, and the fathers of 46 had been priests.[65] Among the Social Revolutionary terrorists of the following generation, the middle- and lower-middle-class element was much more strongly represented, even though there were still numerous terrorists of impeccable aristocratic background. In this respect Russian terrorism resembled the composition of terrorist groups in Latin America in which the sons and daughters of the middle and upper-middle class have traditionally predominated. In Uruguay, as well as in other Latin American countries, available statistics tend to show that the sons and daughters of the administrative middle class are particularly strongly represented — educated persons without independent means, the academic proletariat.[66] The composition of the Argentine ERP seems to be similar, whereas in the Montoneros the lower-middle class and even, to a lesser extent, the working class appear to be more strongly represented. The small West German, Japanese and U.S. terrorist groups consisted to a large degree of university dropouts, and, like the early Fascist movements, of *déclassés, spostati,* socially uprooted elements. The social origins of the membership (and particularly the leadership) of these groups is of considerable interest. Ernst Halperin reaches an interesting quasi-Marxist conclusion when he argues that terrorism in Latin America is "a vigorous reaction against economic stagnation and social putrefaction by the most energetic members of the administrative class, a bid for absolute power in order to give that class the challenging task of totally transforming society." In this way "class interest," idealism and social consciousness neatly complement each other. But it is also true that the smaller the group, the less meaningful the search for common social patterns.

The nationalist-separatist terrorist groups almost always consist of young people of lower social background than the socialist-revolutionary groups; the IRA is an obvious example. Inasmuch as the nationalist-separatist movements have a left-wing fringe, this again consists mainly of intellectuals of middle-class background or white-collar workers; Fatah is more "proletarian" than the more radical PFLP and PDFLP. In the United States up to the First World War, and in Spain up to the Civil War, terrorism frequently accompanied industrial disputes; hence the presence of many workers among the terrorist militants.

Close foreign observers of the Russian scene, such as Masaryk and George Kennan, Senior, noted that the young terrorists were men and women of the highest ethical standards. Most Russians, even their bitterest opponents, tended to agree with them. Dostoyevski's villains are mere caricatures: Pyotr Verkhovenski, a buffoon, slanderer and traitor, and Shigalov with his enormous ears ("all are slaves and equal in their slavery"). Any similarity between the "Possessed" and the terrorists of the 1880s is purely accidental.[67]

The Russian terrorists anxiously questioned whether they had the right to kill, in contrast to many latter-day terrorists with their philosophy of killing for fun and profit. Dora Brilliant, one of the martyrs of the Socialist Revolutionaries, confessed that it was easier to die than to kill; Timofei Mikhailov, who was to participate in the assassination of the tsar in 1881, at the last moment felt unable to do the deed, but he showed no weakness when he was about to be executed. Kalyayev, who set out to kill the Grand Duke Serge Alexandrovich, did not throw the bomb at his first attempt because the intended victim was accompanied by his family, and clearly it was wrong to kill children.[68] For the same reason Angiolilo, the Italian Anarchist,

did not shoot Canovas, the Spanish prime minister, when he first had
the opportunity to do so. Police spies who had been infiltrated into
the ranks of the Russian terrorists and who had been unmasked,
escaped death on more than one occasion by appealing to the humanity of the terrorists, who hesitated to kill them if there was even
the slightest doubt concerning their guilt. These men and women
had little in common with the IRA, the German Freikorps of the
1920s, the Japanese "Red Army" and many other present-day terrorist groups. Killinger, the Freikorps leader who later became a Nazi
Gauleiter, describes with evident relish how he and his comrades
whipped a woman so that there was not one white spot left on her
back.[69] The cruelties committed by Macedonian and Croatian terrorists are well documented, and there was also a cruel streak in Irish
terrorism from an early date. John Devoy, it is true, said on one
occasion that Celtic nature revolted at the mere idea of assassination.
But national character changes and the practice of cutting the victim's Achilles tendon was reported in Ireland as early as 1813, a
system refined in recent years.[70] In the light of historical evidence
it would be wrong to juxtapose the "humane" character of left-wing
terrorism to the "sadistic" terror of the nationalist and right-wing
groups. Criminals have frequently shown greater humanity than
terrorists; they are out for profit, not for psychological satisfaction.
They don't normally torment their victims. Terrorists are fanatics,
and fanaticism frequently makes for cruelty and sadism.

In February 1972, a United Red Army hideout was discovered in
Karuizawa, a mountain spa some eighty miles from Tokyo. There
fourteen mangled and tortured bodies were found; one half of the
group had liquidated the others for antirevolutionary failings, a few
had apparently been buried alive. This has been explained against
the background of unfathomable Oriental traditions, but would
hardly account for the comments of Bernardine Dohrn, leader of the
Weather underground, on the Sharon Tate murder: "First they killed
those pigs, then they ate dinner in the same room with them, then
they even shoved a fork into a victim's stomach! Wild!" The Black
September assassin of Wasfi Tal, the prime minister of Jordan,
thirsted, he said, to drink his victim's blood after having fulfilled
his mission.

The preoccupation with ethical problems, it has been said, was very much a nineteenth-century European phenomenon. In the twentieth century, human life became cheaper; the belief gained ground that the end justified all means, and that humanity anyway was a bourgeois prejudice. Selfless devotion, idealism, courage and the willingness to sacrifice oneself had not disappeared, but these qualities can be found in all parts of the political spectrum. They have been demonstrated by militants of good causes as well as of very bad ones. Right-wing terrorism is not just gangsterism and Brecht's *Arturo Ui* is about as helpful for the understanding of Nazism as *The Possessed* for Russian terrorism. Horst Wessel, paradoxically, is a type out of the pages of Tolstoy or Dostoyevski — the student from a middle-class home who goes to live with a prostitute in order to "redeem her." At another time and in another place he would have been an Anarchist hero; in his life-style he belonged to the counter-culture, not to the establishment. It has been said that the sterling qualities of the members of Narodnaya Volya deeply impressed even their political enemies. But it is also true that the fanatical devotion of some of the Nazi terrorists inspired admiration among many who were opposed to their political beliefs. For, it was asked, how could men possibly fight with such passion for a cause that was all wrong? Karl Radek wrote a famous obituary for Schlageter, the terrorist who was an early member of the Nazi party, in which he said that this courageous soldier of the counterrevolution should be sincerely ad-mired by the soldiers of the revolution. "The fact that he risked death shows that he was determined to serve the German people. . . . We shall do everything in our power so to ensure that men like Schla-geter, willing to go to their deaths for an ideal, should not die in vain but be harbingers of a better world."[71] Radek was later criticized for this indiscretion but he was, of course, right. In other circumstances, Schlageter could have turned with equal ease to the left. The par-ents, the brothers and sisters of Fascist terrorists were as convinced as the families of Russian revolutionaries that their dear ones had died for a "holy cause."[72]

The mystical element has been noted in Russian terrorism, but it is also found in Ireland, in Rumania, and among Japanese, Indian and Arab terrorists. Some of the Social Revolutionary terrorists were deeply religious believers. Rasputina went to church each morning, much to the consternation of the detectives shadowing her; Benevskaya, another Social Revolutionary, became a terrorist precisely because she was a believing Christian. There were more than a few practicing Catholics among Latin American terrorists. It is, however, true that most Russian terrorists had nothing but contempt for the religious establishment, and that most French Anarchists and American terrorists were confirmed atheists. Yet their belief in their cause had a deeply religious quality. The last words of some of those about to be executed — such as Fischer (of the Haymarket trial): "This is the happiest moment of my life" — reveal that these men and women were deeply convinced that upon them, as on Christ, rested the burden of deliverance. They were martyrs for their faith, making the supreme sacrifice for the salvation of mankind; but in contrast to the early Christian martyrs they no longer believed in the commandment "Thou shalt not kill." Describing the spirit with which his comrades, the Russian terrorists, were imbued, Kravchinski frequently drew on illustrations from the Bible.[73] Bjørnsterne Bjørnson, the Norwegian writer, noted in his *Beyond Human Power* that it was among the Anarchists that modern martyrs might be found. The idea of the martyr who has gained eternal life appears in the history of Irish terrorism from its beginnings to the present day. Writing about Russian terrorism, Masaryk detected a "mysticism of death"; the same is true of Anarchism, some Fascist groups and above all of the Rumanian Legionnaires with their rite of calling the names of the dead at parades and answering "Present."

The political issues in nineteenth-century Russia were clear-cut; there was no constitution, no elementary rights, no legal redress against the abuse of power. Elsewhere, the issues were more complex, and terrorists had to persuade themselves that there was no alternative to violence, that democracy was dictatorship and that radical change could be effected only if bombs were thrown and pistols fired. In these circumstances the choice of terrorist means was less obvious, and those opting for them were usually more problematical characters. Emma Goldman, defending the Anarchists in a famous essay, said that they were torn in a conflict between their souls and unbearable social iniquities.[74] Highly strung they certainly were but for their motives one has to look as often as not to their private lives rather than to their political and social environment.

The "propaganda by deed" in Western and Southern Europe was

carried out by individuals acting on their own, mostly men of little education. Some were Herostratic figures; the last words of Bonnot, the leader of a gang of Anarchists and criminals in the Paris of the *belle époque*, were "I am a celebrated man." Some were sick in mind as well as in body, which led Cesare Lombroso into his premature conclusions about the connection between bomb throwing, pellagra and avitaminosis. By the turn of the century, some terrorist groups already included adventurers and even criminal elements. In the later stages of the Russian terrorist movement, there were comments about the dictatorial behavior on the part of some leaders, on their disregard for human life and waste of money; such complaints would have been unthinkable in the days of the Narodnaya Volya.[75]

The less clear the political purpose in terrorism, the greater its appeal to unbalanced persons. The motives of men fighting a cruel tyranny are quite different from those of rebels against a democratically elected government. Idealism, a social conscience or hatred of foreign oppression are powerful impulses, but so are free-floating aggression, boredom and mental confusion. Activism can give meaning to otherwise empty lives. Sofia Perovskaya and Vera Figner were the symbols of one kind of terrorism — Ulrike Meinhof and Patty Hearst of another.

The subsequent fate of some of the leading terrorists of past ages is of some interest. Durruti, the fiery Spanish Anarchist, was killed in the defense of Madrid, Marighella died in a shoot-out with the Brazilian police. Johann Most and O'Donovan Rossa, two of the grand old men of violent action, mellowed a little with age. Joseph Casey, the Fenian leader, faded away in his Paris exile: as Kevin Egan he appears in Joyce's *Ulysses:* "He prowled with Col. Richard Burke, tanist of his sept, under the walls of Clerkenwell and crouching, saw a flame of vengeance hurl them upward in the fog." Kropotkin, Emma Goldman and Alexander Berkman advocated nonviolent action in later life. Of the nineteenth-century Irish terrorists in the United States, some went into American politics, a few became Congressmen or diplomats. Among those who lived to see the emergence of the Irish Free State, many were killed in the subsequent internecine struggle; the survivors constituted the political elite of the new state. Sean Mac Bride, a former chief of staff of the IRA, became a distinguished international civil servant — and winner of the Nobel Prize for

peace. The leaders of the Irgun and the Stern Gang became opposi-
tionist members of the Knesset, the Israeli parliament, others went
into the army or into business. A Russian-Jewish terrorist of earlier
vintage, Pinchas Rutenberg, reappeared in Palestine as a distinguished industrialist and founder of the local electricity company.
Andrea Costa and Paul Brousse, leading anti-parliamentarians in the
1880s, were to enter parliament soon after. Brousse, who had coined
the phrase "propaganda by deed," in later years was to congratulate
the king of Spain on his escape from assassination. Of the surviving
Russian terrorists of the 1880s some subsequently moved to the extreme right, many made a name for themselves as scientists. Kropotkin had been a distinguished geographer all along. Mention has been
made of Morozov and Sternberg, and one should also add to this list
the biochemist A. N. Bach, a member of the Soviet Academy of
Science in later years, the ethnographers Bogoraz-Tan, Yokhelson
and Krol, as well as the bacteriologist Kharkin.[76] Of the Social Revolutionary terrorists of early twentieth-century vintage not one joined
the Bolsheviks; most emigrated from Russia, or did not return to
Russia after 1917. Savinkov, who had served in the Kerenski government, actively fought the Communists, as did Maria Spiridonova; she
had been given a life sentence in Tsarist Russia, and in 1918 again
found herself in prison where she died twenty years later. The heroic
example of the Freikorps terrorists was praised by the Nazis but with
very few exceptions these men were kept at arms' length in the
Third Reich. Pilsudski and Arciszewski, leaders of the Polish terrorist
struggle in 1905–1906, became chief of state and prime minister of
Poland respectively. Ante Pavelic, the leader of the Ustasha was
made the *Führer* (Poglavnik) of an "independent" Croatia during the
Second World War; with the defeat of the Axis his career came to a
sudden end, and he became one of the most wanted war criminals.
It is too early to generalize about the fate of the European and North
American terrorists of our time; some advocates of individual terrorism in the United States have already changed their views and life-
style, having realized that the imperfect system against which they
were fighting was by no means the worst possible.

The search for a "terrorist personality," it was maintained earlier
on, is a fruitless one. The Russian terrorists of 1880 had certain characteristics in common, as had the Irish or the Anarchists or the Pales-

tinians, but to search for a common denominator spanning various countries, periods, cultures and political constellations is no more helpful than attempting a quantitative analysis of the height and weight of terrorists. Some were the sons of well-known revolution-aries — the Russian Balmashev, for instance, or Emile Henry, whose father was a leading communard, or Sean Mac Bride. But the father of young Cabrinovic, who was involved in the Sarajevo plot, was an Austrian police spy, and the large number of sons and daughters of high Tsarist officials in the revolutionary movement of the 1870s and 1880s has already been noted.

Nechaev was totally devoid of moral scruples in his private life, but in this he was an exception among nineteenth-century revolution-aries. Most and O'Donovan Rossa were heavy drinkers, yet many of their comrades were fanatic abstentionists. Some Russian and Ser-bian terrorists suffered from tuberculosis and died young, some en-joyed perfect health. Ravachol, Emile Henry and a few of the Russian terrorists were mystics or believers in the occult, others had not the slightest inclination in this direction. Some contemporary observers noted a suicidal urge among terrorists; they were *todestrunken,* in the words of one observer.* But for every intellectual preoccupied with death there were no doubt several others who enjoyed life as much as the next man. In short, there has always been a great variety in character traits, mental makeup and psychology among terrorists.

All that can be said with any degree of confidence is that terror was (and is) a pursuit of young people, and that in most other respects the differences between terrorists are more pronounced than the fea-tures they may have in common. The character of terrorism, further-more, has undergone a profound change. Intellectuals have made the cult of violence respectable: there had been no such cult among the Russian terrorists. Vengeance played a certain role, but not cru-elty: Emile Henry wanted to avenge Vaillant, who had thrown the bomb in the French parliament; after Henry's execution, Caserio killed Sadi Carnot, the French president, because he had not par-doned Henry. The explosion in the Barcelona opera house (1893) was

*This seems to have been true with regard to some of the French Anarchists and also Orsini who wrote in his famous last letter that he had tried to kill Napoleon III in a fit of mental aberration, that he did not believe in murder and that Italy would not be liberated by attempts to emulate his deed.

to avenge Paulino Pallas who had been executed shortly before. The bomb thrown at the Corpus Christi procession two years later, also in Barcelona, was in protest against the conditions at Monjuich prison. The particular ferocity of LEHI terrorism was no doubt connected with the desire to avenge the death of their leader, Abraham Stern. In the history of Russian terrorism, and also in Rumania and Ireland, repression frequently caused a new wave of terrorist operations.

Not all nineteenth-century terrorists were knightly (or saintly) figures; there were doubtful characters among them and some were half mad. But by and large these were fighters against brutal dictatorships and against hideous persecution. It was surely no coincidence that terrorism was most widespread in Tsarist Russia and Turkey, the two most oppressive regimes in Europe. Nor is there any doubt about the genuineness of the grievances of the Irish rebels, the American workers and the Spanish peasants. Inasmuch as there was indiscriminate terror, it was perpetrated by unstable individuals; it was not a matter of systematic policy. Atrocities were committed, but the ethical standards prevailing in Macedonia around the turn of the century and in Mexico were not quite comparable to those of countries on a higher level of civilization.

The terror of the 1960s and 1970s is different in quality. The more oppressive regimes are not only free from terror, they have helped to launch it against the more permissive societies. The fate of the terrorist of the 1880s and 1890s, when apprehended, was not an enviable one; in contrast, no West European, North American, Japanese or Middle Eastern terrorist of the 1960s or 1970s has been executed (except in some cases by his comrades) and there is always a good chance that he will be released even before serving his term, his comrades having blackmailed the authorities into freeing him. Much of the risk has gone out of terrorism. It is no longer a daylight duel between giants in a kind of Russian *High Noon* as the Narodovoltsy saw it. With time bombs left in public places and the dispatch of letter bombs, the struggle has become anonymous and much of the heroism and sacrifice have gone out of it. Sometimes terrorism has become bureaucratized and at others it is manipulated from afar.

Standards and modes of behavior have changed. The Narodnaya Volya, the French Anarchists or the Irish dynamiters would not have abducted children and threatened to kill them unless ransom was paid, they would not have hired agents to do their own work, nor would they have given parcels with explosives to unsuspecting tourists. They would not have sent parts of their victims' bodies with little notes to their relatives as the (right-wing) Guatemalan MANO and NOA did. They would not have expected a premium of millions of dollars from foreign governments for commissions executed, they would not have tormented, mutilated, raped and castrated their victims, nor would they have engaged in senseless wholesale slaughter of their own ranks. Not all recent terrorist movements have made a fetish of brutality; some have behaved more humanely than others. But what was once a rare exception has become a frequent occurrence in our time. It is still true that, as initially noted, generalizations about the "terrorist personality" are of limited value because there are so many variations. But it is also true that where a common pattern, a general trend, can be discerned at the present time, it is precisely that which has just been noted. When all allowances have been made for the primitive character and the violent traditions of certain societies, there is no escaping the fact that nineteenth-century terrorists acted according to standards very different from those prevailing at present. This is not to idealize the Narodnaya Volya or to denigrate the terrorists of the 1960s and 1970s; Latin American or Arab terrorists may be fervent patriots or feel the injustice done to their people as acutely as the terrorists of an earlier age, but they still belong to a different species. Whatever their motives may be, the "ardent love of others" which Emma Goldman observed is not among them, the driving force is hate not love, ethical considerations are a matter of indifference to them and their dreams of freedom, of national and social liberation are suspect precisely because of their personalities. Nineteenth-century nationalist terrorists were fighting for freedom from foreign domination, but of late appetites have grown; the Basques have designs on Galicia, the Palestinians want not only the West Bank but also intend to destroy the Jewish state, the IRA would like to bomb the Protestants into a united Ireland. The aims of terrorism, in brief, have changed, and so have the terrorists.

4

Interpretations of Terrorism— Fact, Fiction and Political Science

I

The question of terrorist motivation is far from new, and has received an enormous variety of answers. This is hardly surprising, for terrorism has assumed widely differing characteristics from age to age and from country to country. Any explanation that attempts to account for all its many manifestations is bound to be either exceedingly vague or altogether wrong. It has been said that highly idealistic and deeply motivated young people have opted for terrorism when they faced unresolved grievances and when there was no other way of registering protest and effecting change. Dostoyevsky and many others would hardly have agreed. It has also been said that terrorists are criminals, moral imbeciles, mentally deranged people or sadists (or sado-masochists). Sweeping definitions of this kind are bound to provoke scepticism. Terrorist movements are usually some kind of youth movements and to dwell upon the idealistic character of youth movements is only stressing the obvious: they are not out for personal gain and they always oppose the status quo. But political goals are not necessarily wholly altruistic: idealism and interest may coincide, nor are personal ambitions absent: terrorists have also been driven on by impatience and a kind of *machismo* (or, more recently, its female equivalent). Terrorism has occurred with increasing frequency in societies in which peaceful change is possible. Grievances always exist, but in certain cases oppression has been borne without protest, whereas elsewhere and at other times relatively minor grievances have resulted in violent reaction. Nor is the choice of terrorism as a weapon altogether obvious, for frequently there are other ways of resistance, both political and military.

In short, the problem of terrorism is complicated, and what can be said without fear of contradiction about a terrorist group in one country is by no means true for other groups at other times and in other societies. Love of liberty, as well as the ardent love of others, were invoked by sympathetic observers trying to explain the motives of the terrorists of the last third of the nineteenth century — "the last, desperate struggle of outraged and exasperated human nature for breathing space and life."[1] Emma Goldman noted that the anarchist terrorists were impelled to violence not by the teachings of Anarchism but by the tremendous pressure of conditions which made life unbearable to their sensitive natures. Compared to the wholesale violence of capital and government, political acts of violence were but a drop in the ocean: "High strung like a violin string, the anarchists weep and moan for life, so relentless, so cruel, so terribly inhuman. In a desperate moment the string breaks."[2]

Other contemporary observers interpreted terrorism in a less complimentary light: it was altogether evil, a form of madness with perhaps an underlying physical disorder. It was noted that quite a few of the terrorists of the period suffered from epilepsy, tuberculosis and other diseases. Lombroso saw a connection between bomb throwing and pellagra and other vitamin deficiencies among the maize-eating people of southern Europe. Others detected a link with the general nervous overexcitement of the period which also manifested itself by an exaggerated individualism and the spread of decadent literature. The connection between terrorism and barometric pressure, moon phases, alcoholism and droughts was investigated, and cranial measurements of terrorists were very much in fashion.[3]

It is not true, however, that early interpretations of terrorism were merely hysterical and that there were no genuine attempts to understand their deeper motives. Many contemporary observers took a remarkably detached view, arguing, *inter alia,* that the importance of anarchist terrorism should not be exaggerated, that repression was less important than prevention and that capital punishment was not called for.[4] Lombroso had doubts from the beginning about the efficacy of international cooperation against anarchist terrorism and also opposed capital punishment. He argued that punishment was no antidote to fanaticism. If, as he maintained, terrorism was an indirect form of suicide, capital punishment, leading to the desired end, would merely act as a spur.[5] Zenker, one of the earliest historians of Anarchism, suggested that all exceptional ("emergency") legislation against Anarchism should be avoided; it would be far more helpful if the state made an effort to redress social inequalities. But Zenker was too close and objective an observer to be satisfied with facile explanations and solutions; he stated *expressis verbis* that anarchist terrorism could by no means be explained by pauperism alone.[6]

By the turn of the century Anarchism had outgrown its terrorist phase, but terrorist actions did not cease. Compared with other manifestations of political violence, they seemed to be of minor importance and this is perhaps one of the reasons why no serious attempt was made to study the phenomenon. There were other reasons too, such as its fundamentally shocking and disturbing character, which may have inhibited serious study.[7] It is also true that from an early stage terrorism was perceived as a very complex phenomenon, varying from country to country as the result of cultural traditions, social structures, political relationships and many other factors which made generalization very difficult indeed. One of the few attempts to give a definition and explanation was Hardman's entry in the *Encyclopaedia of the Social Sciences,* published in the 1930s. The author defined terrorism as the method (or the theory behind the method) whereby an organized group or party sought to achieve its avowed aims chiefly through the systematic use of violence. Thus terrorism was different in substance not only from governmental terror but also from mob violence and mass insurrection. Hardman regarded the publicity value of terrorist acts as a cardinal point and he noted that the inspiration of terrorism could be left-wing as well as rightist and that terrorism had never attained real success as a complete revolutionary tactic. Some of his other observations, although perhaps correct at the time, clearly show the changes that terrorism has undergone in recent times. Thus the doctrine of indiscriminate terror did not yet exist in the 1930s: "Terrorist acts are directed against persons who as individuals, agents or representatives of authority interfere with the consummation of the objectives of such a group."[8] Nor is it likely that any observer of the terrorist movements of the 1960s and 1970s would still subscribe to the view that "the terrorist does not threaten; death or destruction is part of his programme of action" or "violence and death are not intended to produce revenue or to terrorize the persons attacked." Books on terrorism continued to appear, but these were usually either historical monographs on recent Russian or Irish history or journalistic accounts of exotic movements such as the Macedonian IMRO or studies of the legal implications of terrorist operations.

It was only in the 1960s that social scientists became interested in political violence; some had believed that it was a relatively rare phenomenon; others may have neglected it for different reasons.[9] Most of the research took place in the United States and had a definite connection with the Vietnam war and America's own internal turmoil. The fact that there had always been a great deal of violence outside the United States had somehow not quite registered. With the experience of American suburbs in mind it was widely believed that political life all over the globe was steadily becoming more civilized and that stability could be regarded as the norm and political violence as a regrettable aberration. When it was suddenly realized that this appraisal may have been overoptimistic, the pendulum began to swing to the other extreme and the conviction gained ground that the frequency of violence must somehow reflect the inequities of society — the "system," low income, bad housing, insufficient education and so on. The shock of recognition was apparently so great as to make comment quite incoherent on occasion: "If there is a streak of violence in the national character, then it is precisely that streak which sets itself in opposition to change."[10]

The implied assumption was that a healthy society faced no such problems and that a government which could count on the loyalty of its citizens had no reason to fear terrorist outrages and other perils. These assumptions were at the bottom of the new departures in conflict studies which in turn were mainly based on the work done by Dollard and his collaborators on frustration and aggression just before the outbreak of the Second World War.[11] They had stated that aggression is *always* a consequence of frustration, an assumption which was by no means universally shared. It came under attack, for instance, from ethologists who maintained that aggressive behavior was spontaneous, an inner drive. But most psychologists too found this theory wanting; "War occurs because fighting is a fundamental tendency in human beings," one of them wrote.[12] Anthony Storr noted that the frustration-aggression concept was widely accepted among Americans: perhaps it was true that perennial optimism made it hard for them to believe that there was anything unpleasant either in the physical world or in human nature which could not be "fixed."*

The Dollard concept was widely accepted for a while by students of conflict who regarded protest and violence as the result of discontent caused by frustration. And they saw social discontent as the discrepancy between demand and fulfillment. Or, in more scientific language, the higher the social-want formation and the lower the social-want satisfaction, the greater the systemic frustration. Violence, seen in this light, is the result of socialization patterns which either encourage or discourage aggression and of cultural traditions sanctioning collective responses to various kinds of deprivation.[13] Students of conflict had a rich armory at their disposal to explain protest and violence-causal models, such as factor analysis and multiple regression (multiple regression is a way of predicting the dependent variable from two or more independent variables). Over the following years many dozens of papers and books were published investigating the correlation between violence on the one hand and on the other such variables as literacy, urbanization, caloric intake, GNP, and numbers of newspapers and physicians. This was the so-called frustration index. Its composition was, of course, bound to be highly arbitrary, for it could not be taken for granted that the circulation of newspapers inevitably makes for happiness. Nor was it at all clear whether lack of schooling made for greater discontent than the existence of schools and universities together with an absence of sufficient jobs for their graduates.

By 1968 some 650 American political scientists listed "revolutions

---

*The frustration-aggression hypothesis was refined in the 1960s by Leonard Berkowitz. Frustration, as he saw it, produces an emotional state, anger, which heightens the probability of the occurrence of aggression. Berkowitz was more aware than his predecessors of outside stimuli; even if there was frustration and anger, the probability that aggression will take place still depends on the presence (or absence) of factors restraining aggression. Stated in this more cautious form the hypothesis seemed to be of greater validity but as a tool of empirical research it is still of limited use especially with regard to larger social groups. Leonard Berkowitz, *Aggression* (New York, 1962), and Reed Lawson, ed., *Frustration, the Development of a Scientific Concept* (New York, 1965).

and political violence" as their field of specialization, and although their orientation and approach differed widely, many of them believed that group conflict within nations had common properties and causes that could be compared and explained by way of quantification.*

Within the context of macro cross-national research Rummel investigated dimensions of conflict behavior within and between nations (1946–1959) and Raymond Tanter did the same for a shorter period (1958–1960). This led them into examining the relationship between domestic and foreign conflict behavior and finding, perhaps to their surprise, that there was apparently none. Perhaps there was a third factor that had been ignored, such as the personality characteristics of the national decision-makers or perhaps there was a causal relationship after all that was still obscured by some unknown phenomena. Douglas Bwy examined political instability in Latin America, in many ways a more propitious topic precisely because the author was dealing with societies of roughly similar traditions. But

*T. R. Gurr, "The Calculus of Civil Conflict," *Journal of Social Issues,* I (1972), 29.
Below is a fairly representative but by no means exhaustive selection from this literature:

I. K. and R. L. Feierabend, "Social Change and Political Violence: Cross-National Patterns," in H. D. Graham and T. R. Gurr, *Violence in America* (1969). See also *Journal of Conflict Resolution,* 10 (1966); and J. V. Gillespie and B. A. Nesvold, *Macro-Quantitative Analysis Conflict, Development and Democratization* (Beverly Hills, 1971).

T. R. Gurr, *Why Men Rebel* (Princeton, 1970); also T. R. Gurr and R. Duvall, "Civil Conflict in the 1960s," in *Comparative Political Studies,* 6 (1973).

R. J. Rummel, "Dimensions of Conflict Behaviour within and between Nations," *General Systems Yearbook,* 8 (1963).

R. J. Rummel: "Dimensions of Conflict Behaviour within Nations, 1946–59," *Journal of Conflict Resolution,* X, 65 *et seq.*

B. A. Nesvold, "A Scalogram Analysis of Political Violence," in Gillespie and Nesvold, *supra.*

T. R. Gurr and C. Rutenberg, *The Conditions of Civil Violence: First Tests of a Causal Model,* Center for International Studies, Research Monograph 28 (Princeton, 1967).

W. H. Flanigan and E. Fogelman, "Patterns of Political Violence in Comparative historical perspective," in *Comparative Politics,* 3 (1970).

P. R. Schneider and A. L. Schneider, "Social Mobilization, Political Institutions and Political Violence," *Comparative Political Studies,* 4 (1971).

F. R. von der Mehden, *Comparative Political Violence* (New York, 1973).

G. B. Markus and B. A. Nesvold, "Governmental Coerciveness and Political Instability," *Comparative Political Studies,* 5 (1972).

R. Tanter, "Dimensions of Conflict Behaviour within and between Nations," *Journal of Conflict Resolution,* 10 (1966).

the search did not lead very far, for it was established that there was no obvious correlation between the legitimacy ascribed to a political system and the intensity or frequency of violence. Riots broke out as frequently in highly legitimate as in less legitimate systems.[14]

Some researchers saw the decisive factor in the break-up of traditional society; others concentrated on the unequal distribution of property or land; and a third group took the social consequences of rapid economic development as their starting point. According to some investigators the most modern and most backward societies were the most stable, whereas those in the middle showed a high degree of instability. Sometimes the results were a little unexpected, showing in one case that the citizens of the United States (including blacks) were more content than those of other countries. Perhaps misery and frustration were insufficient to explain riots and anarchy; perhaps the need to prove *machismo* had to be taken into account as well as the desire to raise hell out of sheer exhilaration and habit of lawlessness.[15]

A study of violence in eighty-four countries reached the conclusion that a little repression increases instability, whereas a great deal of it has the opposite effect or, to put it more obscurely, "political instability is curvilinearly related to the level of the coerciveness of the political regime; the probability of a high level of political instability increases with mid-levels of coerciveness, insufficient to be a deterrent to aggression, but sufficient to increase the level of systemic frustration."

Change leads to unrest; modern countries are more stable because they can satisfy the wants of their citizens; the less advanced countries are characterized by greater instability because of the aggressive responses to systemic frustration evoked in the populace. But as there has been dissatisfaction in advanced societies as well as in backward ones, the investigators wisely hedged their bets: the satisfaction of wants may have a feedback effect and may increase the drive for more satisfaction, thus adding to the sense of systemic frustration. It is only when a high enough level of satisfaction has been reached (on the Patty Hearst level, malevolent critics would add) that a country will tend toward stability rather than instability.[16]

The cross-national studies were usually based on the index of the *New York Times* or similar sources; assassinations committed by madmen and terrorist groups were listed side by side; the victims of the Nazi purge of June 1934 were enumerated but not those who had died as the result of the Soviet purge of 1936–1938. The authors of a study on assassination found it directly related, among other things, to external aggression and minority hostility. In these calculations, some of which had a distinctly Alice-in-Wonderland quality, East Germany, Jordan, Guatemala and Paraguay were defined as belonging to the "high external aggression" category; Bulgaria, Czechoslovakia, Afghanistan and Panama (to provide some random examples) were rated "low external aggression." Turkey, Peru, Tunisia and Switzerland were countries with "high minority hostility" and Yugoslavia, the Philippines, Syria and the United Kingdom appear under "low minority hostility."[17]

Other investigators had meanwhile reached the conclusion that their scales were not truly applicable to political violence in communist nations because these countries were not "scalable" and that the models of modernization and its effects did not apply to these countries either.[18] But leaving aside questions of general principle such as the applicability of quantification, it was by no means certain whether Third World countries were "scalable" either, if only due to the difficulty in obtaining reliable data. The researchers were not unaware of the weaknesses of their concepts and conclusions all too often based on shotgun statistical marriages: "Factor analysis has been used to give the appearance of statistical order to what remains conceptual chaos."[19] Yet at the same time, until about 1972, the general feeling was one of great optimism. Thus the Feierabend study in 1966 stated: "Although exploratory in nature the findings are sufficiently striking and persuasive to argue for continuing with additional designs."[20] And Ted Gurr, writing in 1972, believed that the study of civil conflict was on the eve of a major breakthrough: "The accomplishment of these studies to date seem to me to have more than justified their doing. It is problematic but entirely possible on the basis of results thus far, that civil conflict will become one of the first fields of social science outside of psychology and economics in which parameter, etiology and processes are understood well enough to constitute a cohesive scientific field in the narrow sense of that term."[21] This optimism was not shared by all political scientists, let alone by historians. Harry Eckstein, writing in 1964 and again in

1969, expressed scepticism about the conclusions reached up till then. In 1975, Erich Weede, surveying the work of a whole decade, doubted whether there had been any progress at all.[22] Eventually, the authors of the studies of the 1960s, who had emphasized the psychological origins of strife, themselves became dissatisfied with the results achieved so far. New investigations were launched with the emphasis on tension and strain rather than on relative deprivation as in the older studies. Social tensions were now interpreted as the result of persistent strain or short-term stress. These strains were said to be particularly strong where a social system had a long tradition of conflict.

Internal conflict, according to this argument, occurs when injustice and inequality persist and when domestic rule is based on constraints rather than on consensus.[23] This model tries to take into account economic and political discrimination as well as the presence of religious and nationalist-separatist trends and also economic dependence on other countries. Another hypothesis was based on the assumption that protests escalate into internal war as a result of negative sanctions on the part of the government.[24] Protest provokes government repression, which itself helps to produce a fresh and more intense wave of protest and violence. Increased coerciveness offers no likelihood or guarantee of enhancing public order; on the contrary, it tends to undermine it. Thus, in the final analysis, government coerciveness is positively related to political instability. Such findings may have applied perhaps to a few countries but they were obviously wrong with regard to many others. Meanwhile, again from within the profession, some searching studies were challenging the conventional wisdom underlying most of the work that had been done. Was it really true that hardship was always the cause of collective violence and that there was a close correspondence between urbanization, crime and collective violence? Tilly and his colleagues, from studies of nineteenth- and twentieth-century France, reached the conclusion that it was quite wrong to assume that urban growth — by dissolving ties, disrupting existing controls or disorienting newcomers to the city — had a strong and consistent tendency to increase the level of crime, violence and disorder. More important yet, their research showed that there was no general connection between collective violence and hardship "such that an observer could predict one from another . . . and we suppose that the principal, immediate causes of collective violence are political."[25] A monograph on Africa showed that social mobilization on that continent, contrary to expectations, did not generally lead to frustration and violence.

Radical political scientists have sharply criticized their nonradical colleagues on many counts, but so far as methods of explaining political violence are concerned, the differences between them and their colleagues are not readily discernible. Neither believe in history and the scope of the radicals' work is conditioned by the liberal-democratic political regime in which they live; what Marx said about the conditioning of political consciousness is certainly applicable to them. A recent assessment of revolutionary warfare (including political terrorism) by radical political scientists may serve as an example.[26] According to this school of thought, such warfare has acquired unprecedented popularity; it is a "moral explosion" among the disenchanted masses in under-developed countries. It does not break out where there are institutions and mechanisms through which one can hope to influence and change the existing system. The question of legitimacy is crucial: legitimacy comes to governments when citizens actively and meaningfully participate in the processes of government, that is when there is a maximum of self-government. There is little to quarrel with the sentiments expressed: that there should be a maximum of self-government in society, that governments should have legitimacy and that there should be free institutions goes without saying. It may even be true that this concept is historically true with regard to one or two countries, for such is the variety of history that few theories are altogether wrong. But with the occurrence and success of terrorism on a worldwide basis such general propositions have no more relevance than the correlation between the incidence of storks and the birthrate in Sweden. There have been no moral explosions among the disenchanted masses of the underdeveloped countries of late because their new rulers have abandoned the moral inhibitions of the former colonial masters. As far as self-government is concerned, it is unfortunately true that, by and large, the less there has been of it in a country, the more immune the country has been from terrorism. Wherever the means of repression has been most complete and perfect there has been no terrorism at all. These facts are not in dispute, but there is a psychological resistance to accepting the obvious. Seldom has it been admitted that virtue in politics is not always rewarded. One of the few exceptions is Romero Maura in his discussion of Anarchism in Spain. One school of thought, Maura noted, has alleged that Anarchism was the explosive result of a lack of political freedom:

> The safety-valve metaphor is popular but based on a misrepresentation of Spanish modern history, while failing to take into account the plain fact that anarchism and other revolutionary movements have only been strong in conditions where other, more moderate political alter-natives *were* available.[27]

Thus the results of the application of political science to the study of internal conflict, far from proving anything, have been quite negative and no truly scientific (that is, predictive or explanatory) theories have emerged. One can think of a great many reasons why this should have been so, but three major causes immediately come to mind. A quantitative index cannot possibly reflect deprivation which defies "objective" measurement. Secondly, most of the research was unhistorical and thus ignored the fact that political violence has occurred in ages of rapid social change as well as in periods of stagnation; it has happened in countries that were ethnically homogeneous as well as heterogeneous. Terrorism has been sponsored by the left as well as the right. There have been fundamental differences between anarchist and national-separatist terrorisms; "pure terrorism" is not unknown; terrorism has sometimes been merely one weapon among others used by political movements. Indeed, its very character has been subject to change. In short, a good case can be made for the comparative study of terrorism, but it should have been apparent that not everything can be compared with everything else. Finally the analysis of political violence has not only been one-dimensional in time, i.e., synchronic instead of diachronic, exclusively preoccupied with the present age and so ahistorical; it has also implicitly assumed democratic societies to be the norm and ignored modern dictatorships, and this at a time when only a relatively small part of humanity has the good fortune to live in democratic, or quasi-democratic, societies. This curious parochialism has resulted in assertions, such as that regimes resorting to coercion tend to defeat themselves, which cannot be seriously maintained in the light of historical experience, especially that of recent times. History may sometimes reward the virtuous, but this is unfortunately not a historical law; Meriam's dictum, that "power is not strongest where it uses violence but weakest," may or may not apply to certain cases in the past, it is certainly not valid in the age of totalitarian dictatorships. The use of the notion of legitimacy has only served to obscure some quite patent facts of the modern world. What is one to say about a quantitative analysis of 114 countries which indicates that as the legitimacy of governments decreases, internal violence increases or about a state department conference which reaches the conclusion that recourse to repression is a self-defeating tendency because it thereby loses the appearance of legitimacy?[28] Can it be safely maintained that the governments of Uganda, Algeria, Afghanistan, Albania and Czechoslovakia (to chose a random few which know no terror except from above) are that much more legitimate than those of England, West Germany, Canada, France, Italy or Spain, which have been the targets of terrorist operations?

It has been said that even if there existed a valid theory of political instability and civil violence in general, it would still be a long way from a theory of terrorism.[29] In fact, it is not at all clear whether there has to be any connection at all between these phenomena, for terrorism is usually resorted to by small groups of people whose motives may not necessarily be connected with observable "objective" political, economic, social or psychological trends. Even if it could be shown, for argument's sake, that the feeling of relative deprivation is widespread in a certain country, it does not follow that the handful of active terrorists are those most acutely suffering from it. Thus, given the specific difficulties involved in the study of terrorism rather than political violence in general, it is not surprising that there has been no stampede to search for a general theory explaining the phenomenon. Eugen V. Walter, on the basis of a study of some primitive societies, has provided a "general theory of terrorism." But his concern is with the rule of terror, with terror exercised by the holders of power. He excludes from his investigations movements attempting to overthrow established systems of power.[30] Some authors have provided general observations, but these are more in the nature of classification and definition. Thornton has described terror as a symbolic act in an internal war designed to influence political behavior by means entailing the use of the threat of violence.[31] Brian Crozier has noted that terror is usually the weapon of the weak and that it is most suited to national liberation struggles against foreigners. Paul Wilkinson has pointed out that the effects of terrorism are highly unpredictable and that terrorist violence can escalate until it is uncontrollable.[32] All this is probably true but it is not of much help in understanding what causes terrorism. Political science, to paraphrase G. M. Trevelyan, is not something you take to history; with luck it is something you carry away from history. Robert Moss has referred to the sense of relative deprivation and the legitimacy gap. Z. Ivianski has explained the Anarchist terrorism of the 1890s by reference to urbanization, cultural crisis, the breakdown of traditional society and mass migration. (It is quite true that, as Ivianski notes, in the 1890s many of the propagandists of the deed were immigrants, but this has, however, no significance with regard to Russian and Irish terrorism.) Paul Wilkinson has made a small bow to the cross-national studies on political violence of the 1960s. But these are foreign implants in otherwise valuable studies; they are hypotheses, only occasionally borne out by the historical evidence — not conclusions.[33] Both Crozier and Thornton believe that terrorism is associated with the initial phase of guerrilla warfare. It would be easy to think of many instances, past and present, where this has not been the case; nor should too much be made of terrorism as a "symbolical act"; a campaign of systematic terror consists of many acts that are not symbolical at all. Hannah Arendt has noted a connection between terrorism and protest against the anonymous character of modern society.[34] But while *obiter dicta* of this kind contain a grain of truth, it is scarcely new; historians of Anarchism such as Zenker made similar observations many decades ago. On the other hand, it would appear that the anonymity of modern society in no way helps to explain the activities of the IRA, the ETA or Fatah; their complaints have a different character. According to Feliks Gross, a terroristic response arises as a result of foreign oppressive rule and conquest or oppressive domestic rule (the "Sociological factor"). But Gross quite rightly notes that objective circumstances per se are not a sufficient, perhaps not even a necessary condition of terrorism, for oppression must be perceived as such by a particular group. The

formation or existence of a revolutionary party needs definite ideological objectives and also a certain personality type. Gross stresses
the importance of ethnic and ideological-political tensions rather
than economic and social conditions and notes that terror may be
long-lasting and become institutionalized.[35] There is little to quarrel
with these observations as far as they go, but they are mainly based
on the experience of nineteenth- and twentieth-century Eastern
European terrorism; they do not necessarily apply elsewhere and,
furthermore, they merely define conditions in which terrorism
might, or might not, occur.

From what has been said so far, it seems that quantitative research
into the origins and character of political violence has not contributed
much to the understanding of terrorism. The more ambitious the
project, the wider its scope, the more sweeping the hypotheses, the
more reckless the quantification of data, the more disappointing the
results. But this is not to say that the study of terrorist movements is *a
priori* unfeasible and that it should not be undertaken. There is an
accidental element in the emergence of terrorism and for this reason
a truly scientific, predictive study is indeed impossible. But it is also
true that terrorism is more likely to occur in certain social and political
conditions than in others and that there are interesting parallels
between the etiology and the properties of terrorist movements
which have been insufficiently investigated. To compare the Narodovoltsy of the 1870s with the Symbionese Liberation Army or the
Baader-Meinhof Gang would clearly be a waste of time, but a comparative study of "urban guerrilla" groups in Latin America or a juxtaposition of past and present nationalist terrorist groups such as the IRA,
the Basque ETA and perhaps the Macedonian IMRO and the Croat
Ustasha could be of considerable interest.

It is quite likely that the record would not have been so negative
if an idea first suggested in the 1960s had been followed up and
expanded. H. Eckstein noted at the time that etiologies of internal
wars were chaotic and unproductive because, among other things,
they concentrated on insurgents and ignored incumbents. In real
life, internal war results from the interplay of forces and counter-
forces, from a balance of possibilities. There are forces pushing
toward internal war, but there are also prerequisites for and obstacles
to it.[36] The idea that revolutions were as much due to the incapacity

of elites as to the vigor and skill of the challengers of the system had of course been expressed before; but it had not served as a point of departure for the study of terrorism. Such an investigation ranging over the last hundred years would, at the very least, have saved a great deal of time and effort and prevented a great many projects that were doomed to failure from the very beginning. It would have shown that terrorism, however justified the grievances of its proponents, has under no circumstances succeeded against effective dictatorship; it has not managed to weaken it, modify its policies or affect its course of action in any way. If terrorism has had any success at all, it has been against democratic governments and ineffective, meaning obsolete or halfhearted, dictatorships. It has been relatively frequent among separatist-nationalist minorities; it was predominantly "right-wing" in character between the two world wars and it has more often than not been left-wing — with some important exceptions — since the 1950s.

The indiscriminate use of terms such as "left-wing" and "right-wing" and the inclination to take political ideology at face value have made an understanding of the issues involved all the more difficult. Slogans apart, "left-wing" and "right-wing" terrorism have more in common than is usually acknowledged. Terrorism always assumes the protective coloring of certain features of the *Zeitgeist*, which was Fascist in the 1920s and 1930s but took a different direction in the 1960s and 1970s. In actual fact, however, underlying both "left-wing" and "right-wing" terrorism there is usually a free-floating activism — populist, frequently nationalist, intense in character but vague and confused. Writing well before the recent wave of terrorism, the late G. D. H. Cole, a man of impeccable left-wing credentials, noted that in a later age the Anarchist terrorists of the 1890s would probably have been Fascists. Such a generalization may well be unfair toward the Anarchists of the 1890s but it provides food for thought with regard to terrorist politics of a later age. Many Latin American terrorists of the 1960s and 1970s, for instance, would almost certainly have been Fascist, had they been born twenty years earlier.

Accepting the disturbing fact that effective dictatorships are immune to terror but that even the most just and permissive democratic countries are not, it would still be of interest to know why certain democratic societies (Scandinavia, Australia, New Zealand,

Switzerland, Belgium, Holland and a few others) have witnessed relatively little terror. It will be noted that the population of these countries is small, that these states are predominantly Protestant in character, and that their political culture in recent history has been generally peaceful. As for the non-Communist dictatorships, some have managed with comparatively little repression to subdue or prevent opposition, whereas others have had to invest much greater efforts, and this quite irrespective of how far the grievances of the opposition were justified. It would be interesting to know why certain national minorities have accepted their fate *qua* minorities while others have launched into bitter and protracted warfare. In certain cases, separatist terrorism may be explained with reference to outside support but this is not always true, and in the last resort the outcome of such confrontation depends upon the terrorists' determination and that of their opponents. It is doubtful whether studying the impact of economic development on the spread of terrorism will provide many new clues for understanding the phenomenon. The relationship seems to be tenuous in the extreme. Stagnation certainly is not the reason; industrial development in Ulster has been faster than in England, and the same applies to the Basque region in comparison to Spain as a whole. Terrorism in Latin America has occurred in the countries with the highest per capita income such as Cuba and Venezuela and it has been more rampant in developed Uruguay and Argentina than in backward Paraguay or Ecuador. Yet it would not be difficult to think of prolonged and bloody periods of *violencia,* Colombian style, in poor and stagnant societies. To unravel the mysterious character of terrorist movements with reference to general economic trends is like using a giant nutcracker to crack a very tiny object, which might not even be a nut. There should be no illusions about what can be discovered about the origins and the character of terrorism: all that can be established is that terrorism is more likely to occur in certain circumstances than in others and that in some conditions it cannot take root at all.

II

Fiction holds more promise for the understanding of the terrorist phenomenon than political science, but some words of caution are nevertheless called for. Terrorism has figured prominently in works of modern literature, but the novels, plays, poems and films are of unequal value in providing historical evidence and psychological explanation.*

*Some of the novels and plays mentioned subsequently inspired the moviemakers. This refers to *Under Western Eyes (Sous les yeux de l'Occident)*, with Jean-Louis Barrault (France, 1936); *The Secret Agent* [directed by Hitchcock, 1936); Sartre's *Les Mains sales* (1951). The most impressive film was no doubt John Ford's *The Informer*, based on Liam O'Flaherty's novel, with Victor McLaglen in the role of Gypo Nolan, who betrays his comrades. There had been a silent version of *The Informer* directed by Arthur Robinson in 1929. John Ford made yet another film with an IRA background, *The Plough and the Stars* (1937), based on Sean O'Casey's play, but this was much less successful than *The Informer*. Other memorable films with an Irish Civil War background were Carol Reed's *Odd Man Out* (1947), starring James Mason; *Ourselves Alone* (1936), shown under the title *River of Unrest* in the United States; and *Shake Hands with the Devil* (1959), with James Cagney. During the Second World War two films on the Irish underground were produced in Nazi Germany, *Der Fuchs von Glenarvon* (1940), and *Mein Leben für Irland* (1941). More recently Gillo Pontecorvo's *The Battle of Algiers* and Costas Gavras's *State of Siege* offer much of interest to the student of terrorism. The former, a very impressive film "offers a blueprint for other struggles and revolutions," teaching "urban guerrilla warfare" (Piernico Solinas, *Gillo Pontecorvo's "The Battle of Algiers"* [New York 1973], IX). This film of "rare ideological consistency" can be shown in France but not in Algeria, for street demonstrations and the shouts "Free Ben Bella" might well be misunderstood in view of the fact that Ben Bella has been in Algerian prisons for twelve years. The latter film is a quasi-documentary study of the Tupamaros which, however, takes considerable liberties with the historical record — a countrywide vote is taken before the execution of the American hostage (Dan Mitrione). The very first "terrorist" feature film I have been able to discover was Protazanov's *Andrei Kozhukhov* in 1917, with Ivan Moshukhin, known in Hollywood in later years as Ivan Mosjoukine, as the chief hero. This is based on Stepniak-Kravchinski's novel *The Road of a Nihilist* of 1889, of which more below. There was an even earlier short American film *Queen of the Nihilists* (ca. 1910), but it dealt with escape from prison rather than with terrorist operations. A bowdlerized version of Dostoyevsky's *Possessed* was produced in 1915 in Russia; also directed by Protazanov with Moshukhin in the title role (Protazanov was the first Russian producer of distinction). Andreyev's *Story of Seven Who Were Hanged* was produced in Russia in 1920, and there was a film on Stepan Khalturin in 1925. A film on Nechayev was envisaged in the 1920s but the idea had to be dropped for ideological reasons. This is almost the sum total of films on nineteenth-century Russian terrorism, which both during and after Stalin has remained a very delicate subject — very much in contrast to the Russian military tradition from Alexander Nevski to Kutuzov which has provided Soviet moviemakers with a wealth of material. Terrorist operations were the subject of many movies with a Second World War background, most dramatically perhaps Andrzej Wajda's *Kanal* (1957) and *Popiol i Diament (Ashes and Diamonds)*

The main difficulty, however, is that of approach and method. For the student of terrorism, fiction is a quarry in which rich finds can be made; it is no place for leisurely strolls. Above all, it is a most awkward subject for generalizations. It is easy to point to certain common patterns in the study of terrorism as practiced by political scientists, for there are only a very few basic schools of thought with only minor variations within each trend. The conclusions may not be true but they are certainly stated in an orderly unequivocal fashion as befitting a scientific discipline. With the transition from the sciences to the arts we move from the level of certainties to the realm of impression. To provide a coherent framework of orderly and lucid argument, to single out common patterns becomes well nigh impossible. It can be done but only by singling out certain themes in certain books (or plays or movies) at the expense of others. Literature as a source for the study of terrorism is still virtually *terra incognita;* a survey of a hitherto uncharted field may be more profitable at this stage than the attempt to impose a single clear pattern on the stories of individual heroes and villains.

(1958). The setting of *Kanal,* the fate of a unit of the *Armia Kraiowa* forced into the sewers of Warsaw, was used in Aleksander Ford's *Piatka z ulicy Barskiej (The Five from Larska Street).* Fritz Lang's *Hangmen Also Die,* on the assassination of Heydrich, also might be mentioned in this context. The *Molly Maguires* (1969) with Richard Harris and Sean Connery was shot on location in Eckley, Pennsylvania, to give it greater authenticity; Eckley was said to be the ugliest town in America. Some critics complained that they found it impossible to identify with either warring side. This may be an excellent testimony for the historical accuracy of the film but it did not make it a box office success. There was a renewed interest in terrorism in the late 1960s and early 1970s, as manifested, for instance, in Chabrol's *Nada* or in Alan Resnais's *La Guerre est Finie* with Yves Montand, the story of the old Spanish revolutionary who finds it difficult to accept the changing world: *Trente ans sont passés et les anciens m'emmerdent . . .* The same motif, the inability of the Anarchist released from prison in the 1880s to adapt to the new political mood, recurs in Taviani's *San Michele* (1971). There was a recent Swiss film on Nechayev in which the hero, contrary to historical evidence, has an affair with Natalie Herzen; a French movie on the exploits of the Bonnot gang in pre–World War I Paris; the Taviani brothers in Italy produced movies on various nineteenth- and twentieth-century terrorist groups and Brazilian filmmakers operating in Chile (under Allende) and in Mexico chose similar topics. Some of these films were not widely shown and there are by now, in any case, far too many of them for enumeration. Some are listed in Guy Hennebelle, *Cinema Militant* (Paris, n.d.), and in *Guide des films anti-imperialistes* (Paris, n.d.).

THE OUTSIDERS

For the student of terrorism, as distinct from the lover of literature, Ropshin (Savinkov) the Russian ex-terrorist turned writer, is as of much interest as Dostoyevsky and Liam O'Flaherty is more revealing than Henry James. O'Flaherty's preoccupation is not with the art of the novel but with the authenticity of the account. O'Flaherty served with the IRA whereas the author of *Princess Casamassima* later wrote that his novel "proceeded quite directly from the habit and the interest of walking the streets of London."[37] ("Hyacinth Robinson sprung at me out of the London pavement.") The streets of London have a great deal to offer but there are obvious limits to what they can teach about terrorists, their motives, thoughts and actions. Henry James and Joseph Conrad were attracted by certain specific facets of terrorism, the most dramatic, grotesque or fascinating ones for the student of the human soul. They also used it, as did Dostoyevsky, to juxtapose destructive terrorism and their own philosophy. Among the most dramatic (and politically most interesting) aspects of terrorism is of course the Judas Motive. It has been noted that Mr. Leopold Bloom thinks on not less than three occasions of Carey, the small-time building contractor and the chief organizer of the Phoenix Park murders who became a witness for the prosecution; and this in a book *(Ulysses)* written more than two decades after the event.[38] Terrorism inspired Borges to outline a plot on the theme of the traitor and the hero "which I shall perhaps write someday."[39] Betrayal is the main motive in Joseph Conrad's *Secret Agent* and *Under Western Eyes* and countless other novels. It is of course true that few, if any, terrorist groups escaped defectors and traitors in their ranks. However, the heavy emphasis on treason to the detriment of other motives is bound to distort the general picture. It may result in a brilliant work of fiction, but then the novelist is preoccupied with the fate of the individual, whereas the historian pays more attention to social and political movements. Robert Louis Stevenson and G. K. Chesterton were attracted by the grotesque element in terrorism. The hero in Stevenson's *The Dynamiters* is the redoubtable Zero, who wants to bomb Shakespeare's statue in Leicester Square but instead blows up the home of an inoffensive lady, believing that this will shake England to the heart and that "Gladstone, the truculent old man, will quail before the pointing finger of revenge."[40] Gabriel Syme, the writer-hero of Chesterton's *The Man Who Was Thursday*, is involved in the exploits of a group of anarchists, all of whom are police agents spying on each other. One of the high points of the novel is a chase through London on the back of an elephant.[41] Joseph Conrad made his views on Russia quite clear in his introduction to *Under Western Eyes*. His heroes are the "apes of a sinister jungle"; one of them, Nikita, is the "perfect flower of the terrorist wilderness." Conrad noted of his character: "What troubled me most in dealing with him was not his monstrosity but his banality." The behavior of the terrorists reflects the moral and emotional reactions of the Russian temperament to the pressure of tyrannical lawlessness "which, in general human terms could be reduced to the formula of senseless desperation provoked by senseless tyranny." Mr. Conrad clearly did not love Russians; nor did he like Anarchists, who, without exception, are depicted as degenerates of ludicrous physique or madmen like the "Professor" in *The Secret Agent*, who always left home with a bomb in his pocket so that at a moment's notice he could blow up himself as well as the policeman trying to arrest him.

Anarchism was a riddle as far as Western European public opinion at the time was concerned. The newspapers reported the existence of a mysterious society of ruthless men who had as their watchword the murder of monarchs and the overthrow of governments.[42] About the origin of these wild men there was, at best, speculation. Were they socialists or nihilists (whatever that meant), misguided idealists, criminals or madmen? Henry James could not make up his mind. In *Princess Casamassima*, Hyacinth Robinson is a young skilled worker who joins the Anarchists because of vague social sympathy (the same motive broadly speaking applies to the princess herself). He commits suicide when asked to murder on behalf of a cause in which he no longer believes. Hyacinth is a mere fellow-traveler, "divided to the point of torture" by sympathies pulling him in different directions. In the same novel a few real revolutionaries such as Muniment and Hoffendall make their appearance and so far as they are concerned it is not at all clear what causes them to act as they do. It has been said that there is no political event in the novel which is not confirmed by multitudinous record (Lionel Trilling). But although

Henry James read about Fenians and Anarchists he was, of course, dealing with a world with which he lacked intimate contact. Ricarda Huch, a German Neo-Romantic writer, knew, if possible, even less at first hand about terrorists than Henry James and her novel *Der letzte Sommer (The Last Summer)*, written in 1910, seemed at the time altogether unreal. It is the story of Lju, a young teacher who joins the household of a high Tsarist official, one of his functions being the protection of Jegor, the governor. He comes to like and respect the family but this does not prevent him from carrying out his mission, which is to kill his employer. A most ingenious method is used: the letter "J" in the official's typewriter is the fuse for a bomb which explodes the moment Jegor signs the letter he has written to his children. This needless to say is also the end of the novel.*

A fairly realistic picture of "propaganda of the deed" emerges from several semi-documentary novels of varying literary quality published around the beginning of the century. Zola's *Paris* (1898) is not one of his outstanding works but it conveys interesting impressions of the age of spectacular assassinations. The reader is subjected to a lecture on explosives, pursues the Anarchist through the Bois de Boulogne, watches his trial and execution.[43] London is the scene of Mackay's *The Anarchists*, which is mainly devoted to disputes between advocates of physical violence (Trupp) and those (Auban) who argue that the terrorists simply play into the hands of the authorities.[44] Mackay, born in Britain, grew up in Germany and wrote in German. His subsequent literary and political career led him far away from the Anarchist ideas of his youth. Mackay's novel is now virtually unreadable, but this is by no means true with regard to two other novels, one in Spanish, the other in Czech, which have unfortunately remained quite unknown outside their own countries. Pio Baroja's *Aurora Roja*, which takes place in Paris and Madrid around the turn of the century, is full of discussions about socialism and Anarchism, the future of Spain and the use of dynamite. It is a far

*Sixty-six years later Ana Maria Gonzalez, aged eighteen, worked her way into the family of General Cardozo, chief of the Buenos Aires police, and became a close friend of his eldest daughter, Graciela. The general was warned by his own informants about Miss Gonzalez but disregarded these warnings. She often slept in their apartment and eventually planted a bomb under the general's bed. Cardozo was killed; the corpse of Miss Gonzalez, a member of the ERP, was found a few days later in the streets of Buenos Aires. (*New York Herald Tribune*, June 22, 1976.)

more vivid novel than Mackay's work, not only because a great many historical figures make their appearance.[45] The hero, Juan Alcazar, is a young painter and sculptor who reaches the conclusion that he must fight for women and children and for all weak and defenseless people. For their sake society must be destroyed and the social fabric brutally cauterized. All ways, all means are good if they lead to revolution, *un Aurora de un nuevo dia.* But the idealistic young hero fails in a world in which base egotism prevails; a comrade says at his graveside that he became a rebel because he wanted to be just *(fue un rebelde porque quiso ser un justo).*[46]*

Even closer to historical events is a Czech novel, Marie Majerova's *Namesti Republiky.*[47] This is the story of a young Polish-Jewish tailor, Jakub Goldshmid ("Luka Vershinin"), who moves to Paris and joins the Libertad terrorist group. Disappointed by the false freedom of French republicanism on the one hand and repelled by the cynical attitude of Libertad on the other, he decides to do something that (he hopes) will trigger off a revolutionary rising. On May 1, 1905, he shoots three officers on the Place de la République. But, far from rising, the masses want to lynch him and he is saved only by the arrival of the police.[48] Frank Harris's *The Bomb* (1908) is also based on a well-known historical incident — the Haymarket bombing in Chicago in 1886. Harris, who lived in America for several years, tells the story of Louis Lingg, one of the main defendants in the subsequent trial, through the device of the recollections of one Rudolf Schnaubelt, who, for the purposes of the novel, is the man who threw the bomb. Schnaubelt, a recent immigrant, joins Lingg's Anarchist circle, having been shocked by the exploitation of foreign workers. Lingg says that he believes in force, the supreme arbiter of human affairs: "One cannot meet bludgeons with words, nor blows by turning the other cheek. Violence must be met by violence." Much of the material used by Harris is drawn from contemporary newspaper accounts; the

---

*The Spanish Anarchists of the 1930s in Ramon Sender's novel *Siete Domingos Rojos (Seven Red Sundays)* are Tolstoyans and vegetarians, but they have no hesitation about throwing bombs; furthermore, there is a substantial dose of egocentrism in their *Weltanschauung.* Thus Samar, the Anarchist, calls to the "naked crowds": "I hate you all! The unhappy and the happy! I hate you and despise you! For the imbecility of your outlook, for the feebleness of your passions." He dies when the prison is stormed, shouting, "Freedom or death," for death, "metaphysically and actually, is the only possible freedom."

Anarchists are depicted in a sympathetic light and *The Bomb* has been considered by later critics as a little masterpiece. It has been given high marks by left-wing reviewers, despite the somewhat unstable convictions of the author.

In the 1890s there was already the vision of terror and counterterror leading to universal disaster. In Ignatius Donnelly's *Caesar's Column*, New York is burned to the ground in the Brotherhood of Destruction's rebellion against a small oligarchy which maintains itself in power with a fleet of dirigibles armed with gas bombs; this is a remarkable piece of science fiction considering that the novel was written in 1891. In Part Two of Bjørnson's *Over Aevne (Beyond Human Powers)*, Elias Sang, the leader of the striking workers, confronts the brutal and arrogant Holger, representing the interest of "grand capital." He too decides to use dynamite as his *ultima ratio;* Sang is killed in the process and Holger crippled, but the last act witnesses a not altogether convincing reconciliation. Bjørnson did not like Anarchists but he noted that they were the modern martyrs, welcoming death with a smile because they believed like Christ that their martyrdom would redeem humanity.[49]

Terrorism as a moral problem continued to preoccupy some of the leading writers of the 1930s and 1940s. Brecht, as so often, was an exception; he was fascinated by violence and wanted to shock the public: the young comrade (in *Die Massnahme*) has to be killed because out of foolish pity and a misplaced sense of honor and justice he had revealed his own identity and so endangered the whole conspiratorial group: "Hence we decided to cut off our own foot from the body." True, the Communists are unhappy ("it is horrible to kill") and before committing the deed they ask the victim's permission.[50]

The dilemma of terrorism reappears in Sartre's *Les Mains sales (Dirty Hands)*, and Camus' *Les Justes.* The action in Sartre's play takes place in a south European country. Hugo decides to kill Hoederer, the party secretary. Although there are political reasons, his real motives are personal: he wants to be recognized by his comrades not only as a journalist but also as a doer. In the end, after many hesitations, he does kill Hoederer, but only after finding his wife in Hoederer's arms. Hugo knows full well that he too will now be liquidated and that this has given meaning to his action. Though dramatically effective, *Les Mains sales* is confusing; like Brecht's play it was sharply attacked by the Communists, much to Sartre's dismay, but it has remained one of his great popular successes.

Moral issues are more clear-cut in Camus' play which takes Kalyayev's assassination of the Grand Duke Serge as its starting point.[51] The first attempt has failed because Kalyayev did not want to kill the Grand Duke's children who were with him. There is a bitter quarrel among the terrorists: Dora, Annenkov and Voinov justify his action because the new and better world should not be inaugurated by the murder of children. On the other hand Stepan, the iron Jacobin, argues that in the scale of the fate of humanity the lives of two children weigh lightly when measured against the thousands who will die every year of starvation — unless the system is destroyed. But Kalyayev does not accept the argument: certainly the Grand Duke has to die and he has to do the deed. But murder is wrong; all life is sacred and the crime has to be expiated by the death of the murderer. And so, after the assassination, Kalyayev does not ask for a pardon which he might have been given. When the news of his execution arrives, Dora, his mistress, announces that she will be the next to throw a bomb.

TERRORISM IN RUSSIAN LITERATURE

Dostoyevsky's *Besy (The Possessed)*, written in 1871–1872, is the best known "terrorist" novel in world literature and is largely based on the Bakunin-Nechaev affair. Pyotr Verkhovenski, possessed by the idea of destruction, kills the student Shatov, a fellow conspirator, allegedly because he represents a threat of denunciation. In fact he kills him out of pure boredom. In Ivan Leskov's *Nekuda (Nowhere to Go)* (1864) the Nihilists, with one exception, are all either infantile characters or degenerates, and in *Na Nozhakh (At Daggers Drawn)* (1870–1871) they act as "contract killers," murdering a rich husband to enable his widow to inherit. They promote murder, theft and corruption in every possible way. Leskov was accused by his more progressive contemporaries of having been commissioned to write this novel by the secret police. He himself claimed that he had simply provided a "photographic rendering of reality."[52]

The terrorist motive fascinated many Russian writers of the second half of the nineteenth century; the avant-garde defended the "Nihilists" but, in view of Tsarist censorship, this had to be done in Aesopian language. In contrast the anti-Nihilist novels and plays (of Klyushnikov, Markevich, Ustryalov, Prince Meshcherski) were far more outspoken. This entire literature is now deservedly forgotten with the exception of the works of Turgenev, whose Nihilists were not, however, terrorists.

More intriguing are the books published outside Russia and in Russia after 1905, when censorship was considerably relaxed. Serge Stepniak Kravchinski, a leading Narodovolets, was the author of several indifferent novels, but he also wrote the classic account of the terrorist movement of the late 1870s.[53] *Underground Russia* was clearly a labor of love; his heroes, the leading members of the Narodnaya Volya, are without exception idealists of the highest moral standards.* Stefanovich was an atheist, but his closest relationship was with his father, an old village priest. Lisogub is described as a "saint," Vera Zasulich as a woman of "great moments and great decisions" and Sofia Perovskaya as a revolutionary of "iron will, iron self-discipline who always went first into the fire." True, there are passing references to Ossinski's feverish excitement and to the fact that he loved women and was loved by them. It is also made clear that Klements was a charismatic leader but quite unsuited for work in a small conspirational group. On the whole, however, there were few shadows in this story of heroic and virtuous people and there is reason to assume that the picture is true to life: the men and women of the Narodnaya Volya were indeed most attractive human beings. This also emerges from other contemporary accounts. Young Vera Barantzova in Sophia Kovalevsky's novel follows her terrorist husband to his Siberian exile: "Are you weeping for me?" she said with a cheerful smile. "If only you knew how I pity those who are left behind."[54] There is always the motive of sacrifice by the chosen few

---

Underground Russia was basically an autobiographical account, the first of a great many. The recollections of Morozov, Frolenko, Vera Figner, Gershuni, Savinkov and others are one of the most important sources for the study of Russian terrorism. This is also true for some other terrorist groups; the autobiographical accounts of Natan Yalin-Mor and Geula Cohen are of greater interest than the novels written about Irgun and LEHI.

and the belief in final victory. For example, one novel by Stepniak closes with a declaration that though the hero, Andrei Kozhukhov, has perished, the cause for which he died still lives: "It goes forward from defeat to defeat towards the final victory, which in this sad world of ours cannot be obtained save by the sufferings and the sacrifice of the chosen few."[55] The Narodovoltsy appear in a similar light in Leopold Stanislav Brzozowski's *Plomienie (Flames)*, which has remained almost totally unknown in the West.[56]

Where Conrad saw nothing but an "imbecile and atrocious answer of a purely Utopian revolutionism," Brzozowski invoked high moral pathos when describing the thoughts and actions of the handful of young heroes who challenged the overwhelming power of the Tsarist regime. Where Conrad saw a strange conviction that a fundamental change of heart must follow the downfall of any given human institution ("these people are unable to see that all they can effect is merely a change of names"), his fellow Pole was dazzled by the vision of the emergence of a new man and a new society. Brzozowski's novel is in the form of a diary kept by a young Polish nobleman, Michael Kaniowski, who throws his lot in with the revolutionaries of the 1870s. Nechaev, Mikhailov, Zhelyabov, Goldenberg and many others make their appearance, sometimes under hardly veiled *noms de clef* (Tikhonravov = Tikhomirov), and the author, on the whole, sticks fairly closely to the historical record. The reader follows the hero on his revolutionary grand tour to the Paris Commune, to the workers of the Swiss Jura and to Italy. But above all it is the political, cultural and social life of Russia of the period which constitutes the canvas of the great epic which ends with the release of Kaniowski from the Schlüsselburg fortress where he has been a prisoner for many years. *Flames* was clearly a labor of love: the Narodovoltsy are seen, as in so many other accounts of the period, as knights engaged in a hopeless struggle on behalf of a cause that will triumph only at some future date: the blood of the martyrs is the seed of the church. The religious elements of the novel are reflected in chapter headings such as *Dies Illa* or *Dolori et Amori Sacrum*. Despite certain literary weaknesses, *Flames* is one of the most vivid accounts of the Narodovoltsy ever written and perhaps the most inspiring, yet the book never had the success it deserved. Written in Polish it remained a work of marginal interest in Brzozowski's native country because it dealt with the revolutionary tradition of the oppressor nation. The Russians were reluctant to look for inspiration to an author whose own credentials were not above suspicion; some years after the novel was written, Burtsev, the indefatigable sleuth of the Russian revolutionary movement, declared that the novelist had been a Tsarist police spy. But Burtsev, though the first to make it publicly known that Azev had been a police agent, was not infallible: Brzozowski's friends all stood by him and defended him against the accusations.[57] Burtsev's informant was Bakaj, an official of the Okhrana in Warsaw with no conceivable personal motive for denouncing Brzozowski. Could *Flames* have been written by a police informant? The affair continued to preoccupy Polish literary circles throughout the 1920s and 1930s and although the evidence is perhaps not altogether conclusive, there is some reason to assume that Brzozowski (who died in Florence in 1910) may have acted at one time as a police informer.

All this refers to the heroes of the 1870s and 1880s. The Russian terrorist movement of the early twentieth century was less fortunate in its authors — but it is also true that reality had become more complex and that the motives of terrorists were often less obvious. True, there were admirers of the movement from Gorky to Leonid Andreyev, but those with more intimate knowledge provided less flattering pictures. Boris Savinkov (Ropshin), the onetime leader of the terrorist organization of the Social Revolutionaries, is a good example. When planning assassinations in 1905 he was not plagued by doubts on the rightness of his cause; the terrorist-hero of his novel four years later is a very different character, describing himself as bored by his own thoughts and desires: "People and their lives bore me. There is a wall between them and myself. Let love save the world. I need no love. I am alone. Damned be the world. . . ."[58] Yet at the same time there is a preoccupation with moral issues: the choice, says the hero, is either to kill all the time or never to kill at all. Why should he be eulogized for having killed the police chief, and why should the colonel be a villain for hanging the revolutionaries? Did not he too act out of conviction and not for material gain? And, if so, who made these rules? Marx, Engels and Kant, who had never killed a man in their lives? In Savinkov's *Pale Horse*, a story in diary form, each of the five heroes is driven by different motives: Vanya is a religious fanatic; Genrich is a socialist; and Fyodor is an "emotional terrorist" who opted for revolutionary violence, having seen a woman killed by the Cossacks during a riot. Erna participates because she loves George, the main hero, who does not believe in anything or anyone. *The Pale Horse* created a minor storm in Russian left-wing circles and was severely condemned by Savinkov's erstwhile comrades. The storm became a major scandal in 1913 with the publication of Ropshin-Savinkov's second novel *To chevo ne bylo*.[59] Now the moral chaos is absolute; beneath a Nietzschean veneer there is only emptiness, crime and betrayal. The leader of the group, Dr. Berg (Azev?), a police agent, is killed by Abram, a Jewish terrorist.[60] The whole atmosphere is one of hopelessness: the struggle cannot possibly be won, the government is bound to prevail. Savinkov's subsequent fate is of some interest. He served in the French army during the First World War, was for a short time governor-general of Petrograd under Kerensky in 1917 and committed suicide or was killed in a Soviet prison in 1924, after allegedly having organized terrorist operations against the Bolsheviks.

THE INSIDER

Savinkov was a unique case among the Russian writers of his day; French and English literature on Anarchism, with some notable exceptions, reveals more about those who wrote it than those who engaged in it. Irish literature is far more rewarding in this respect.

In Irish plays, novels and short stories one is never far from the bomb and the sniper — and this refers to Yeats and Joyce as well as to Brendan Behan, who at sixteen, arrived in Britain on the eve of the Second World War with a few bombs.[61] It appears in Yeats's *Easter 1916* and his *Rose Tree*, that needs but to be watered to make the green come out again, or in the "Sixteen Dead Men" loitering there to stir the boiling pot. What Auden said about Yeats ("Mad Ireland hurt you into poetry") is perhaps even more true for the writers of the following generation. Sometimes the allusions are obscure (as in Yeats's *Second Coming*) and the experts are still hard at work interpreting them. Nor are they always complimentary; in *Ulysses* and *Finnegans Wake* the heroes of a past age usually appear in a lurid light, but then Joyce was never the paradigm of an Irish patriot. The "terrible beauty" is in any case balanced by a great many ugly things. But Yeats too was irked by the fact that the "Young Irelanders" treated literature as subservient to political doctrine, as an instrument for politics. And it has been noted that when Yeats justified the *Easter Rising* he did so on other than moral grounds — "A terrible beauty is born," not a terrible virtue.[62] There is Sean O'Casey's moving epitaph to the heroes of 1916:

> They had helped God to rouse up Ireland: let the people answer for them now! For them now, tired and worn, there was but a long, long sleep; a thin ribbon of flame from a line of levelled muskets, and then a long sleep. . . . But Cathleen. the daughter of Houlihan, walks from now, a flush on her haughty cheek. She hears the murmur in the people's hearts. Her lovers are gathering around her, for things are changed, changed utterly:
> A terrible beauty is born,
> poor, dear, deadmen; poor W. B. Yeats.[63]

But there is little of that pathos in O'Casey's plays: the women are fanatics; the men fight because they are afraid to admit their fear or, worse, in order to plunder.[64] Above all, almost everyone is given to boasting. In *The Shadow of a Gunman* Minnie, the admiring young woman, asks Davoren ("poet and poltroon"): "Do you never be afraid?" Davoren: "I'll admit one does be a little nervous, at first, but a fellow gets used to it after a bit till, at last, a gunman throws a bomb as carelessly as a schoolboy throws a snowball." But eventually Minnie gets out in the streets, shouts "up the Republic" at the top of her voice and is killed, while Davoren goes on hiding.[65]

The case of Jack Cliteroe in *The Plough and the Stars* (1926) is also quite revealing: "Why doesn't Cliteroe have anything to do with the Citizens Army?" "Just because he wasn't made a Captain of. He wasn't goin' to be in anything where he couldn't be conspicuous. He was so cocksure of being made one that he bought a Sam Browne belt an' was always puttin' it on an' standin' at th' door showing it off in." There was a public scandal at the first performance and O'Casey had to leave Dublin for London. In *Juno and the Paycock* (which also became a film in 1930), young neurotic Johnny Boyle is executed by IRA fanatics for having betrayed his neighbor to the police. The Irish writers, playwrights and poets were awkward witnesses, perhaps doubly so because they knew the terrorists so well. Most of them came to agree with what O'Leary had said on an earlier occasion about the dynamiters: "There are things no man should do, even to save a nation." Yeats' *Cathleen ni Houlihan* includes the old woman's promise to those who die for Ireland: "They shall be remembered for ever." In this play Ireland appears in the guise of an old woman but in the end she is transformed into her true likeness: "Did you see an old woman going down the path? I saw no old woman, but a young girl and she had the walk of a queen." When in 1939 Yeats lay dying he remembered these words with a certain horror and asked himself the question, "Did that play of mine send out certain men the English shot?"[66]

The real heroes in Sean O'Casey's plays and in O'Flaherty's novels are (noncombatant) women; the men are dubious types more often than not. Sean O'Faolain's Leo O'Donnell is an anti-hero and Commander Dan Gallagher in Liam O'Flaherty's *The Informer* tells his girlfriend that "they talk at headquarters about romanticism and leftism and all sorts of freak notions. What do they know about the peculiar type of hog mind that constitutes an Irish peasant?" Yet O'Flaherty, Frank O'Connor and Sean O'Faolain all fought in the ranks of the IRA (the last-mentioned was its director of publications) and O'Casey was a Communist of sorts. Whatever their professed politics, most terrorists are really mystics and the idea of martyrdom obsesses them. It is the central theme in one of Liam O'Flaherty's novels. Crosbie, the martyr, is a strange mixture of mystic and Nietzschean, recalling some of Savinkov's heroes. He is, in his own words, "a light shining in the darkness," he needs no guide to heaven: "I'm waiting on the mountains in Europe and the whole of Christendom is waiting for the resurrection when the brazen gods of money and sensual pleasure shall be burned in the dust and Christ, our Saviour, again enthroned as the King of Kings. There will be peace between all men. There will be no hunger, no disease and the only suffering will be the craving of souls for union with God."[67] All this from a terrorist engaged in indiscriminate killing after the war against the foreign occupier has already been won.

The question of motive reappears time and again in the books written by insiders. There are the conventional explanations: to

serve people, to save the nation, to redeem mankind. But there is also
the bad conscience of the intellectual as described by Regis Debray.
Frank, his hero, never finds real identity with the guerrillas; he
joined them because he had pangs of conscience.

> Où étais-je le jour où des paysans en sandales donnèrent l'assaut à
> Dien Bien Phu? Le jour où Frank Pais s'écroula, criblé par les flics de
> Batista sur un trottoir de Santiago de Cuba? . . . Tout occupé à siroter
> un vin de pays, à caresser les seins d'une brune un peu fugace. . . .

There is much talk about Gramsci and Lukacs, but in the end:

> 'Peu m'importe en effet la destination — socialisme ou autre — voire
> même le sort des autres voyageurs. Pourvu que ça roule.[68]

When the Macedonian revolt broke out around the turn of the
century, Pejo Javorov was a young Bulgarian poet groping for the
meaning of life. "All my interior world is in ruins," he wrote to a
friend; "I am lost if I do not find a new religion to inspire me."[69] He
found it in the ranks of the IMRO and saw action on Ilin Den; he
wrote some fine poems as a result. The enthusiasm lasted for a year
or two, and then he was back to depression, hopelessness — and
symbolist poetry in the French style.

The motive of the intellectual who vainly yearns to be a terrorist
appears also in Arthur Koestler's *Thieves in the Night.** Joseph is told
by the terrorist commander that he has that intellectual squint which
makes him see both sides of a medal — "a luxury we cannot longer
afford. We have to use violence and deception, to save others from
violence and deception." But despite his moral scruples Joseph asks
permission to take part in an action — "even if only one." It is so
much easier for the young boy who, when asked what made him join
the Freedom Fighters, answers: *Exodus* twenty, one, *Deuteronomy*
nineteen, one, "Block out the remembrance of Amalek from under
heaven." "Thine eye shall not pity." "I will make mine arrows drunk
with blood." Koestler's Joseph is a democratic socialist who turns to

---

*Koestler was not, of course, an "insider." But he knew and admired Jabotinsky who
had been until his death in 1940 the supreme authority of Irgun. He also met some
of the Irgun and LEHI commanders.

terrorism because he has realized that a nation of conscientious objectors cannot survive and that "if we left it to them we shall share the fate that befell their comrades in Germany, Austria, Italy and so on." Hence the necessity to speak "the only language universally understood from Shanghai to Madrid, the new Esperanto that is so easy to learn — the gun under the leather jacket."

The Bible provided constant inspiration to Avraham Stern ("Yair"): God himself is a warrior *(Ish milkhama Adonai zvaot)*, armed struggle and bomb throwing are acts of praise to God *(Halleluya be Kravot ubepezazot)*. The kingdom of Israel, the central and somewhat vague concept in Yair's thought, will be reached only by way of the valley of the shadow of death. The theme of death appears in almost every one of Stern's poems, including the anthem of LEHI: "Unknown soldiers without uniform, we have joined for our whole life — around us only horror and the shadow of death."[70]

Joseph, Koestler's hero, graduates from democratic socialism to terrorism. Gyorgy Kardos, another novelist of Hungarian origin, wrote a novel showing what made one terrorist give up the armed struggle — not weakness, but because he found fulfillment in another way of life. The action takes place in Mandatory Palestine in 1946 or 1947. David is on the run: the British chase him as a terrorist; Irgun is after him for failing to carry out an assignment. He hides on the farm of one Avraham Bogatyr, and his contempt for those who have opted for nonviolent resistance gradually turns into admiration.[71]

The Irish, Irgun, LEHI and Debray's hero Frank, were bothered by a great many problems, but the question of purpose was not among them. The struggle against oppression was their overriding concern; right and wrong were certainties, they were fighting for a sacred cause. They would have been incapable of understanding the (mainly platonic) advocates of terrorism in America of a later generation, who saw their heroes in Bonnie and Clyde; indeed, any such argument would have appeared blasphemous. The very concept of destruction as instant theater would have been demeaning if not altogether incomprehensible.* This was the language of pseudo-ter-

---

*"When in doubt, burn. Fire is the revolutionary's god. Fire is instant theatre. No words can match fire. Burn the flag, burn the churches. Burn, burn, burn." Barely five years later, Cleaver and Rubin were changed men, burning the gods of violence they had once worshipped.

rorists. Yet in a strange way the nihilist syndrome was by no means new and it appeared on the right as well as among the left. Chen, the terrorist in Malraux's *Condition humaine,* has ceased to believe in humanity long ago: "I do not like mankind to be so indifferent towards all the suffering." Yet in the end he throws himself with his bomb in front of the car in which he mistakenly believes Chiang Kai-shek is driving.

The question of purpose never bothered Ernst von Salomon and his comrades who assassinated Rathenau.[72] "What do you want?" they were asked. "We could not answer because we could not even understand the question. We did not act according to plans and well-defined aims." They were certainly not fighting "so that the people should be happy"; they were propelled into action by some inner force. From one excitement they went on to the next. Kern, the leader of the group, told them that he had been dead since November 9, 1918 — Armistice Day, the day of national disgrace. All that remained was the work of destruction: "We want the revolution. Our task is the 'push' not the seizure of power."[73] When asked what kind of motives they should admit to if caught by the police after the assassination, Kern answered, half bored, half amused: "Oh God, how little does it matter. Say that he was one of the Elders of Zion or that he let his sister marry Radek — who cares. . . ." They feared one thing only — that the dead Rathenau would suddenly appear as a witness in their trial . . .

The nihilistic mood pervades much of the right-wing literature of the early 1920s. Schlageter, in Hanns Johst's play of the same name (dedicated to Adolf Hitler in "loving admiration") is not troubled by metaphysical question; since the French are occupying the Ruhr, it is the duty of every German patriot to resist them in every possible way — ethical problems do not bother the former soldier. If he has doubts at first, they concern the effect of terror:

> Politics can't be created with one bundle of Ekrasit, that's just playing at terror: every action must have a purpose. . . . Twenty-five pounds of dynamite won't free so much as a square yard of German soil. Individual *Sturm und Drang* without mass support is nonsense.
> ÜBERNITZ: No, our utter desperation should sweep away the slave mentality, the profit motive, and all petty bureaucracy.

SCHLAGETER: If so, all Germany will be a cemetery.
ÜBERNITZ: Better a decent cemetery than a fifth-rate old clothes shop.
SCHLAGETER: That's a matter of opinion.

But eventually he joins his friends in terrorist operations.

> What does it matter whether I die of a bullet at twenty, or of cancer
> at forty, or of apoplexy at sixty. The people need priests who have the
> courage to sacrifice the best — priests who slaughter. . . .[74]

Arnolt Bronnen's heroes, the Freikorps fighters in Upper Silesia, are
cut from the same cloth. Bronnen, once a friend of Brecht and, like
him, attracted by violent action, moved sharply to the right. To the
Nazis, however, he always remained somewhat suspect and, while
using him, they kept him at arm's length. The same is true of Hans
Fallada, who wrote a semi-documentary account of the bomb-throwing peasants of Schleswig-Holstein and who hoped that their violent
actions would draw attention to their plight.[75]

In Salomon's story, which has been mentioned earlier, Otto, the
leader of a Communist fighting group, makes an appearance. He is
a sympathetic young man, a fighter like the right-wingers to whom
he shows a natural affinity: "Soon we were friends." Such apparently
incongruous friendships were by no means rare; activists, after all,
have a great deal in common. In his autobiography Milovan Djilas
relates that in prison the Communists soon found a common language with the Croat Ustasha, "national revolutionaries and fanatical
believers." They had a common enemy — the government — and
they despised the democratic opposition for its lack of daring. The
Communists certainly did not approve of the links of the Ustasha
with Fascist Italy and with Hungary, but neither did they condemn
them.[76] Theirs was a "conditional friendship."

For the Narodnaya Volya, the Irish or the Macedonians, sexual
problems did not exist or, if they did, there was general agreement
not to discuss them in public. Underground life in theory, if not
always in practice, involved members of the group refraining from
any close relationship; some even preached asceticism: everything
that would deflect the terrorist from his main assignment was repre-
hensible. Whether this was repression, sublimation or simply the
reaction of a generation with different values and standards is a

question which could no doubt be discussed at great length. Sexual problems have indeed figured very prominently in the writings of contemporary terrorists, mainly in the United States and in Germany, and the explosion of a bomb has come to be regarded as something like an ersatz orgasm. Michael Baumann, a former member of a terrorist group, has even maintained that the choice or rejection of terrorism was "programmed" — the individual's unavoidable reaction to the presence or absence of a fear of love: most terrorists, if not all, escaped from that fear into total violence. From his own experience, as well as the writings of Malatesta and Fromm, he reached the conclusion that revolutionary (meaning terrorist) practice and love could not coincide.[77] He may well have been right with regard to the European and North American terrorism of the 1960s and 1970s; whether one can draw more far-reaching conclusions from statements of this kind is less certain.

TERRORISM AND PROPAGANDA

There is a literature on terrorism that sees its sole function in uplifting morale. The fight is total, the aim the destruction of the enemy; seen in this light, literature is also a weapon in the sacred struggle. A Bulgarian novel, critical of IMRO, would have been sacrilege about the turn of the century;* an Arab novel or play showering less than fulsome praise on Fatah or PFLP would be treason. However deserving the cause, books inspired by such terrorist groups can seldom or never be called literature, nor will they tell us much about the terrorists themselves. For, if there are no inner conflicts, no troubled consciences, if the heroes have no private lives and no weaknesses, if, in short, everyone does his duty, the only remaining problems are technical in character and more effectively tackled by military experts than by novelists or playwrights. This is true even with regard to the most accomplished novels produced by Palestinian writers such as

---

*There were anti-IMRO novels, including one or two good ones, but they were written by Turks or Greeks. *Bombc*, a classic of modern Turkish literature, describes the misfortunes that befell the family of a Bulgarian freedom fighter who decided the time had come to give up the armed struggle.[78]

Ghassen Khanafani, the editor of *Al Hadaf*, a periodical sponsored by the PFLP, who was killed in Beirut by a booby trap in his car. His main theme is that "there is nothing to say. . . . This matter can be settled only by war" (*Return to Haifa*, 1970).[79] That Palestinian authors show no detachment in their novels is perhaps only natural; what makes their novels less than credible is the absence of a wish to understand the enemy. The Palestinians are described as fearless patriots and handsome paragons of every manly and womanly virtue; the Jews more often than not are pimps and ugly prostitutes making love in mosques and graveyards when they are not engaged in killing Arab civilians as sadistically as possible.[80] Moen Basisu provided an up-to-date version of Samson and Delilah, with Samson as a brutal Israeli officer defeated by Delilah, the self-sacrificing Arab patriot. In another novel *(Sahra min Dam)* even the Arab informer realizes the wickedness of his ways and joins the resistance. True, there is frequent criticism of non-Palestinians who show little sympathy for the cause and visit the refugee camps as a tourist's curiosity (Sharqawi). Just as the villains in these novels and plays are unconvincing, so are the heroes and some Arab critics have asked: if all Israelis were pimps and prostitutes, how could they have defeated us? The only Jews appearing in somewhat better light are those of Oriental ("Arab") origin, which is a little ironic because it is precisely among these circles that goodwill toward Arabs is strictly limited, whereas the attitude of "European" Jews has been traditionally one of indifference rather than hate.*

What has been said about Arab literature on Palestinian terrorism refers, *mutatis mutandis,* to much of Third World writing on terrorism. There were some exceptions in India, no doubt because public opinion was divided on whether terrorism was the most effective means in the struggle against the British, and also among some French-speaking North African writers who live in France.

*Hebrew literature on the terrorist groups of the 1930s and 1940s is not of outstanding interest. The most ambitious novel from a literary point of view is Haim Hazaz' *Bekolar ehad* (freely translated: *Together* [Tel Aviv, 1962]), a *roman à clef* describing the last days in prison of two young terrorists, Feinstein and Barsani, who blow themselves up on the eve of their execution. Yigal Mossenson's *Derekh Gever* (*The Way of a Man* [Tel Aviv, 1950]) has the early postwar period as its background and the ambivalent attitudes of members of the Hagana toward the "dissidents" (i.e., terrorists). Some interesting and psychologically revealing novels by writers of a younger generation have appeared recently — for instance, Yizhak Ben Ner's *Mischakim bechoref* (*Games in Winter* [Tel Aviv, 1976]).

In Latin America there is a long-established tradition of revolutionary songs, the *cancones de protesta*, to which guerrilla and terrorist groups have made a significant contribution in recent decades.[81] There was a similar tradition in pre-revolutionary Russia; some of the members of Narodnaya Volya, such as Morozov and Klements, wrote and composed songs which became quite popular. They ranged from ironic comment on Drenteln, the head of the Tsarist political police, to funeral songs for comrades who fell in the struggle for freedom, expressing the conviction that one day an avenger would arise — variations on Virgil's *Exoriare aliquis.* . . .[82] At this point the literature of and on terrorism begins to merge with its folklore, an intriguing topic but not the subject of the present study.

It has been shown how the terrorists of the nineteenth and twentieth centuries made their way into world literature just as Brutus and Wilhelm Tell, Judith, and Charlotte Corday had attracted writers of earlier generations and for similar reasons. Sometimes it was the liberating deed rather than the ethical dilemma which fascinated the writers: Judith and Wilhelm Tell were in no danger of moral censure. With Caesar we move on to more uncertain and psychologically more interesting ground: the admiration for the great statesman is tempered by criticism for the man who destroyed the tradition of freedom, and the tragedy of Caesar is also the tragedy of Brutus. Charlotte Corday is the first truly modern terrorist heroine: a vile reactionary in the eyes of the Jacobins, she is a figure of great courage and angelic purity for all those who dreaded and despised the extremists. Her personality expressed itself in a political act, but politics do not explain her personality; Jeanne d'Arc had acted on what her voices told her, but what had inspired Charlotte Corday? The great German writer Jean Paul, writing less than a decade after Marat's assassination, saw the roots of her behavior partly in her education and reading: the heroes of ancient Rome had been her great example. But intellectual adventures alone were clearly insufficient as an explanation; a great many young people had read Plutarch, but she had killed Marat. Perhaps it was because as a woman she was not free to develop her strong personality, or because she was not distracted by (or had not found fulfillment in) love or marriage. Jean Paul's *Halbgespräche* appeared in 1801; it would be a long time before nineteenth- and twentieth-century terrorists were treated with similar perception. Novels and plays are not an ideal vehicle for long ideological discussions as various abysmal failures demonstrated (Mackay). But literature was ideally suited to deal precisely with those vital issues for which there was no room in the learned treatises on the history of Anarchism and kindred political movements: the question of motive, the analysis of character.

This proved to be exceedingly difficult in the case of the Anarchists, for they constituted a subculture (as it would now be called) on the fringes of society, far removed from the circles in which writers usually moved. Those who wrote about them drew, like everyone else, on newspaper reports rather than on personal experience. The Anarchist figures in the novels of the period are usually unconvincing, strange or sick people, marginal characters, outsiders, eccentric or perverse. All this may have been true, but it was not very satisfactory, nor did it make for a clearer understanding of why these people had banded together and engaged in actions which shocked society so profoundly. Was it only their tortured inner life and some Herostratic impulse which impelled them to go out and knife kings and presidents and throw bombs in cafés and parliaments? They were clearly dissatisfied with society and wanted to take a kind of revenge. But at this point personal and political motives somehow merged, and the how and why usually remained a mystery. Furthermore, some of our Anarchist heroes and villains had not been mistreated by society: their childhood had been reasonably happy; they were by no means disadvantaged, so that personal revenge was certainly not their central motive. Nor were they particularly unbalanced or wicked or ambitious — which made it all the more difficult to understand them.

With a few exceptions the Anarchists appeared as sinister or pathetic miscreants in the literature of the period, fascinating, perhaps, but hardly ever true to life, and in the last resort inexplicable. A decade or two were to pass until Anarchists became more credible: the initial shock had passed (and so had the Anarchists-terrorists), a younger generation of writers had appeared, more familiar with their habits and ideas, more inclined to regard them as well meaning but misguided failures rather than as *hostes humani generis*.

It was easier for the Russians to understand their own terrorists. True, there was the same generation gap, the same consternation as young people began to adopt a strange life-style, propagate incomprehensible ideas and finally engage in dastardly actions such as killing the tsar. But in the final analysis they were flesh of their own flesh, the generation gap was not vast. And if Dostoyevski found terrorism in 1871 a sinister enigma, this was at least in part due to forgetfulness; two decades earlier he would have found it much easier to understand the Narodovoltsy. The interpretation of terrorism in the Russian novel varied, of course, with the politics of the writer. Hence the total rejection in the works of Dostoyevski and Leskov, for whom it was nothing less than the anti-Christ, the incarnation of all evil, the negation of all values. Hence, on the other hand, the boundless admiration of the progressive intelligentsia; in this climate of adulation a psychological analysis of the personal motives of these heroes and martyrs would have been as much out of place as an investigation into the sex life of a saint in an official Church history. Again, some time was to pass before the initial excitement died away and a calmer approach made it easier to rethink and refeel the motives which had induced young people to engage in desperate actions.

These were no déclassé Bohemians or outcasts of society, but, quite often, the offspring of the elite; clearly their idealism could not be denied, they had no personal accounts to settle with society. On the other hand some specifically Russian features were evident: this, after all, was not the first generation of rebellious young intellectuals. But whereas their predecessors had talked revolution for nights on end, they were the first to act and did so with a frenzy quite un-Russian: Oblomov had passed away. But this had not come easily to them, nor were they really "nihilists." On the contrary, they were very much preoccupied with moral questions and had an ethical code of behavior stricter in many ways than that of established society with its dual standards. Only a few among them were strong and resolute characters and even they wavered and quarreled; sometimes they were unhappy and occasionally they gave up or even betrayed the cause. In short, they emerge as credible human beings from Russian literature.

Savinkov's books shocked his left-wing contemporaries not merely because these were the novels of a man just about to renege the cause. The critics could not possibly accept the unflattering accounts of men and women who had daily risked their lives in the struggle against Tsarist despotism. Many of them had, in fact, made the ultimate sacrifice. Perhaps the critics were right, perhaps the heavy emphasis on personal passion and prejudice distorted his descriptions, perhaps one who had lost hope could not do justice to those who had not. But Savinkov had really been a leading terrorist, whereas his critics — were critics. They had never made a bomb, let alone killed anyone, and the most important decision facing them was the topic of their next essay.

Eventually the critics realized that though there were wonderful young men and women among the terrorists, the new generation was not quite comparable to that of 1880. Among the Narodovoltsy there had been Hamlet-like figures and some foolish young men who thought they could outwit the police while collaborating with them. But there had been no Azev. After the archtraitor had been unmasked, the old innocence of terrorism had gone, it was no longer a subject on which one could write with ease. But the personality of Azev, too, remained an impenetrable mystery. It would have been easy to solve the enigma had he just been a police spy out to get the maximum of money from the chiefs of the Okhrana. But he was an agent on the greatest scale, he took their money and frequently delivered. Yet he was not their tool; he had political aims and ambitions of his own which by no means always coincided with the views of the Okhrana. He played a double role so complex that its threads could never again be unraveled once the game was over.

The books on the Russian terrorists of 1905 were the first to raise some of the issues that were to recur ever after. They showed how difficult it was to separate real heroism and the lust for adventure, steadfastness and routine, how in certain conditions the borderline between loyalty to the cause and betrayal becomes almost invisible. They showed that most terrorists were bound to ask themselves sooner or later whether the game was worth the candle, and not merely because of the many losses in their ranks. Above all, they raised the moral question of the right to kill.

This dilemma did not trouble many later writers on nationalist terrorism. There were exceptions, above all Irish literature with its ambivalence about terrorism. "No people hate as we do," Yeats had written. But he had also said that everything he loved had come to him through the English language. For a while, toward the end of the last century, the political and the literary movements in Ireland coincided or ran concurrently but later there was a parting of ways — the philistine character of Irish society and the hostile reception of their works drove some of the writers from Ireland and deeply wounded others. Most of them were to rally to the cause in 1916 and again in 1919, but with the establishment of the Free State there came a new wave of introspective criticism. Examples have been given for the spirit of candor with which former terrorists wrote about their past, their friends and their comrades-in-arms; it made the Irish literature of the 1920s and 1930s uniquely revealing for the comprehension of patriot and reformer alike.

The uses of fiction as a source for the understanding of terrorism are not unlimited. A witness recently advised a U.S. congressional committee that Joseph Conrad's *Secret Agent* should be made mandatory reading for every police officer in the United States: "Conrad tried to get into the human mind of an anarchist living in London in the early 1900's. If a police officer could read this, he could start understanding how much a revolutionary is really motivated by political ideology and how much by individual needs."[83] Such recommendations, though well meant, are, of course, a little naïve. Police officers (and not only they) will benefit from reading a book that has become a classic of world literature. It is equally clear that they will not draw any immediate profit for coping with the problems facing them in their work. Conrad's hero, Adolf Verloc, it will be recalled, is a police agent; after his death Winnie, his widow, looks for help. Ossipon, the Anarchist and womanizer to whom she turns in utter despair, disappears with her savings and drives her to suicide. There have been Verlocs and Ossipons at all times and in all countries, but an analysis of their thoughts and actions, however intrinsically interesting, is of no help in understanding why a young man or woman may join a Latin American terrorist group, the IRA or Weatherman. Nor does it explain what makes them commit acts of heroism and betrayal, what induces them to continue a hopeless struggle or to surrender. The writer, it must be emphasized once more, deals with the individual and his motives, putting the stress on boredom or ambition or selfless devotion as he sees fit. He cannot possibly provide an identity kit picture of the "typical" terrorist. There are, in any case, infinite varieties, and as terrorism has changed during the last century, so have those practicing it. Everyone is impelled by considerations transcending the self as well as by motives of a personal character. Fiction cannot offer a master key to the soul of the terrorist; the most one can hope for is to detect certain common patterns in the character and mental makeup of the *dramatis personae* who acted as a group at a certain time and place. To accomplish even this modest task a great deal of empathy, psychological understanding and creative mastery is needed. Once this has been accepted a great deal can be learned about terrorism from contemporary fiction, provided these books, plays and films are not regarded as manuals for the study of terrorism, aspiring to photographic exactitude and universal applicability.*

*There are, of course, many more novels, plays and movies of interest to the student of terrorism than have been mentioned here. Some have been inaccessible to the author; this refers, for instance, to Ramon Sempau's *Los victimarios* (1906), an important document for the history of Spanish Anarchism around the turn of the century. Sempau was an active terrorist, sentenced to death by a military tribunal; he was later acquitted by a civil court. Others were written in languages with which I am not familiar — novels on Bengali terrorism, for instance, or on the Rumanian Iron Guard. Of late a great many novels have been published dealing with the most recent phase of terrorism; Klaus Rainer Röhl's *Die Genossin* (Munich, 1975) is an unflattering portrait of the late Ulrike Meinhof by her ex-husband. Another interesting documentary novel dealing with the kidnapping of the FLQ is Brian Moore's *The Revolution Script* (London, 1972). But there was no intention in the first place to provide a comprehensive survey of "terrorist literature"; in any case it is doubtful whether, after a certain point, further reading will throw any new light on terrorism.

5

Terrorism Today

The postwar wave of urban terrorism began in the late 1960s and has now continued, on and off, for about a decade. It has occurred in many countries and taken many different forms but, broadly speaking, it can be divided into three different subspecies. First, there is separatist-nationalist terrorism, such as in Ulster or the Middle East, Canada or Spain, an old acquaintance from past ages. Second, Latin American terrorism, the trendsetter and, in many respects, a phenomenon *sui generis*. The continent has seen more civil wars, coups d'état and assassinations than anywhere else, but systematic urban terror was an innovation. Last, there was the urban terrorism in North America, Western Europe and Japan, which grew out of the New Left or, to be precise, the failure of the New Left in West Germany, Italy, America and Japan, and which on occasion was also practiced by quasi-Fascist groups. The terrorists of the New Left mistakenly assumed that methods used in Latin America would work elsewhere or that Latin American conditions could be created artificially in the more developed countries, and this at a time when these methods had not even been too effective south of the Rio Grande.

It was perhaps accidental that the emergence (or reemergence) of these three strands of terrorism coincided in time for basically they had little in common. Neither the IRA nor Fatah owed anything to the New Left; Latin American terrorism certainly developed quite independently. As the terrorist wave gathered momentum, there was a certain amount of cooperation between terrorist movements (on which more below) and also some cross-fertilization: West German terrorists, for instance, freely admitted that they had been influenced by the example of the Tupamaros and learned from their experience.[1] Other groups took the battle for Algiers as their model, even though it had ended in failure for the insurgents.

There were important differences between the terrorism of the 1960s and 1970s and previous terrorist waves. Above all, there was the fact that most of the terrorist groups of the 1960s were left-wing in orientation or, in any case, used left-wing phraseology in their appeals and manifestoes. Right-wing terrorist groups operated in Turkey, Italy and Guatemala, in Argentina and Brazil, but their impact was felt on the domestic scene only.

The use of certain slogans is admittedly not sufficient evidence of the real character of a political group. This is not to imply that left-wing slogans were used to deceive the public; most "left-wing" terrorists no doubt genuinely believed that they were the heirs of the French Revolution, of Marx and Lenin. But it is also true that their policies differed in essential aspects from those of the traditional left. They were certainly radical in the sense that they opposed the "system," the "establishment," that they wanted violent change. But their belief in the historical mission of a small group of people had more in common with voluntarist and idealist traditions than with Marx; they were not radical democrats, and the cult of violence propagated by them resembled Fascism rather than socialism.

Another major difference was the intervention of foreign powers, directly or discreetly, who provided help to terrorist movements. There had been some precedents before the Second World War, with Italy and some Balkan countries as the main wirepullers. But this had been the exception; it was only in the 1960s that this new form of warfare by proxy really came into its own, thus opening entirely new possibilities for terrorism. Operations in third countries became far more frequent; in past ages it had been the rule that Russian terrorists would limit their attacks to Russia, and the Irish to Ireland (or England). In the 1960s, on the other hand, Palestinians would operate in Paraguay or France; Japanese terrorists in Kuwait, Israel and Holland; Germans in Sweden or Uganda. This new multinational terrorism was bound to create occasional confusion with regard to the identity of the attackers and the purpose of their action.

Last, mention has to be made of the new weapons and techniques which had not existed before.

While political violence became intellectually respectable in the 1960s in some circles, the ability of the authorities to counteract terrorism was more restricted than in the past. Up to the Second World War, terrorists who had been apprehended by the authorities faced, at best, lengthy prison terms. With the dawning of the permissive age, it became far less risky to engage in terrorism, except in a few less-enlightened countries. Where terrorism would have been dangerous, it was rare. If the judiciary was reluctant to impose draconian penalties on its own citizens, the foreign terrorist could expect to get away with light sentences if his case reached trial at all,[2] for his imprisonment would have exposed the "host" country to retaliation, to fresh terrorist attacks, to the seizing of hostages and blackmail. Few Western leaders were willing to accept this risk even if their own nationals had been killed; the outcome of the contest between the philosophy of the bomb and the philosophy of the permissive society was predictable. Thus the general climate seemed more auspicious from the terrorists' point of view than ever before: if there were no mass support and no prospect of gaining it in the forseeable future, there were other factors that seemed to work in favor of terrorism. But to some extent these advantages were deceptive as the terrorists found out to their cost. It was relatively easy to provoke a Latin American government, to discredit it and cause its overthrow, but it was far more difficult to survive the backlash of a military dictatorship. Even in Western countries terrorism became distinctly unpopular the moment it ceased to be a nuisance and caused real inconvenience to society. Once this point had been reached, governments had no difficulty in introducing more stringent laws to combat terrorism. These laws did not always have the expected results because there were fairly narrow limits to the measures that could be applied by the security services in a democratic society, even in an emergency. Above all, the international character of the new terrorism provided backing and reassurance, both moral and material, so that terrorist groups would continue their campaigns where in the past they would have given up the struggle.

These generalizations apply to most terrorist movements but not to all; conditions, as stressed more than once in this study, varied from country to country. To establish these distinctions one has to look more closely at the three main varieties of terrorism.

LATIN AMERICA

In the 1950s and the early 1960s terrorism seemed all but forgotten, although there was no shortage of guerrilla warfare in Asia, Africa and Latin America, which proceeded, however, according to a very different pattern. Underlying the guerrilla warfare were the assumptions that a revolutionary movement would develop in some distant province of the country and gradually gather strength and that eventually, in the final phase, as happened in China, the "countryside" would envelop the cities. The prevailing idea was that a contest of this kind ought to be based on mass participation. The concept that a small group of people could and should be the main agent of political change was rejected for both doctrinal and practical reasons. This then was the rule, and if there were a few exceptions, they could easily be explained as a result of unique local conditions: Cyprus was a small island, easy to control by the rulers — it was impossible to establish a "National Liberation Army" in the countryside and, in these circumstances, the use of urban terror was quite natural. But tactics used in an island of half a million inhabitants were not thought to be applicable elsewhere. Equally, the incidence of urban terror in the struggle for Algeria was explained as part of the political mobilization of the masses in the capital of the country; demonstrations and propaganda were part of it, but bombs had also much to recommend themselves. The city of Algiers, in any case, was not really considered the main battlefront; the defeat of the ALN in the capital did not, in the event, affect the outcome of the struggle.

The transition from rural guerrilla warfare to urban terror came after disaster overtook Ché Guevara in Bolivia; it was also connected with the radicalization of sections of the New Left in industrialized countries, and reached its climax in the years 1969–1972. If this was the general trend on a global scale, the situation in individual countries did, of course, vary. In a few places urban terror had been launched well before 1967 and it had already petered out by the time it reached its climax elsewhere. In other places, the fashion arrived after some delay, and in these countries urban terror continues to the present day.

The earliest and, in some ways, most interesting manifestation of urban terror on a substantial scale was in Venezuela in 1962–1963 — well before the wave had spread elsewhere. Venezuela seemed in some way predestined: about two-thirds of the population lived in urban centers and urban terror had the support of the activist wing of the local Communist party, which had persuaded itself that an "objective revolutionary situation" existed and that only a little push was needed to topple the regime. The cadres were mainly students with a sprinkling of the urban working class or, to put it less charitably, the *Lumpenproletariat* of the *barrios* (slums) of Caracas. True, urban terror was considered only one of three approaches to be tried simultaneously: the rebels also endeavored to win over sections of the army, in an attempt to stage a military coup; nor did they rule out rural guerrilla warfare. The Venezuelan urban terrorists had no specific doctrine to guide them — they acted by instinct — but their repertoire was nevertheless a wide one, ranging from bank robberies to hijacking planes and ships to the kidnapping of prominent personalities (including the Argentine soccer star di Stefano). They understood perfectly well the paramount importance of gaining publicity for their struggle. It has been said that the whole arsenal of the urban guerrilla operations, later used in many other countries, was in fact developed with much imagination in Caracas.[3] But it was the misfortune of the MIR "urban guerrillas" that they faced, not an inefficient dictatorship such as Batista's in Cuba, but a regime that had come to power in free elections; it was headed by Betancourt, leader of the Acción Democrática. Betancourt's countermeasures against the terrorists seemed halfhearted; there was no massive police repression or army counterattack. He acted decisively only when the terrorists became more and more of a nuisance to the general public, causing disruption to daily life in the capital, and after a popular ground swell against the terrorists had developed. With insufficient support from the middle class and even less from the workers, the terrorists found themselves isolated, only to be told by the older Communist cadres that this was the inevitable result of their adventurist tactics. Following a particularly senseless and counterproductive attack against an excursion train, forceful action was at last taken by the government and this finally broke the terrorists' will to continue the struggle in the city; rural guerrilla fighting continued for a number of years.

Events in Venezuela seemed to confirm what Castro and Guevara had taught the revolutionaries all along — that in underdeveloped Latin America the countryside was the basic area for armed fighting. They had to establish rural *foci*, which could not overthrow the system but would act as a detonator. The countryside, according to the Cubans, had much to recommend itself, both from a political point of view — with its enormous untapped revolutionary potential — and also militarily, because access to the rural areas was much more difficult for the government troops. Fidel's slogan had been, "All guns, all bullets, all reserves to the Sierra"; the idea of leading a guerrilla movement from the city seemed altogether absurd, for an urban terrorist group could not develop into a revolutionary force, it could not transform itself into a people's army and ultimately seize power. The "urban guerrilla" (the Cubans, in fact, frequently used the derogatory term "urban terrorism") was at best an instrument for agitation, a tool for political maneuver and negotiation. But, lacking any central command in the cities, the guerrillas were forced to disperse and this was bound to weaken the insurgents far more than the governmental forces. Moreover, there were sound political and psychological reasons militating against the "urban guerrilla." The Cubans and, following them, Régis Debray, regarded the urban working class (not excluding the Communist parties) as an essentially conservative element. The city, as Castro put it, was the "grave of the guerrilla." Debray was even more outspoken: life in town is tantamount to an "objective betrayal," for the mountain proletarianizes the bourgeois and peasant elements, whereas the city embourgeoises the proletarians.[4] Living conditions in the towns were fundamentally different from those prevailing in the countryside; even the best comrades were corrupted in the cities and affected by alien patterns of thought. This sounded more like Rousseau and the twentieth-century *Kulturkritiker* than Marx and Lenin, but from a military point of view it seemed to make sense, at least for a while.

It was only after 1967 that guerrilla doctrine was adjusted: the Venezuelans and the guerrillas in Peru and Colombia had been defeated; the death of Guevara in Bolivia in 1967 and the arrest of Debray highlighted the failure of rural guerrilla practice. The age of urban terror dawned with Uruguay, Brazil and Argentina as the main scene.

The Uruguayan MLN (*Movimiento de Liberación Nacional* — the Tupamaros) was founded in the early 1960s; in the beginning they displayed only sporadic activity. Their very first operation was an attack against a Swiss rifle club in July 1963. Their activities reached a peak in 1970–1971; the following year they were decisively defeated.

In Brazil there were several urban terrorist groups — the ALN *(Ac ão Libertadora Nacional)*, the VPR *(Vanguarda Armada Revolucionaria)* and the VAR-Palmares *(Vanguarda Armada Revolucionaria)*, all considerably smaller than the Tupamaros. They launched an urban terrorist campaign in 1968 which was to last for three years. In Argentina, too, the urban terrorists were split into several factions; the main group, the ERP, started its activities in 1970, as did the left-wing Peronist FAR *(Fuerzas Armadas Revolucionarias)* and the Montoneros, whose first publicized operation was the kidnapping and murder of ex-President Aramburu, also in 1970. In addition there were a great many other small groups in various Latin American countries. From time to time there would be reports about bank robberies, kidnappings and assassinations in Mexico, Guatemala, Colombia, the Dominican Republic and other places; a detailed analysis of these countries' terrorist groups is of considerable importance for the student of Latin American politics, but on the whole they were politically ineffective and a detailed review of their activities would not add much to the understanding of the general phenomenon of terrorism.[5] For, in the present context, Latin American terrorism is of interest mainly in so far it throws some new light on the possibilities and limitations of terror as a political weapon in modern conditions.

The upsurge of terrorism in Uruguay occurred against a background of a deep economic structural crisis and the same is true, *mutatis mutandis*, with regard to Argentina; in Brazil, on the other hand, it took place precisely at the time of a major boom. The Tupamaros confronted a liberal government; they suspended their activities during the elections of 1971. The Brazilians, on the other hand, faced an army dictatorship and their terrorism, in some ways, was "defensive." In Argentina, urban terror developed in the period preceding Peron's second coming, after years of inefficient military rule. But the return of the popular leader by no means induced the ERP to cease their activities, whereas their main rivals, the Montoneros, stopped operations for a while. Tupamaros terrorism was far more discriminating and sophisticated than the operations carried out by their Brazilian counterparts; no doubt this reflected the less violent political culture in their country. Cold-blooded murder was not approved of by public opinion in Uruguay and the Tupamaros were well aware of this fact. They mainly raided banks, businesses, offices and arms stores; on occasion they distributed stolen goods and published documents they had seized revealing corruption in high places. In February 1970 they raided a leading gambling house and stole a quarter of a million dollars, but later distributed the money among workers and employers. After 1970 their operations became more violent. Foreign diplomats and local officials were kidnapped and Dan Mitrione, an American police adviser, was killed.[6] A further escalation in violence took place in 1972 when it was decided to launch a "direct and systematic attack against the repressive forces"; an army officer and several police officials engaged in countersubversion were killed in hit-and-run attacks against army personnel. It quickly appeared that the attempt of the Tupamaros to establish a real "alternative power" (people's courts and people's prisons) to the government had less support than they thought. "The Tupamaros are the people and the people are the Tupamaros" was a fine slogan; but the *Frente Amplio,* which the Tupamaros supported in the elections of November 1971 (and which was also backed by the nonterrorist left), polled less than 20 percent.

Terrorist operations in Argentina likewise were at first on a modest scale (bank raids, kidnappings), but by 1970 the first assassinations had occurred.[7] The ERP and the Montoneros claimed that this was in retaliation for the Rawson jail escape (in Patagonia) when sixteen out of nineteen recaptured prisoners were shot while allegedly trying to escape for a second time. But this massacre did not take place until August 1972, whereas the killing (by the ERP) of Dr. Sallustro, general manager of Fiat, had been committed five months earlier and the Montoneros had killed ex-President Aramburu in May 1970. Later on murder became quite indiscriminate; the victims included moderate trade union officials, who were accused of having betrayed the working class. True, the ERP stopped their assassinations for a short time when, in December 1974, some of their militants had murdered the small daughter cf an army captain together with her father, but there is reason to believe that they were more concerned with the impact on public opinion than with the purity of their souls. Meanwhile, Santucho (killed in a shoot-out with the police in July 1976) and Firmenich, the leaders of the ERP and the Montoneros, had met and coordinated the activities of their organizations which, since 1974, had spread to the countryside. While the Montoneros were the far larger group, with the whole left wing of the Peronist movement as its base and (allegedly) some 25,000 armed members, it had little political cohesion or discipline and the smaller ERP, with a mere 5,000 members (but better and heavier military equipment), was a more dangerous foe for the government. During 1975 and the first part of 1976 there was an escalation of terrorist attacks and government repression, and Argentina became one of the very first cases in history of terrorism turning into urban guerrilla warfare.

In Brazil, where government repression was strongest, the character of the terrorist campaign was also the most cruel. The terrorists were accused, even by the extreme left wing, of "militarist deviation" in trying to crush the enemy rather than win over the masses, and of neglecting "armed propaganda."[8] The Brazilian security forces, like those of Uruguay, were quite unprepared in the beginning to cope with urban terrorist tactics, but after a year or two they too gained experience. Carlos Marighella, the leader of the ALN, was killed in a police ambush in São Paulo in November 1969, Camara Ferreira, his successor, in October 1970; in December 1970, Fujimora, one of the leaders of the VPR, was shot. By that time the number of active terrorists had fallen to fifty and Carlos Lamarca, a former army captain and the leader of the VPR, was hunted down in the countryside and shot in the state of Bahia in September 1971. Most of the terrorist operations took place in Rio de Janeiro and São Paulo and the number of victims, excluding terrorists, was relatively small — about one hundred killed over a period of five years. But the terrorists had an excellent flair for publicity and good connections with the media and their exploits were extensively reported all over the globe. There is no reason to disbelieve the reports about systematic torture used against captured terrorists; but it is also true that the terrorists had few, if any, scruples; their victims included farm workers who had stumbled on terrorist hideouts, motorists killed by terrorists who needed their cars, and boatmen cut down after a getaway at gunpoint.[9]

Latin American urban terrorists developed a doctrine, but more by instinct than on the basis of sociopolitical analysis. They realized that a strategy that had worked in China (and in Cuba) would not be successful in countries in which the majority of the population lived in cities. Latin America, after all, had the fastest rate of urbanization in the world; to talk about the "encirclement of the city by the village" in Uruguay or Argentina was to invite ridicule. The political as well as the military and economic centers of power were in the big conurbations; hence the decision to attack the enemy there, not on the periphery. True, all Latin American "urban guerrillas" stressed the importance of building up rural guerrilla *foci* but this resolution remained a dead letter in most cases and almost their entire effort was concentrated in the cities.

The two chief ideologists of urban terrorism in Latin America were Abraham Guillen (a refugee from Spain) and Carlos Marighella. Guillen's writings initially influenced both the Tupamaros and the Argentinian ERP but he did not belong to either organization, criticized their strategy on various occasions; there is no reason to assume that he ever had any decisive influence on their strategy. Guillen advised the terrorists to engage in many small actions and thus to compel the security forces to cede terrain. His ideal cell consisted of five people who had to decide whether to launch an attack without referring the matter to the high command. Guillen explained the subsequent setbacks of the Tupamaros as the result of their decision to engage in big ("Homeric") battles as well as the establishment of "fixed fronts" (supply depots, hospitals, "people's prisons," etc.). Guillen advocated constant mobility and clandestine existence but at the same time insisted on the importance of political work so as to gain mass support. This was excellent advice but not very practical, since a movement observing strict rules of conspiracy could not possibly engage in political and propagandistic activity at the same time.

A similar contradiction pervades the writings of Carlos Marighella. Marighella had been a leading member of the Brazilian Communist party but left in disgust over its "reformist" character. His reputation spread after his death in battle; the *Minimanual* was translated into many languages and almost as often banned by the authorities, even though it contained little that was not known. If Guillen was preoccupied with the politics of guerrilla warfare and condemned senseless murder, Marighella was predominantly interested in military (i.e., terrorist) action: the more radical and destructive, the better. He advocated a scorched-earth strategy, the sabotage of transport and oil pipelines, and the destruction of food supplies. His assumption was that the masses would blame the government for the resulting calamities. True, he also wrote that "urban guerrillas" should defend popular demonstrations, but this was hardly ever done. Typical for Marighella and also for the Argentinian terrorists was the burning conviction that shooting was far more important than any other activity — especially intellectual discussion. There was contempt for ideology and "politics" — the future society (Marighella wrote) would be built not by those who made long-winded speeches or signed resolutions but by those steeled in the armed struggle. His writings are permeated with a fanatical belief in the justice of his cause and the single-minded advocacy of "the revolution"; political details were of little importance. For this anti-intellectual and even irrational attitude there were perhaps mitigating circumstances: the sterile and unending ideological debates of the Latin American left, usually a rehash of ideas imported from France. The Tupamaros, too, for years scrupulously refrained from issuing specific political statements, remaining deliberately vague with regard to their aims, stressing that "words divide us, actions unite us." The contempt of the Argentine ERP for the doctrinal hairsplitting of their erstwhile Trotskyite mentors has already been mentioned. Such ideological vagueness was partly tactical but, to a large degree, it was genuine, reflecting the prevailing state of ideological confusion: for many of these young men and women "nationalist," "socialist," "revolutionary" and "anti-American" were more or less synonymous. Erstwhile leading members of quasi-Fascist organizations, or Peronist ideologists could switch to the Castroite-Trotskyite camp with the greatest of ease.[10] When the Montoneros first appeared on the scene in 1970 with the murder of ex-President Aramburu, their political character genuinely puzzled outside observers: some commentators called them a movement of the extreme left, others wrote that they belonged to the far right.[11] Both, in a way, were right.

Like the early Russian Narodniki, Latin American terrorists assumed that the intelligentsia, especially the students, constituted the revolutionary vanguard, even though lip service was paid to the central role of workers and peasants. Sabino Navarro, the chief of the Montoneros in 1970–1971, was a worker, but he was the exception, not the rule. From other, earlier, terrorist movements they borrowed the concept of provocation; violence would produce repression, repression would result in more violence; by constantly harassing the government, they would compel it to apply even more draconian measures. Thus, the establishment would have to shed its liberal-democratic "façade" (Venezuela, Uruguay) or quasi-populist-front (Argentina) and antagonize large sections of the people. At the same time, attacks against the army would push the officers to the right and prevent a left-wing military takeover — such as in Peru — which the terrorists considered a major danger. This theory of increasing polarization was based, as the Tupamaros and the Brazilians admitted after their defeat, on a serious overestimation of their own strength and the underestimation of the "forces of repression." The Tupamaros had intimidated (and infiltrated) the police but the moment the army took over the combat against terrorism, their strategy no longer succeeded. The Brazilian terrorists were also quite unprepared for the intensity of the government's backlash. Torture evoked much protest but it did not provide new recruits; the heroism of a Marighella and a Lamarca was admired among intellectuals but not emulated and, in the end, even the left came to consider the terrorist tactics quite pointless. Conditions in Argentina were more promising inasmuch as the social basis of the terrorist movement was somewhat broader; they had the support of some trade unions, which were considerably stronger than in Brazil or Uruguay. Furthermore, the terrorists benefited from the political vacuum caused by a succession of ineffective military juntas and the equally incompetent interlude provided by Peron and his widow. Thus the ERP and the Montoneros grew stronger but eventually all they achieved was the overthrow of a quasi-democratic regime and its replacement by another military dictatorship.

The innovations of Latin American urban terrorism were in the practical field rather than in producing any new concepts. Like the Palestinians, the Latin Americans realized that the mass media, domestic and foreign, were of paramount importance; on various occasions they seized radio and television stations and broadcast their propaganda. They were the first to engage in the systematic kidnapping of foreign diplomats and businessmen, correctly assuming that such operations would both embarrass the local government and attract worldwide publicity. It should be noted in passing that hardly any prominent political figures (other than foreigners) were killed by Latin American terrorists. This may have been accidental; more probably it was part of their strategy, based on the assumption that acts of violence against foreigners would always be more popular. On a few occasions the Tupamaros engaged in major military operations (the seizing of public buildings in 1969, the occupation of police stations and airports in some provincial towns in 1971–1972), as did the ERP and the Montoneros on a few occasions when they attempted to storm army camps. This was in line with their doctrine of escalating individual terror to mass action. But these operations were never quite successful; sooner or later the terrorists returned to the small-scale raids, kidnappings, bank robberies and hit-and-run attacks which were less risky and not necessarily less rewarding.

The most interesting innovation made by Latin American terrorists was the foundation of a "Junta of Revolutionary Coordination," a terrorist international of sorts established by the Argentine ERP, the Tupamaros, the Chilean MIR and the Bolivian ELN. The ERP contributed an initial five million dollars to the Junta's budget, which was used for arms production and procurement, operations in Europe (the assassination of Latin American diplomats) as well as the publication of a journal *(Ché Guevara)*. However, since among the four associates of the Junta only one was in a position to provide money and strength, the establishment of the new body only meant that the center of gravity of Latin American urban terrorism moved for a few years to Buenos Aires.

TERRORISM: NATIONALIST AND SEPARATIST

Of the nationalist-separatist urban terrorist groups of the last decade the Irish and the Palestinians have received more publicity than any others. There were many such groups — the Basque ETA and the Quebec FLQ, to mention only two, and, of course, countless nationalist-separatist groups in Asia and Africa which predominantly engaged in rural guerrilla warfare. The Ulster and Palestinian terrorists received greater publicity because of their greater visibility and their international connections. Both groups have certain features in common, such as the great impact of religion, even though they have absorbed a great deal of revolutionary verbiage; this is true, in particular, with regard to the Official IRA and the Arab PFLP and the PDFLP. The conversion to Leninism was no doubt genuine so far as the orientation of some intellectuals was concerned, but the motivation of the great majority of the rank and file was nationalist-religious, the desire to unite Ireland or the wish to destroy the "Zionist state." While the ideological pronouncements of these groups should, of course, not be ignored, they should not be attributed undue importance. There is no systematic exposition of the uses and purposes of terrorism in their writings. In theory, they are engaged not in terrorism but in a "people's war." The history of armed struggle for Irish independence did not end with the establishment of the Free State; the fight had to go on, as some Irish nationalists saw it, until the six counties of Northern Ireland are united with the rest. The fact that Catholics in Ulster are politically discriminated against, and that many of them are socially underprivileged is not in dispute. But the attempt to describe the clash in Ulster mainly as a class war is unconvincing, since the terrorist organizations of the Protestants are also predominantly working class. Class struggles have hardly ever led to terrorism in the twentieth century, and in any case, it would not explain the particular bitterness of the terrorist struggle which developed around 1970 following several years of a Catholic civil rights campaign. The specific character of Ulster terrorism has its roots in the nationalist mystique of the anti-British struggle on one hand and Protestant fears on the other. Furthermore, free-floating aggression has been a frequent phenomenon in Irish history. The nineteenth-century "faction fighters" were in the tradition of the old warrior clans of Ulster; they fought each other savagely: "I never saw fellows more determined on the destruction of each other," wrote a British army lieutenant stationed in County Limerick in 1824, having watched one of these faction fights, which had no other visible purpose than the desire to fight; neither politics, nor religion nor social factors were involved.[12] It ought to be noted, at least in passing, that many acts of violence in the recent Troubles have also been quite motiveless.

The history of the IRA is well known and need not be retold; we are not concerned, in any case, with its activities after the end of the civil war of the 1920s or the resurgence in 1938–1939, and again in the late 1960s.[13] For these were mainly guerrilla raids across the border; systematic terrorism which began with the formation of the Provisional IRA in 1970 was of very different character indeed. It was initiated by the Provisionals, the Official IRA did not engage in individual terror before 1972 — and the Protestant counterterror (headed by the UDA and UFV) also began only in that year. Both IRA Provisionals and Officials have always maintained that the character of their struggle is not sectarian, that the enemy are not the Protestants but the British army (which was originally sent to Ulster to protect Catholics against Protestant mobs). But in fact many more civilians were killed in the Troubles than soldiers and, furthermore, Provisional and Officials also engaged from time to time in assassinating each other. In brief, what happened in Ulster was to all intents and purposes a civil war. The presence of the British army imposed certain limitations and this was perhaps the main reason that terrorism rather than open street fighting became the prevalent mode of struggle. What distinguishes Ulster terrorism from most other terrorist groups is the social composition of the movements, which, as already mentioned, is predominantly working and lower middle class on both sides; it is one of the few terrorist campaigns in which middle-class intellectuals (students, in particular) have not played any significant role. It was precisely the sectarian character of the terrorist groups that gave them a good deal of popular support, more than any social-revolutionary terrorist group could ever count upon. Thus, almost uniquely in terrorist history, the IRA established "no go zones" in some urban areas for Protestants and the British army, which in any case was inhibited in its operations by the doctrine of graduated response. The Protestant terrorists tried, with varying success, to do the same. With a little imagination these "liberated areas" could be compared to the *foci* of the rural guerrilla movements.

Terrorism was indiscriminate; it was not directed against the leaders of the enemy camp; but, on the other hand, bars, stores and public transport were among the favorite aims of bomb attacks both in Ulster and in England. It was perhaps because terrorist operations were so easy that the IRA did not engage in some of the more far-fetched terrorist techniques, like the hijacking of planes, that were so popular among terrorist movements elsewhere. IRA terrorists could cross into the Irish Republic without much hindrance and this was of invaluable help. The Irish government and the great majority of the population in the south were far from enthusiastic about the activities of the IRA, but, on the other hand, there were obvious limits to cooperation between Dublin and London in combatting terrorism. The IRA, however, confined its operations in the south to such actions as the liberation of prisoners or the occasional assassination of a prominent Englishman, correctly assuming that any other course of action would deprive them of their sanctuary, training ground and supply base.

What distinguishes the most recent phase of Irish terrorism from all previous outbreaks is on the one hand its greater efficiency and on the other its even greater cruelty. Up to the days of Michael Collins, Irish terrorists almost always bungled their operations; there was an appalling lack of secrecy, of discipline and of planning. Of late, Irish terrorists greatly improved in this respect, though it is, of course, also true that they have had less reason to fear the British security forces, which could no longer respond as they had done in a less civilized age. But if army and police had to act more humanely the terrorists of both sides behaved with almost pathological cruelty, which was not in the tradition of even the most extreme Irish freedom fighters of past generations who had advocated and practiced terrorism. For this particular viciousness the key is not to be found in an analysis of social and economic statistics of Ulster.

Comparisons have been drawn between the situation in Ulster and Israel; both the IRA and the Palestinians intend to liberate a country

against the desire of the majority of its inhabitants. The comparison
is of doubtful value, for the differences are far more pronounced than
the common patterns. The history of the Palestine resistance can be
briefly recapitulated: Palestine militants did not accept the existence
of a Jewish state and organized armed resistance against it. There had
been small scale hit-and-run operations in the 1950s; in 1964 the PLO
(Palestine Liberation Organization) came into being, and acted as
the cover organization for Fatah and smaller terrorist organizations
such as Dr. Habash's PFLP (which had 500 militants in 1975), Naif
Hawatmeh's PDFLP (300), the Syrian sponsored *Saiqa* (2,000) and
others. Their bases were outside Israel though they had, of course,
members and sympathizers inside the Jewish state. Attempts to set
up a rural guerrilla movement in Israel, shortly after the Six Days'
War, failed — the terrain was unsuitable, the Israeli security forces
too watchful. A little more successful was an early attempt at urban
terror in the refugee camps of Gaza in 1968–1969; but by resettling
the refugees in new camps the Israeli authorities soon regained the
initiative and terrorism ceased. Since then the Palestinian organizations have engaged, roughly speaking, in three kinds of operations:
shelling Israeli settlements from beyond the border; hit-and-run attacks by small units against Israeli transport or settlements, sometimes combined with an attempt to obtain hostages; and attacks
against Israeli and Jewish individuals and offices in third countries
and the hijacking of third-country planes. These operations launched
outside Israel were of considerable importance in view of the publicity they received.[14] While Fatah and *a fortiori* PFLP and PDFLP
doctrine stressed the participation of the masses in the Palestinian
revolution, there was near total divergence between theory and
practice; the masses, for obvious reasons, could not take part in terrorist operations such as hijacking or the attack at the Munich Olym-
pic Village in 1972. But such inconsistencies between doctrine and
reality are frequent in the history of terrorism and it may be unfair
to single out the Palestinians in this respect. There are certain unique
features distinguishing Fatah and the other Palestinian movements
from all other terrorist groups. One is the great financial support
provided by Arab governments, to which attention has already been
drawn, another is the size of Fatah. It has kept between 10,000 and
15,000 men under arms, first in Jordan and later in Lebanon. How-

ever, only a very few of these were trained for or participated in
terrorist actions. Furthermore, Fatah and the other Palestinian organizations received more massive outside political support than any
other terrorist movement. That the Palestinians had legitimate
grievances against Israel was not the decisive issue; many millions
lost their homes in the three decades following the Second World
War, or lost their independence. But whereas the Lithuanians, the
Kurds, the South Moluccans or the inhabitants of Biafra looked in
vain for international support, the Palestinians were backed by the
whole Arab world, including some of the world's leading oil producers. This explains an apparent paradox, the disproportion between
the size and number of the terrorist operations, which were relatively few and on a small scale, and the political achievements, which
were considerable. Fatah operated in conditions that were altogether unique and it would be misleading to draw far-reaching conclusions from its successes. Israel, a small country, found itself in
virtual isolation, not as the result of Fatah operations but because of
the hostility of the Arab world and its unwillingness to accept a
non-Arab state in its midst. It may well be true that the PLO would
have had the same achievements even if its supporters had not fired
a single shot: it was the political support that mattered. On the other
hand, a few spectacular operations were of great help both as a moral
uplift for the Palestinians and to demonstrate to the world that there
remained an unsolved political problem in the Middle East. Thus the
actions of the Palestinians, even more than those of other terrorist
groups, have to be considered in the context of their publicity impact. While the Palestinian organizations were not the first to hijack
planes, they carried out some of the most spectacular hijackings
(Dawson's Field, September 1970). In later years the practice was
only infrequently employed; Dawson's Field led to the expulsion of
Fatah from Jordan. Summarizing the experience of eight years of
hijacking, a leading Arab journal wrote that, far from harming Israel,
past Palestinian hijackings had strengthened her and aroused hostility to the Palestinians in particular and the Arabs in general.[15] It
would perhaps be more correct to conclude that while the hijackings
and similar operations were not popular in the democratic countries
of the West, they were always of some value in view of their news-
worthiness. The figure of the hijacker-kidnapper was usually one of

fascination rather than horror (Leila Khaled, Carlos et al.); there was as much sympathy for him as for his victim, always on the assumption that if people committed atrocities they surely had good reasons for doing so, that people willing to die for a cause must have pure hearts and lofty ideals. One of the main problems with these spectaculars was that frequent repetition reduced their publicity value.[16]

Like most Latin American terrorist movements, Fatah (in contrast to the smaller PFLP and PDFLP) kept its political program deliberately vague. For this it was sharply criticized, especially from the left, but the strategy had much to recommend itself. Helped by the inherent vagueness of the Arab political language, the leaders of Fatah stated their aims in a way that they could appeal to the left as well as to the right, both domestically and on the international scene. The fact that the quasi-Marxist PFLP and PDFLP were more outspoken in their ideological pronouncements hardly mattered in practice. They would invoke death and damnation on the head of the "reactionary circles" in the Arab world, yet in practice they would do little or nothing to annoy or provoke them. Thus the PFLP in its platform stated that it fought for a "popular war of liberation by arming and mobilizing the people in popular militias so that the war can be fought on the widest possible front . . . protracted war waged by a mobilized, self-reliant people, armed with proletarian ideology is the sole road for national socialism. . . ."[17]

If the PFLP had stuck to its program, its place would not be in the present study, the subject of which is urban terrorism rather than "war on the widest possible front."* But it did not; the main operations of the PFLP were the hijacking and derouting of air planes to Dawson's Field, the attack at Lod Airport, the attempt to blow up oil installations in Singapore (January 1974), the OPEC kidnapping (December 1975) and the Entebbe hijacking. Some of the actions were carried out by foreigners, others by mixed Arab-German, Japanese or Latin American teams, hardly an example of mobilizing the people, popular militias and a national war of liberation.

The fact that the Palestinian resistance was split hindered its oper-

---

*The PFLP, according to its own accounts, progressed from Fascism via Nasserism to an extreme left-wing ideology. See, for instance, *Harakat al quawmiyyin al arab min al fashiyya ila al nasiriyya* (Beirut, 1970), *passim*. The ideological emphasis has undoubtedly changed; to what extent the substance has is open to doubt.

ations to the extent that there was no central planning and little coordination between the various organizations. There was much verbal battling, but until the outbreak of the Lebanese Civil War (1975–1976) there was little actual fighting between the various groups. The Palestinians were among the first to develop two new important techniques. They enlisted foreign nationals: terrorist groups from various nations had cooperated on occasion in the past — the collaboration between the Macedonian IMRO and the Ustasha was only one such case. Such cooperation was, however, to a great extent perfected and systematized by the PFLP. The Lod Airport massacre (May 1972), carried out by members of the Japanese Red Army, is perhaps the best-known example, but there were many others in which sundry Latin Americans, Frenchmen, Germans, Turks and others took a prominent role, not to mention the involvement of foreign governments and secret services. Thus a new "international brigade" came into being, able and willing to participate in national liberation struggles all over the globe, provided the political context of these struggles happened to be of interest and profit.

The other important innovation was the foundation of ad hoc organizations for the execution of operations that were either particularly gruesome or involved international complications. Hence the establishment of "Black September" and other less well known groups which suddenly appeared on the scene, only to vanish equally rapidly. It was argued that these groups were constituted of particularly dangerous and radical militants, over which the more responsible Arab groups had no control. This technique was used on many occasions, not only in the West but also in operations in Arab countries such as the murder of Wasfi Tal, prime minister of Jordan, and the murders at the Saudi Arabian embassy in Khartoum (March 1973). Thus the attack against a train carrying Jewish immigrants from the Soviet Union to Vienna was executed by a group calling itself "Eagles of the Palestinian Revolution," whereas five Saudi Arabian diplomats were kidnapped in Paris by a group called "Al Iqab" of which no one had heard before or since. The fiction was maintained even though the Sudanese and the Jordan governments published documentary evidence that Black September was not an independent new group but a section of Fatah and that it was supported by Libya, and after a leading Black September member had confirmed this on Jordan television. For, given the advantageous international constellation, the division of labor (for which, of course, there were precedents in the history of terrorism) had invaluable advantages: it made it possible to pursue the terrorist struggle while the political leadership of the movement could at the same time dissociate itself from such operations. On a few occasions there were genuine splits and the sorcerer's apprentice became truly independent — but these were the exceptions.

Mention has been made of the fact that Fatah had a wider social appeal than its rivals: intellectuals and students congregated in the quasi-Marxist PFLP and PDFLP. In contrast to terrorist groups of earlier periods, or the Latin American terrorists of our time, the leaders of the Arab groups hardly ever took part in operations. In fact, among those who participated in terrorist operations inside Israel there were few educated young people; actions outside Israel, on the other hand, usually demanded some skills.

Of the many separatist-nationalist groups operating in Europe and North America, some are of no relevance in the context of the present study because they used terrorist tactics only on rare occasions (this refers, for instance, to the various separatist groups in France, Britain or Italy). Among those who opted for "urban guerrilla" tactics the FLQ in Quebec, the Basque ETA, the Croatian Ustasha and the Puerto Ricans were the most prominent. The FLQ *(Front de Libération de Quebec)* was founded in 1963: its operations reached its peak in October 1970 with the kidnappings of Cross and Laporte. After that date, following energetic government action, terrorism ceased, even though the Quebec problem continued to exist. The Basque ETA first launched terrorist attacks in 1968; its most spectacular exploit was the assassination of Prime Minister Carrero Blanco in December 1973, and it continues its operations to this day. While FLQ and ETA acted from within their respective countries, the Croat Ustasha concentrated its activities on attacks on Yugoslav representatives abroad, such as the killing of the Yugoslav ambassador to Sweden (April 1971) and of numerous other Yugoslav diplomats. Attempts were also made to infiltrate agents into Yugoslavia, sometimes individually, sometimes in groups. Puerto Rican terrorists, mainly concentrated in the FALN, have killed policemen in Puerto Rico, bombed hotels on the island, and blown up taverns and offices in New York and other American cities. In all these cases terrorism evolved out of separatist movements that had existed for many years. In some cases social grievances reinforced the nationalist demands: the average income of French-speaking Canadians in Quebec province is 30 to 40 percent lower than that of English-speaking Canadians. On the other hand, the Basque region is among the more prosperous parts of Spain, and Croatia is one of the most developed parts of Yugoslavia. In these instances national-cultural (and/or religious) factors were obviously of decisive importance; the Croats and Quebeçois, in contrast to their neighbors, are Catholics. Most of the separatist terrorists could count on at least some public sympathy; even if the majority dissociated itself from violent actions (the revulsion among French-Canadians after the Laporte murder in 1970), there was a vague feeling of solidarity, a tendency to forgive unforgivable deeds because the motive had been sincere. Where such sympathy was not much in evidence (Puerto Rico had overwhelmingly voted in 1967 in favor of association with the United States) there was outside (Cuban) help as a countervailing factor.

The strong impact of religion on Irish militants and the Palestinians has been noted; religious roots of Ustasha terrorism are also unmistakable and it has been said that the Basque clergy kept their language, the main vehicle of Basque nationalism, alive so that their flock should be unpolluted by modern ideas such as liberalism and socialism.[18] The link between religious fanaticism in Ulster, the Basque regions, the Middle East and Croatia is too obvious to be ignored; fanaticism persisted even when the belief in religion had been eroded and when the terrorists had been excommunicated. Religion, like terrorism, offers certainty; religion, like terrorism, asks people to sacrifice themselves for a cause greater than themselves. When traditional religion is discarded, its place is taken by a new faith, be it nationalism or Communism — but the underlying intensity of belief is still deeply religious in character.

Terrorist tactics varied greatly: the FLQ during its early years directed its attacks against establishments rather than persons. If there were a few victims, this was apparently not planned. ETA's first operations were aimed at the security forces, but from 1973 on it also engaged in bank raids and abductions of businessmen — in one famous case in 1975 the victim was killed when the money demanded for his release was not forthcoming. ETA had a sanctuary in neighboring France, but the movement was split on lines resembling the IRA internal division — with the populist ETA V resembling the Provisionals, and the quasi-Marxist ETA VI (1970) and a more recent group ETA VI-LCR (1973) [*Liga Communista Revolucionar*] comparable to the IRA Officials. ETA V, with its broader nationalist appeal and its greater militancy, has been responsible for most terrorist operations and has pushed its rivals of the extreme left into the background. For both the FLQ and ETA the Algerian war of liberation served as the great model, even though the situation there had been altogether different: Spaniards and English-speaking Canadians were not, after all, French *colons.*[19]

It is impossible to deny the validity of at least some of the demands, grievances and fears of the separatist-nationalist movements, from which these terrorist groups sprouted. The real difficulty facing them was that they were not simply dependencies to be decolonized by expelling the foreign rulers. Given the heterogenous ethnic composition of most modern nations, it is frequently impossible to fulfill the demands of one group, however justified, without discriminating against another. Not every ethnic group or minority can have a viable state of its own, and their problems can be solved only on the basis of a reasonable compromise. History unfortunately provides a great many precedents for the absence on both sides of the desire to compromise; the reappearance of separatist movements in the 1960s and 1970s is not therefore a matter of great surprise.

COMMUNISM AND TROTSKYISM

Official Soviet spokesmen have always condemned international terrorism. It has been denounced as adventurist, elitist, objectively serving the interests of the class enemy and the forces of international reaction. Yet at the same time the Soviet Union has provided arms, financial aid, military training and, on occasion, political support to various terrorist groups. In practice, as distinct from doctrine, the Soviet attitude has been one of selective support to "national liberation" movements employing terrorist means and it has also assisted some groups that even by stretching a vivid imagination cannot be classified as belonging to the national liberation camp. This ambiguity stems from the fact that the Soviet attitude to political terrorism is dictated not by humanitarian principle but by political expediency. The ambiguity is reflected even in the legal discussions on terrorism that have kept the United Nations busy for several years. On the one hand the Soviet Union stated in 1973 in the U.N. Ad Hoc Committee on International Terrorism that it had no objection to the adoption of an international convention which would impose definite obligations on states to prevent such illegal acts.[20] But on the other hand the Soviet representative stressed that it was quite unacceptable to give a "broad interpretation" to the term "international terrorism" so as to cover national liberation movements which, it maintained, were justified from the viewpoint of international law. In the Soviet view, some national liberation movements are "just" whereas others are not. Soviet spokesmen would certainly take a dim view of any suggestion that Lithuanian, Ukrainian or Tadjik movements advocating political independence might be worthy of support. According to Soviet doctrine, only those national liberation movements should be supported which are part of the "world revolutionary process," which weaken the West and promote Soviet interests. For a variety of reasons, the Soviet Union would probably prefer these groups to apply means other than terrorist, since such actions are usually difficult to control and, if they fail, their defeat has an adverse effect on the Communist parties. If on the other hand they succeed, the Chinese or some ultra-left group may claim the credit. Terrorism, in any case, is problematical from the Soviet point of view, for there is always the risk that the example may be emulated and that terrorist operations may be used against Soviet representatives abroad, or even within countries belonging to the "Socialist Camp."

The ambivalence vis-à-vis terrorist movements dates back to the days of Marx, Engels and Lenin: their opposition to Bakuninist, Blanquist and Mostian techniques is well known, but there was always room for some exceptions. Special allowances were made for the Fenians and the Narodnaya Volya. In a similar way, Soviet leaders may have reservations about the uses of terrorism today but, given the existence of such groups, assistance has been given whenever thought expedient. On the other hand, the Soviet Union cannot

openly support terrorist groups without harming its image of responsible statesmanship and complicating its relations with the United
States and other countries. This, then, in brief outline, is the Soviet
dilemma facing terrorism at the present time.

Soviet relations with the PLO were relatively uncomplicated,
since this body received wide international recognition after 1968.
The Soviet attitude to the PLO was initially fairly cool; prior to 1968
the militant Palestinians were sometimes even denounced in the
Soviet press as reactionary, adventurist and ultra-revolutionary.[21]
After that date the attitude became gradually much more friendly,
weapons were liberally supplied, training was given and PLO leaders
have fairly regularly conferred with Soviet leaders. The reasons for
the rapprochement were obvious; the PLO had been recognized by
China as early as 1964 and while the Chinese could not do much for
the Palestinians, there was always the danger of a pro-Chinese orientation developing unless Moscow were more forthcoming. Soviet
setbacks in the Middle East and the close cooperation between the
PLO and the pro-Soviet regimes in the Arab world also helped the
rapprochement. But the Soviet Union, directly and indirectly, also
supported the PFLP and the PDFLP which, in contrast to Fatah,
made no claims to moderation and statesmanship.

Similar problems existed in Latin America: the Venezuelan Communist party opted for urban terrorism in the early 1960s; there is
reason to assume that this was their own decision, not Moscow's, but
on the other hand the Soviet Union could not dissociate itself from
the sister party. Among other Latin American Communist parties
which have engaged in terrorist operations during the last decade
are those of Colombia, Guatemala, Haiti and the Dominican Republic. These were small parties and their attitude was not representative; in Latin America, only the Dominican Communist party
refused to sign the Moscow manifesto of Communist parties in 1969,
on the grounds that it was not sufficiently revolutionary. (The
Dominicans changed their views in 1972.) The FARC terrorists in
Colombia were orientated toward the Soviet Union and received
some assistance; their leader was Manuel Marulanda, a member of
the Central Committee of the Colombian Communist party. But
again, as far as the Colombian Communist party was concerned,
terrorism was only one form of the political struggle. On the other

hand, there were declarations by leading Latin American Communist spokesmen sharply condemning the "desperate adventures of ultra-leftists" who engaged in kidnappings and attacks which had no working class support and which contributed nothing to the revolutionary cause.[22] Rodney Arismendi, leader of the Uruguayan Communist party, said in an interview with the Italian *Unità* that his party considered the Tupamaros sincere, honest and courageous revolutionaries and that they had defended them on occasion. But in the final analysis Tupamaro tactics did not correspond to the needs of Uruguay. To make the overall picture even more confused, it ought to be added that some Soviet help has apparently been extended to the Tupamaros, the ERP and other such groups without the mediation and probably even without the knowledge of the local Communist party.

Until about 1969–1970 the Cubans gave more or less indiscriminate support to Latin American guerrilla and terrorist movements. Doctrinally, the Cubans should have assisted only rural guerrillas but, in fact, they also supported urban terrorism, especially after the collapse of most Latin American rural guerrilla movements.[23] Cuban support became somewhat more selective after 1970, partly no doubt under Soviet pressure, partly in view of the realization that the "revolutionary wave" of the 1960s had passed and that it was only desirable to normalize Cuba's relations with other Latin American governments. This led to bitter recriminations on the part of the more militant Latin American guerrilla and terrorist groups, which claimed that Cuba had sacrificed (if not betrayed) the revolutionary cause. These charges were, on the whole, unjustified, since Cuba continued to provide training, arms and money to Latin American terrorists — as well as to some groups in other parts of the world; this emerged quite clearly after the expulsion of several Cuban "diplomats" from France in connection with the "Carlos" affair in 1975. The Soviet Union did not act only through the good offices of the Cubans; Soviet diplomats were expelled from Mexico in March 1971, from Bolivia in March 1972 and from Colombia in August 1972, after evidence of links with local terrorist groups had been revealed. By and large, however, a division of labor has been established, with the Soviet Union gradually disengaging itself from direct involvement and with Cuba and North Korea taking over a large share of the burden. Beginning in 1938–1969, terrorist training centers were established in North Korea: the trainees have been traced to, and in some cases apprehended in, Latin America (Mexico, Brazil, Bolivia, Colombia and other countries), the Middle East (PFLP) and Asia (Sri Lanka, Malaya, Indonesia) and Africa. Cuba has concentrated its activities on Latin America and the Latin American emigration in Europe and Spain. At the same time, Soviet links with various terrorist movements such as the Croatians, various Paris-based groups and others farther afield have not apparently been altogether discontinued.[24] There seems to have been some coordination between the Soviet bloc and Algeria and Libya, the other two main supporters of terrorist movements. Algeria has provided shelter and assistance to North American terrorist groups as well as to the ETA and most African and Middle Eastern terrorists. The list of groups that have received Libyan support is long, even though Libyan promises have been even more numerous. While Cuba and North Korea have acted in close contact with Moscow, Soviet coordination with Algeria and Libya has been looser

The question of the armed struggle has figured prominently in the internal debates of the world Trotskyite movement. If the Communist camp has become polycentric over the last two decades, Trotskyism was split into several groups almost from the beginning, and this makes generalizations almost impossible. The Ninth World Congress of the Fourth International (April 1969) accepted a resolution on the armed struggle in Latin America, calling its supporters not only to "increase the number of rural guerrilla nuclei but also to engage in actions in the big cities aimed at striking at the nerve centres of the regimes."[25] Individual Trotskyite leaders have approved of the FLQ kidnappings in Canada, the Weathermen in the United States, the activities of the IRA and the Basque ETA and even the Munich massacre.[26] While rejecting the Baader-Meinhof style of terrorism, Trotskyite spokesmen such as Livio Maitan (the movement's main expert on Latin American affairs) and Daniel Bensaid justified "urban guerrilla" tactics as consistent with the struggle of the workers' movement.[27] The *Red Weekly* (January 11, 1974) announced that it gave total support to the assassination of Carrero Blanco, the Spanish prime minister, by Basque nationalists; Livio Maitan commented that "critical support" would have been a more appropriate term in this context. On two occasions, money from Latin American kidnappings is said to have been transferred to Trotskyite groups abroad; $100,000 of the proceeds of the Beilinson kidnapping in May 1973 and an unspecified sum seized in a bank raid in Guatemala, which went to the Posadistas, a Trotskyite splinter group. The French section of the Fourth International engineered some minor attacks in 1972 such as those against the Argentine embassy in Paris and the local offices of Honeywell-Bull. As a result, the French section of the Fourth International was outlawed by the French government. However, the majority faction inside the Fourth International somewhat modified its position at the Tenth World Congress which took place in Sweden in February 1974 and was mainly devoted to discussions on Latin America. The pro-guerrilla, pro-terrorist resolution adopted five years earlier was criticized as abstract, vague and hasty.[28] The new resolution made it clear that it applied only to Latin America; the activities of the Krivine group in France were denounced. American Trotskyites, who in their majority had opposed the armed-struggle orientation all along, found the new resolution insufficient inasmuch as it was no real retreat from the position taken in 1969 but "simply an attempt to make it more palatable." It still implied that "violent actions initiated and carried out by small groups could serve as examples for the masses."[29]

Leaving aside Pabloites and Posadistas, the "International Committee," the Lambertites and a dozen other small factions, and concentrating on mainstream Trotskyism, the following approximate picture emerges: at the one extreme there is the Argentinian PRT *(Combatiente)* which set up the ERP in 1970. Beginning with "expropriations" this group matured to straight urban terrorism and eventually left the Fourth International, partly under Cuban influence. Closest to them is the French Section of the Fourth International, the "Communist League," which has been, however, by and large, stronger on the theory than the practice of terrorism. The International Executive Committee of the Fourth International (Mandel, Maitan, Tariq Ali et al.) have taken a "centrist" position. Between 1969 and 1973 they provided theoretical justification for guerrilla warfare and urban terrorism in certain conditions.[30] Since then they have to a certain extent retreated from this position. The majority of the Socialist Workers Party in the United States has favored rural guerrilla warfare combined with political work, such as practiced by Hugo Blanco in Peru in 1965. But it has sharply denounced urban terrorism as both anti-Leninist and counterproductive and it has criticized Mandel, Maitan and Tariq Ali for uncritically supporting such manifestations of the "armed struggle."

The discussions on the desirability of urban terrorism continued for years in the Fourth International; while Pierre Frank of the French section argued (quoting Trotsky) that a bomb was an excellent thing in certain circumstances, this was contested by Joseph Hansen and his friends in New York. Altogether these debates have scarcely more than academic interest, for, with the one exception of the Argentine ERP, Trotskyites did not engage in terrorist operations on a major scale.[31] The ERP was both the pride of the Fourth International and the source of much worry from the very beginning. Founded in July 1970 as the military wing of the Trotskyite PRT (*Partido Revolucionario de los Trabajadores*), it was subject to various conflicting influences.[32] From the outset, it had only a tenuous relationship with the Fourth International, whose leadership it criticized as weak and lacking a military orientation. It regarded Ché Guevara as its spiritual mentor and among its prominent members was Joe Baxter, who only a few years before had been a leader of the neo-Fascist *Tacuara*. Baxter, as well as other ERP leaders, had received his military training in Cuba; when Mario Santucho, the head of the ERP escaped from an Argentine prison in August 1972, he found asylum in Cuba — not known for its sympathies for Trotskyism. All this was a little suspect even considering the usual Latin American ideological confusion and it did not therefore come as a great surprise when in the spring of 1973 ERP broke off relations with the Fourth International altogether. The year before, the ERP had kidnapped Oberdan Sallustro, a Fiat executive, and killed him when the money for his release was not delivered in time. The Fourth International leadership had not condemned the action *expressis verbis;* this provoked a violent reaction on the part of the American Trotskyites, who accused the "United Secretariat" of justifying terrorism under the euphemism "urban guerrilla war." In the following year, the (European) Fourth International leadership broke its silence and offered some friendly criticism to the ERP — suggesting

that their operations were premature since a full-fledged revolutionary situation did not yet exist.[33] But the ERP was in no mood to take
advice from Paris and London; they, after all, knew best whether a
revolutionary situation existed, and if it did not exist, why assume
that it could not be created? Their interest in doctrinal discussions
had always been limited: they believed in action and they were to
provide much of it in the years to come.

Some Anarchist groups, too, have reverted in recent years to terrorist practice. The leading spokesmen of the movement had dissociated themselves from individual teror ever since Kropotkin published his strictures about the mindless assassinations of the 1890s.
This is still true with regard to the older leaders today; it is no longer
correct with regard to some activist groups which came into being
in the late 1960s on the fringes of the Anarchist movement. In 1968,
a German Anarchist publisher reissued the text of Bakunin's *Words
to the Young Generation,* in which the use of the dagger and poison
was recommended. The brochure had first been published a hundred years earlier but the reissue was obviously no mere act of academic commemoration. Even earlier, in the early 1960s, the Spanish
Anarchists had established a terrorist underground with the help of
some British and French comrades. Toward the end of the decade,
the Baader-Meinhof faction, the Valpreda group in Italy and the
London "Angry Brigade" came into being, as well as some other
groups elsewhere opting for "direct action." "Direct action" did not
necessarily mean terrorism; the decision of the German "Red Army"
(Baader-Meinhof) to wage "urban guerrilla warfare" was widely criticized in Anarchist circles — the very choice of the name showed that
the group, whatever their original inspiration, had broken with liber-
tarian socialism. Some of these terrorist groups remained faithful to
their original Anarchist, anti-authoritarian principles, others moved
on toward an ideological synthesis of all the revolutionary programs
of our time, even if mutually exclusive, or joined the flying circus of
multinational terrorism.

The motives which induced Libya, Algeria, Somalia, Iraq, South
Yemen and other countries to sponsor and support terrorist groups
had nothing to do, needless to say, with Anarchism or Marxism-
Leninism. Colonel Khadafi may have genuinely cared about Muslim
rebels in Israel, Chad and the Philippines; but whether Catholics or

Protestants gained the upper hand in Ulster was neither a matter of doctrinal nor of vital national interest for Libya. However, giving support and shelter to terrorists enhanced the international status of otherwise not very important countries: it made their rulers feel influential and it seemed worth the expense of these foreign ventures. True, beyond a certain stage vicarious support tended to become embarrassing, and as a result Algerian assistance to terrorists, other than Arabs and their foreign aides, has become more selective in recent years.

THE NEW LEFT

The aid given by Communist and Arab countries was operationally invaluable, but the inspiration for the last upsurge of terrorism in the Western world came from a very different source. The late 1960s and early 1970s witnessed the rise and decline of the New Left, which became the leading force on the university campuses; since there were millions of students, and since they were among the politically most active members of society, their radicalization was bound to have political consequences. It was this force which helped to defeat an American president and almost overthrew the Gaullist regime in France. The New Left was of mixed parentage: on the one hand there was genuine idealism, anti-militarism, revulsion against the inequities of modern industrial society, of poverty, hunger and exploitation in the Third World. But there was also boredom, aggression and the free-floating extremism of every growing generation. Seen in retrospect, the New Left produced much interesting material for the student of social and cultural trends. Politically it was not a very innovative movement; its gurus such as Marcuse were men of an older generation — some of them were no longer alive. The ideas they advocated had been floating around for many years: Gramsci, Lukacs, the unorthodox German Marxists of the 1920s, Reich — there was little that was not known to the student of left-wing ideology, nor had it anything to do with terrorism. Perhaps the only significant new admixture was Frantz Fanon's concept of the liberating influence of violence. Fanon had written for Africans, but it was precisely in Europe and in North America that his ideas found many admirers. He argued that violence not only unified the people, but that it was a cleansing force, freeing the native from his inferiority complex and from his despair and inaction: "It makes him fearless and restores his self respect. . . . When the people have taken violent part in the national liberation they will allow no one to set themselves up as 'liberators.' "[34] It was, in a way, Morozov's vision of systematic terror as a safeguard against would-be dictators after liberation. Fanon's vision was overoptimistic, for the history of Africa after his death can be summarized, *grosso modo,* in a line from Yeats: *The beggars have changed places but the lash goes on.* True, it was now a native lash, but this hardly bears out the predictions about the curative properties of liberating violence.*

The New Left lasted for three or four years, after which some of its proponents converted to orthodox (Soviet-style) Communism while others continued to read the works of the Frankfurt School, of Korsch, Bloch and Benjamin; a few turned to Anarchism; others to Maoism, *situationisme* and a variety of small sects. In the United States the great majority opted out of politics while retaining a vaguely liberal (American-style) orientation. In Western Europe, on the other hand, the process of depolitization did not go so far.[35] When the rapid decline in the fortunes of the New Left set in, a few of its members opted for terrorism. Thus, more or less simultaneously, the United Red Army developed in Japan out of *Zengakuren,* the extreme student organization; the American SDS gave birth to Weatherman; and some of the German students of the far left founded the *Rote Armee Fraktion* (Baader-Meinhof) and the *Bewegung 2. Juni.* There were smaller groups in Italy *(Brigate Rosse)* and in England *(Angry Brigade).*

There has been an unending stream of publications on these various groups and by their members, on their views, moods, beliefs, motives and aims; seldom in history has so much been written about so few and so little. Their doctrine has been minutely analyzed,

*Fanon's basic concept was not all that original. Patrick Pearse, leader of the Dublin Easter Rising in 1916, had written: "Bloodshed is a cleansing and sanctifying thing, and the nation which regards it as the final horror has lost its manhood." Similar motifs can be found in Mazzini's writings and elsewhere. A generation lacking interest in history had to rediscover some well-trodden paths in the history of radical ideas.

although this did them a grave injustice, for they were not really an ideological movement but eclecticists borrowing certain concepts from Marxism-Leninism (such as the Leninist theory of imperialism), others from Anarchism; above all they believed in the "primacy of action." As the German RAF put it, only the practice of terror would show whether an armed opposition could be built up and united. This voluntaristic concept had been taken from Mao, even though in other respects the life-style of the New Left terrorists was the negation of everything the Chinese and the Cubans stood for.

"Armed action" in West Germany began with an attempt to burn down a Frankfurt department store in 1968. It continued with various bomb-laying activities against German institutions and United States army installations (1970), the assassination of the president of a Berlin court (von Drenkman in 1974) and of a "traitor" in their own ranks (Ulrich Schmücker), the attack on the West German embassy in Stockholm, as well as a few other operations — not an impressive balance sheet for eight years of activities. The two groups which engaged in terrorism were small and consisted almost exclusively of students, or ex-students, of impeccable middle-class backgrounds. As in the United States, there were apparently more women than men in their ranks and the women were the more fanatic. The parents of Ulrike Meinhof were art historians, and she was brought up by another well-known historian; Gudrun Ensslin's father was a Protestant clergyman, Baader's father was an academic, Holger Meins's father was a wealthy Hamburg merchant. The parents of others were university professors, writers, professional people. But at this point any similarity with Narodnaya Volya ends. Their policy was not to fight for the "oppressed and exploited" in their own country but to "destroy the islands of wealth in Europe," to act as agents of the Third World. Hence their collaboration with Third World terrorists; Horst Mahler, one of their early leaders, later had second thoughts on whether this was the correct way to make friends and influence people. But his former comrades stuck to it notwithstanding. Their frequently invoked "concept of urban guerrilla" was, as they admitted, of Latin American origin — "the revolutionary method to be used by weak revolutionary forces."[36] It was their firm belief that this method could be used at all times and in all places.[37]

The ideological antecedents of the Japanese United Red Army

were similar to those of the Germans, but there were also native traditions at work.[38] They derived from, on the one hand, the ideological disputations of the student left of the 1960s, on the other hand the traditional spirit of Bushido. It was perhaps no coincidence that in their very first major action, the hijacking of a Japanese aircraft in March 1970, the attackers used Samurai swords and daggers. Subsequently there were a few murders and acts of sabotage inside Japan, but on the whole it was, as in West Germany, a self-perpetuating cycle of arrests, of new attacks, of new arrests, and so on. Thus in January 1974 the United Red Army attacked a Shell refinery in Singapore; those involved were captured by the police. Ten days later, to effect the release of the prisoners in Singapore, the URA struck at the Japanese embassy in Kuwait. In September 1974 they attacked the French embassy in The Hague, demanding freedom for one of their comrades who had been arrested in France. The Japanese terrorists, even more than the West Germans, took a prominent part in "transnational terrorism," frequently in collaboration with Palestinians, but also with the "Carlos" gang (Yutaka Furaya) and other such groups.

Organizationally, American terrorism developed out of radical white and black groups; on one hand there was SDS (Students for a Democratic Society), the extreme wing of which went underground after a "war council" in Flint, Michigan, in December 1969.[39] Three years earlier the Black Panther party had been formed in California by Huey Newton (subsequently its "minister of defense") and Bobby Seale. It was later joined by Eldridge Cleaver whose *Soul on Ice* had sold two million copies and who became its "minister of information." Black Panther thinking was inspired, in its own words, by Ché Guevara, Malcolm X, Lumumba, Ho Chi Minh and Mao. But undue importance should not be attributed to such pronouncements; it was not as if the works of Mao had been carefully studied; all that their proponents knew of Mao was that power grew out of the barrel of a gun. They saw the *Lumpenproletariat* as the main revolutionary force, although they had little success in mobilizing it, and they rejected collaboration with the Weathermen, whose members came from a very different social milieu and whose preoccupations with ego trips, women's lib and various manifestations of the counterculture were not to their liking. On the other hand, the Black Panthers put strong emphasis on cultural nationalism. It was not in the beginning an openly terrorist group; urban terrorism was first advocated by Cleaver from his Algerian exile and by George Jackson, who was killed in August 1971 while trying to escape from San Quentin. Jackson thought of himself as a Communist, had widely read terrorist literature in prison ("I no longer adhere to all of Nechaev's revolutionary catechism"), and stated that the objective was the destruction of the city-based industrial establishment by creating perfect disorder and by disrupting the manufacture and distribution of goods.[40] There were a few shoot-outs between members of the Black Panthers and the police and some bomb attacks, but the Black Panthers succumbed to "perfect disorder" well before American society. Cleaver, who had been the first to advocate the armed struggle, became disillusioned following his painful experiences, first in Cuba and later in Algeria. Huey Newton and his friends opted for community action from within the system, and Stokely Carmichael, who had retreated with his wife, a well-known singer, to a comfortable existence in Africa, advocated political struggle. There was no direct link between the Black Panthers and the Symbionese Liberation Army, which also originated in Berkeley. Consisting of a few students and criminals, it committed some murders of white and black people, robbed a few banks and, following the involvement of Patty Hearst, attained worldwide notoriety. Counting about a dozen members, it was one of the smallest and most bizarre terrorist groups. Like the Manson family it can perhaps be understood against that specific Californian background which has remained a riddle to most foreigners. The name "Symbionese" was defined as meaning a "body of harmony of dissimilar bodies and organisms living in deep and loving harmony and partnership in the best interest of within the body." Its emblem was a seven-headed cobra, a 170,000-year-old sign signifying God and life.

The motives that induced young blacks to join a terrorist group were, of course, altogether different from the motives which had driven white middle-class youngsters underground. On one side there was the despair of the black ghetto, unemployment, poverty and the misery of broken families — on the other, the crisis of identity, suburban boredom, the desire for excitement and action, a certain romantic streak, in short terrorism as a cure for personality problems. All this was enmeshed in immense intellectual confusion, an absence of values, the conviction that everything was permitted; all the bitter things the Weathermen said and wrote about American society and American culture were *a fortiori* true with regard to themselves, for in their violent opposition to this society and culture they were still its offspring, embodying some of its negative features. It was not just their style which set them apart from previous generations of terrorists — the obscenity of their language and their cruelty — the style in this case was the man, or the woman: a very inferior species of revolutionary indeed.

While the black youngster could point to very real social problems, the white suffered mainly from personal hangups. Yet any attempt to engage in generalizations about the behavior of a handful of young men and women is of doubtful value, since the overwhelming majority of their contemporaries, whether they perceived their surroundings in a similar light or not, did not turn to terrorism. And so the Weathermen, even more than the Black Panthers, remained a marginal phenomenon; whatever they did in the underground, it did not affect American life. The statistics still showed a great number of bombings and attacks during the years after 1970 and some of these were undoubtedly the work of the Weathermen, but most of them were perpetrated by lunatics or criminals — a few operations more or less by Bernardine Dohrn and her comrades made no difference.[41]

Manifestations of urban terrorism were reported during 1968–1975 from many parts of the globe, excepting always the Communist countries and other effective dictatorships. Italy and Turkey were beset by both left-wing and right-wing terror: the left was first off the mark, but the right retaliated with a vengeance. The semi-anarchist *Brigate Rosse* began their activities in the factories of Milan and Genoa, committing acts of sabotage, burning the cars of their political enemies, engaging in kidnapping and maturing to the point of killing judges (Genoa 1976). Neo-Fascist terrorists planted bombs at anti-Fascist meetings, killing eight in Brescia (1974); there were twelve victims when a bomb exploded the same year on an express train. If there was any thought behind this and similar actions (which cannot be taken for granted), its aim was to bring about a breakdown of public order, economic ruin and general dislocation. But since the *Brigate Rosse* were no more interested in a Communist victory than the neo-Fascists in Christian Democratic rule, the purpose of these actions remained obscure. Italian left-wing terrorism was initially predominantly working class with a heavy emphasis on sabotaging industrial machinery, but "radical chic" was not missing. Feltrinelli, the head of one of Italy's most distinguished publishing houses and a multimillionaire, blew himself up while trying to destroy a pylon.

In Turkey, the TPLA (the Turkish People's Liberation Army) was an offshoot of *Dev Genc*, the cover organization of left-wing students in the country; it killed a few American soldiers and an Israeli consul, kidnapped a young girl and engaged in a few more activities of this kind, helped by the left-wing Palestinian organizations which provided arms and trainings. Right-wing Turkish terrorism was allegedly inspired by a retired colonel, Alpaslan Türkes, who had founded the Nationalist Action Party; its more militant members were trained in Fatah camps. Its professed aim was Panturkism, the abolition of Kemalist laicism, the destruction of the democratic system, and above all the liquidation of their enemies on the left. Assassinations of left-wing students reached a peak in 1975, by which time right-wing terrorism was definitely more widespread than political violence sponsored by the left.

Terrorist groups, supported originally by Iraq and subsequently by Libya and the Palestinians, were active in Iran. They ranged from the far left to religious fanatics of the extreme right, united by their hate against the Shah and his autocratic rule. From time to time a few American officers would be assassinated; this would be followed by the destruction of a *Siahkel* unit (the most active of the terrorist groups) by *Savak*, the ruthless Iranian political police which, unlike their European colleagues, had no reason to fear public opinion if they overreacted in their fight against terrorism. Terrorists would seldom survive a shoot-out with the police; those who did faced a death sentence, or at best a long prison term. Most other Third World terrorist groups were to concentrate their activities in rural areas, although like the Maoist Naxalites in India or various Mexican terrorist groups they would from time to time transfer the scene of their operations to the cities.[42]

The achievements of the small terrorist groups which had evolved from the much broader New Left movement in Europe, Japan and the U.S.A. were few and far between. True, it was easy to burn down a department store or a factory, to kidnap a diplomat or to hijack a plane. Robbing a bank was child's play and leaving a time bomb in a crowded place was a task that could safely be left to a half-wit — as in Joseph Conrad's novel. The forces of law and order, preoccupied with combatting different sorts of crime, seemed altogether incapable of tracing and arresting young people with no previous criminal record. Nor was it difficult to get money and arms through connections with likeminded friends in other countries or the good offices of one of the pro-terrorist governments. It was easy to get publicity for almost any action or threat of action, for manifestoes and appeals. But all this activity, however often repeated, had no political impact, nor was there any support beyond a small fringe of intellectual sympathizers. Meanwhile the police improved their methods and leading terrorists were captured from time to time. Urban terror became self-perpetuating: a major operation would be staged to seize hostages so as to assure the liberation from prison of some leading comrades. Meanwhile there would be fresh arrests and new operations would have to be planned to effect their release. Neither workers, nor peasants, nor even the intellectuals would show any sympathy, and after hundreds of bombs and thousands of lead stories in the media, the surviving terrorists, sadder and wiser men and women, would have to face a balance sheet that was almost entirely negative. If it was their intention to undermine the system and bring about its downfall, there were obviously more effective ways to do so. Normally, this should have been the end of the terrorist wave. If it nevertheless continued on a small scale, this was partly because of foreign power support, partly because there would always be a few dozen people in favor of terrorist action, quite irrespective of whether or not it served any useful purpose.

The small New Left groups withered away or were absorbed in the new multinational terrorism. The other two main strands of terrorism, the Latin American and the nationalist-separatist, were, on balance, more successful, but not very much so. It is of course true that, as an American study has maintained, quite a few governments have been embarrassed by terrorist activities forcing them to release captured terrorists, for instance. In a few cases governments were even overthrown because they proved incapable of coping with terrorism.[43] But democratic governments can survive a great deal of embarrassment, and the new rulers in Uruguay and Argentina were hardly to the terrorists' liking. Terrorism certainly contributed to the growing international status of the PLO, but much less than Arab oil. Democratic societies were compelled to divert some resources to defense against terrorist attacks but these were minute measured by any standards. There has been a tendency to exaggerate out of all proportion the cost in manpower and resources needed to combat terrorism.[44] The human toll of terrorism, domestic and international, however tragic, was relatively small; from 1966 to 1976, between 6,000 and 8,000 men and women were killed, more than half of them in Argentina and Ulster. This is far less than the number of those killed in one year of the Lebanese Civil War or in one month in Cambodia. If terrorism nevertheless attracted so much attention it was, of course, mainly owing to its dramatic character. It fascinated millions of people, but it directly affected the life of only a handful. If one disregards events in Ulster and Argentina, there has been a substantial decrease in terrorist operations since 1973; many of the groups of the late 1960s and early 1970s ceased to exist, or were reduced to impotence. This refers to Venezuela, Brazil, Uruguay, the United States, Canada and Japan, as well as other countries. The decrease has been most striking with regard to hijacking; between July 1974 and the end of 1975 there were no more than half a dozen such cases. Political terrorism did not, of course, come to a sudden halt in 1973 and it was only to be expected that the exploits of the small groups of remotely controlled international terrorists would continue. Nor were the activities of gangsters and the lunatic fringe affected by the downward trend. And yet, with all these reservations, the wave of political terrorism was unmistakably receding.

Conclusion

A few days before Christmas 1975 a group of terrorists of unknown provenance broke into the OPEC building in Vienna and kidnapped the representatives of the chief oil-producing nations. Coming soon after the attacks of the South Moluccan separatists in the Netherlands, the incident occasioned great consternation among leader-writers in the Western press, who were anxiously concerned about the power concentrated in the hands of a few individuals and who made harrowing predictions about what all this could mean for the future. The incident monopolized the headlines: clearly it was an event of world-shaking consequence. Yet only a few days later when the shooting was over, when the terrorists had temporarily vanished from the front pages and the small screen — until the next hijacking or some other such action should take place — it appeared that the operation, however meticulously prepared, had been one of the great nonevents of the year. Its purpose was anything but clear: the terrorists seemed to have only a hazy notion of what they intended to achieve. They induced the Austrian radio to broadcast the text of an ideological statement which, dealing with an obscure topic and formulated in left-wing sectarian language, might just as well have been read out in Chinese as far as the average, baffled Austrian listener was concerned.

At first the Vienna terrorists were said to be Palestinian, driven by despair and poverty, demonstrating against the loss of their homeland. Later it appeared that the unit was led by Germans and Latin

Americans; there might have been Arabs among them, but they were neither poor nor desperate. Their leader was "Carlos," a Venezuelan, who had been trained in Moscow and been connected with the Cuban secret services in Paris. The raid was certainly not a spontaneous action, and it was not at all clear who was behind it: according to the Egyptian press this operation, like many others, had been paid for by Colonel Khadafi of Libya, who, however, claimed that he had never heard of Carlos in his life and was against terrorism anyway.[1] But what was its aim — was it indeed another action in the struggle for the national and social liberation of suffering mankind as the hijackers claimed? Modern terrorism, with its ties to Moscow and Havana, with its connections with Libya and Algeria, bears a certain resemblance to the anonymous character of a multinational corporation: whenever multinational enterprises sponsor patriotic causes, caution is called for.

The purpose of the operation has not become clearer to this day. It is most unlikely that the policy of the oil-producing countries would have been affected in any way, even if the terrorists had killed all their victims. Had there been mass murder in Vienna on that Sunday before Christmas, long obituaries on Sheikh Yamani and his colleagues would have been published. Within twenty-four hours, ambitious and competent men in Tehran and Caracas, in Baghdad and Kuwait, would have replaced them and would have, *grosso modo,* pursued the same policies. Hence the futility of the enterprise. Terrorists and newspapermen share the assumption that those whose names make the headlines have power, that getting one's name on the front page is a major political achievement. Publicity, needless to say, is important; people pay a great deal of money and go to great lengths to achieve it. But, unless the publicity is translated into something more tangible, it is no more than entertainment.

Seen in retrospect, the OPEC hijacking in Vienna was only a footnote in the annals of international terrorism — dramatic, but without political consequences. Terrorist operations have continued since, not all of them quite as mysterious as the OPEC incident. But what happened in Vienna in December 1975 is still a convenient starting point for a summing up because in many respects it highlights the historical changes that have taken place in the character of terrorism and its political role.

A review of political terrorism, written before the outbreak of the First World War, would have concentrated on Russian terrorism and Irish, as well as on the Anarchists of the 1890s with perhaps some passing observations on the national struggle of Macedonians, Serbians and Armenians. It would have reached conclusions on terrorists' motives and aims very different from those propounded by an author writing in the 1930s, when Russian and Anarchist terrorism belonged already to distant history and when the terrorism of the extreme right was of considerably greater importance. A study of political terrorism, undertaken in the 1970s will again reach different conclusions in the light of events in the recent past. Its earlier manifestations cannot be ignored; terrorism can be understood only in its historical development, not through facts and figures fed, more or less indiscriminately, into computers. But equally, the terrorism of the 1970s is no longer that of the Narodnaya Volya; an overall assessment of terrorism has to take into account, above all, its most recent manifestations, and the same goes, *a fortiori*, for any comment on its future perspectives.

During the last decade urban terrorism has by and large superseded guerrilla warfare. As decolonization came to an end, there was a general decline in guerrilla activity. Rural guerrillas had learned by bitter experience that the "encirclement of the city by the countryside" was not the universal remedy advocated by the Chinese and the Cubans. With the transfer of operations from the countryside to the cities, the age of the "urban guerrilla" dawned. But the very term "urban guerrilla" is problematical. There have been revolutions, civil wars, insurrections and coups d'état in the cities, but hardly ever guerrilla warfare. Urban guerrilla warfare can occur only if public order has completely collapsed and if armed bands freely roam the streets of the cities. Such a state of affairs does happen, but only very rarely and, according to past experience, it never lasts longer than a few days: either the insurgents overthrow the government in a frontal assault, or they are defeated. The term "urban guerrilla," in short, is a public relation's term for terrorism; terrorists usually dislike being called terrorists, preferring the more romantic guerrilla image.

There are basic differences between the strategy of rural guerrilla warfare and urban terrorism: mobility and taking cover are the essence of guerrilla warfare, and this is impossible in towns. It is not true that the slums (or the rich quarters) of the cities provide equally good sanctuaries. Rural guerrillas frequently operate in fairly large units and gradually transform themselves into companies, battalions, regiments and even divisions. They carry out political and social reforms in "liberated zones," openly propagandize, and build up their organizational network. In towns, where this cannot be done, urban terrorists mostly operate in units of three, four or five; the whole terrorist 'movement' consists of a few hundred, often only a dozen, members. There have been a very few exceptions of urban guerrilla groups counting more than a thousand. Their small number is the source of their operational strength and their political weakness. For while it is difficult to detect small groups and, while they can cause a great deal of damage, their political effect is limited. Only a few years ago, newspaper readers in the Western world were led to believe that the German Baader-Meinhof group, the Japanese United Red Army, the Symbionese Liberation Army or the British "Angry Brigade" were substantial movements that ought to be taken very seriously. Their "communiqués" were published in the mass media; there were earnest sociological and psychological studies on the background of their members and their motivation; their "ideology" was analyzed in tedious detail. But these were groups of between five and fifty members, and their only victories were in the area of publicity. Even the more substantial groups, such as the Tupamaros and the Brazilian ALN, the Black Panthers and the Weatherman, were very small indeed and had no significant public support — hence their sudden collapse and disappearance. Elsewhere, terrorists had been more successful, either because their nationalist-separatist appeal guaranteed them wider popular support, or because they received massive assistance from a foreign power (or powers) or, last, because in a very few cases the government of the country was in an advanced state of decay, no longer capable of mobilizing the vastly superior resources of the state against the terrorists. With a few exceptions, the terrorist wave of the late 1960s and early 1970s has abated but the shock waves are still felt and its causes have largely remained obscure. In this sense it resembles public reaction to the Anarchist wave of the 1890s — the near panic of the mass media on one hand and the quaint theories of criminologists, early sociologists and political scientists on the other.

During the last decade a mythology of terrorism has developed, which in all probability is likely to persist for some time. Some of these misconceptions were mentioned at the beginning of this study; in an attempt to disentangle truth from mythology, it is necessary at the cost of some repetition to restate some essential facts.

(1) Contrary to widespread belief, terrorism is not a new and entirely unprecedented phenomenon. It is frequently argued that terrorism in past ages was sporadic and had no doctrine. But the Narodnaya Volya and the Russian Social Revolutionaries were as well organized as any contemporary movement, even if their weapons were less advanced; their ideological and political sophistication was, if anything, higher. There is little in contemporary terrorist literature, other than more recent technological guidance, that cannot be found in the Russian brochures of the last century, in the writings of Most and the volumes of his *Freiheit.*

(2) Terrorism, it is argued, is a "politically loaded term," which should be discarded because one nation's terrorism is another people's national liberation. This is quite correct but no more helpful than noting that many Americans supported F. D. Roosevelt in 1933 and that many Germans admired Adolf Hitler in the same year. That terrorism has been in certain circumstances a liberating force goes without saying. But whereas the terrorism of the Narodnaya Volya and similar such groups was directed against despotic regimes, this is no longer so; today it is directed almost exclusively against permissive democratic societies and ineffective authoritarian regimes. Having been the *ultima ratio* of the oppressed, it has all too often become the *prima ratio* of a motley crowd of people of varying motivations. It is no longer directed against the worst types of dictatorships; there were no terrorist movements in Nazi Germany or Fascist Italy nor are there any in the Communist regimes. The nationalist terrorism of a bygone age aimed at liberation from foreign rule. In our time, more often than not, terrorism is simply one form of nationalist or religious strife.

(3) Terrorism is widely believed to be "left-wing" or "revolutionary" in character. Terrorists, it is true, have usually claimed to act on behalf of the masses but they also believe that the "liberation of the masses" is the historical mission of a chosen few. If at the present time most guerrilla manifestoes are phrased in left-wing language, a

past generation of terrorists gravitated toward Fascism. Nationalist-separatist movements have at various times in their history flirted with Fascism and with Communism. The ideology of many terrorist groups encompasses elements of far-left doctrine as well as those of the extreme right. Slogans change with intellectual fashions — they should neither be ignored nor taken too seriously. The real inspiration underlying terrorism is usually a free-floating activism that can with equal ease turn right or left. Terrorism in any case is not a philosophical school — it is always the action that counts.

(4) Terrorism is believed to appear wherever people have genuine legitimate grievances. Remove the grievances, remove poverty, inequality, injustice, lack of political participation, and terror will cease. The sentiments are praiseworthy and are shared by all men and women of good will. As a cure against terrorism they are of limited value; as experience shows, societies with the least political participation and the most injustice have been the most free from terrorism in our time. There are always grievances and, given the imperfect character of human beings and social institutions, they can be reduced but not eradicated altogether. But only in democratic societies can grievances be more or less freely voiced. It is perception that counts in this respect: a major grievance may be fatalistically accepted whereas at another time (or elsewhere) a minor grievance may produce the most violent reaction. Some grievances can be remedied but very often the demands of nationalist groups are mutually exclusive. Acceding to the demands of one group may result in injustice to another; it may lead to the creation of nonviable states and the crippling of society. Elsewhere, as in Latin America, terrorists have been fighting for greater political freedom and social justice. Their grievances may be perfectly legitimate; whether there would have been more freedom in Brazil under Carlos Marighella or Carlos Lamarca, or in Colombia under Fabio Vasquez or some other Castro-type caudillo is a question open to doubt. Last, there is the terrorism directed against the democratic governments of Western Europe, North America and Japan. The shortcomings of their political systems are well known, but to suggest, for example, that the members of the Baader-Meinhof Gang are more qualified by character or intellect to lead the way to a better life than the Social Democrats is to invite ridicule. However democratic a society, however near to per-

fection the social institutions, there will always be disaffected and alienated people claiming that the present state of affairs is intolerable and there will be aggressive people more interested in violence than in liberty and justice.

(5) Terror, it is frequently argued, is highly effective. Terrorism has indeed resulted in political change, but it has had a lasting effect only in fairly rare circumstances when political mass movements used terrorist tactics in the framework of a wider strategy. There is no known case in modern history of a small terrorist group seizing political power; society usually tolerates terrorism only so long as it is no more than a nuisance. Once insecurity spreads and terror becomes a real danger, the authorities are no longer blamed for disregarding human rights in fighting terror: violence triggers off counterviolence and greater repression. The means of repression at the disposal of the state are infinitely more effective: the terrorists' only hope is to prevent somehow the authorities from using their powers. If the terrorist is the fish — following Mao Tse-tung's parable — the permissiveness of liberal society and the inefficiency of an autocratic regime is the water which the terrorist needs for survival. A government may be so weak and irresolute, a society in a state of such advanced decay, that it is no longer capable of defending itself against a terrorist challenge. But these are rare exceptions; the basic question is not whether terrorism can be defeated; even third-rate dictatorships have shown that it can be put down with great ease. The real problem is the price that has to be paid by liberal societies valuing their democratic traditions. This is the danger that terrorism poses at a time when free societies are on the defensive and in any case facing grave internal and external challenges to their survival.

(6) Terrorists, it is said, are idealists. They are more humane and intelligent than ordinary criminals. Such statements, true or not, contribute little to the understanding of terrorism. The essential humanity of the early terrorists in Russia is not questioned. But this is no longer true with regard to many terrorist movements that have appeared in recent decades and, in any case, some of the worst horrors in the annals of mankind have been perpetrated by those whose idealism was never in doubt. The love of adventure is an important motive in a world devoid of thrill and excitement. Terrorists in Latin and North America, in Europe and in some of the nation-

al-separatist groups have a higher education; they may be well read and articulate. But this is not to say that they have shown greater maturity. With some notable exceptions, they have displayed great political naïveté. Larger issues and future perspectives are of little interest to them; frequently they have been knowingly or unknowingly manipulated by foreign powers. The early terrorist groups abstained from acts of deliberate cruelty. But with the change in the character of terrorism, "left-wing" and "right-wing" alike, humane behavior is no longer the norm. The ordinary criminal does not believe in indiscriminate killing. He may torture a victim, but this will be the exception, not the rule: he is usually motivated by material gain, not by fanaticism. The political terrorist of recent vintage may preach the brotherhood of man and sometimes even practice it. More often he has liberated himself from moral scruples and persuaded himself that all is permitted since everyone is guilty but himself. It is the terrorist's aim not just to kill his opponent but to spread confusion and fear. He believes that the great aim justifies all means, however atrocious.

(7) Terrorism is described as the weapon of the poor. This was certainly true with regard to the nineteenth-century terrorist movements; the militants were usually of middle- or upper-class background, but as a group they were indeed without means. As the targets of terrorism have changed, striking differentiation has taken place. Terrorist groups without powerful outside protectors are still poor. The South Moluccans, for instance, belong to this category; their struggle for national independence happens to be of no interest to outside powers. They will get no weapons from Russia, no instructors from Cuba, no money from Libya or Algeria, because they belong to the wrong religious or ethnic group, or because their aspirations do not coincide with big-power interests. They are the proletariat of the terrorist world. On the other extreme there are the groups kept by outside powers, the aristocracy of the terrorist world, among whom many millions of dollars change hands, who have offices in luxury hotels and bank accounts in Switzerland. This abundance of funds makes it possible to engage in all kinds of costly operations beyond the reach of the poor terrorists. At the same time, the surfeit of money breeds corruption. In between these extremes there have been groups such as the Argentine ERP or the Mon-

toneros who had no lavish outside support but who managed to amass considerable fortunes through bank robberies and extortion — they, too, did not have to live on a starvation diet and operate on shoestring budgets while the going was good.

The most recent wave of terrorism offers a number of lessons to terrorists and governments alike, which run counter to conventional wisdom. Terrorists have been slow in accepting the obvious fact that terror is almost always more popular against foreigners than against their own countrymen (or co-religionists). Most terrorists in our time who have had any success at all had the support of a specific national or religious group; it was the sectarian appeal that counted, not the revolutionary slogans — a fact that the Irish, Basques, Arabs and others found out by trial and error. Terrorists have been quicker in accepting the other chief lesson, that the media are of paramount importance in their campaigns, that the terrorist act by itself is next to nothing, whereas publicity is all. But the media, constantly in need of diversity and new angles, make fickle friends. Terrorists will always have to be innovative. They are, in some respects, the superentertainers of our time. Thus for maximum impact the timing of an operation is of the greatest importance. Western authorities usually call on the good services as mediators of psychiatrists, social workers and clergymen, ever eager to assuage and to mediate. These men and women of good will have the reputation of knowing more than others about the mysteries of the human soul and of having the compassion required for understanding the feelings of "desperate men." The real danger facing the terrorist is that of being ignored, of receiving insufficient publicity, of losing the image of the desperate freedom fighter and, of course, of having to face determined enemies, unwilling to negotiate regardless of the cost. Fortunately, from the terrorist point of view, there are few such people in authority in democratic societies. Leaders who might not hesitate to sacrifice whole armies at a time of war appear willing to make almost any concession to save a single human life in peacetime, even knowing that these concessions will lead to new outbreaks and fresh victims of terror. When an Anarchist tried to kill the Italian king around the turn of the century, Umberto noted that this was the professional risk facing kings. Such philosophical resignation (or sense of duty) is no longer universal. Diplomats, it is reported, have protested against the hard line vis-à-vis terrorism taken by their government, because they fear for their life if taken hostage by terrorists.

To succeed terrorist demands have to be "realistic," i.e., limited in character. Democratic authorities instinctively give in to blackmail, but they can afford to do so only up to a certain point. Thus, the demand for money or the release of some terrorist prisoners is usually a realistic demand. But there are limits beyond which no government can go, as terrorist groups have found out to their detriment. The long-run strategic losses from concessions usually exceed the momentary gains, capitulation is a short-lived palliative.[2] If the terrorist demands are altogether unreasonable they are bound to lead to extreme countermeasures and even the don't-let's-be-beastly-to-the-terrorists-but-tackle-the-roots-of-the-evil school will no longer be able to help them. Terrorists may not be able to survive the anti-terrorist backlash unless they have sanctuaries abroad and strong support from a neighboring power.

The lessons to governments are equally obvious: if governments refused to give in to terrorist demands, terrorism would be much reduced in scale. The attitude of Austrian Chancellor Bruno Kreisky and his minister of the interior, who shook the terrorists' hands after these had killed an Austrian policeman, was not only aesthetically displeasing, it is also usually counterproductive. But all democratic governments have at one time or another acted in a similar way, compromising with the terrorists: The British and the Germans have released imprisoned terrorists, Americans and French have paid ransom, and even the Israelis have freed terrorists who were in their hands. International cooperation against terrorism is almost impossible as long as some sovereign states sponsor, train, finance, equip and offer sanctuaries to terrorist groups. Spokesmen for democratic societies will continue to proclaim that terrorism is condemned by the "whole civilized world"; but the whole civilized world covers no more than about one-fifth of mankind, and it is not at present expanding. Specific bilateral agreements such as the U.S.-Cuban pact, may limit certain forms of terrorist activities. But a really effective drive against international terrorism would be possible only if there were the determination to adopt the strategy first advocated by the Narodnaya Volya, to "hit the center," meaning the main sponsors of international terrorism. It has been maintained that such unorthodox action would result in a tremendous loss of prestige on the part of those rash or foolish enough to undertake it. Advice of this kind is manifestly wrong but again given the inertia of democratic government it can be taken for granted that such a course of action will not be adopted as long as terrorism remains a relatively minor problem. If on the other hand some major disaster were to occur as the result of international terrorism, pressure for "hitting at the center" will become overwhelming: this then is the dialectic of international terrorism. Meanwhile the debates about counteracting international terrorism will continue in the Sixth Committee of the General Assembly of the United Nations and other forums; they have gone on for many years and there is no reason why they should not go on indefinitely. The various international conventions to combat terrorism may be of considerable interest to international lawyers and insurance agents, they are of no practical importance.[3] There is no dearth of well-meaning suggestions such as the establishment of an international court to deal with terrorist activities — an idea first mooted in the League of Nations after the murder of King Alexander of Yugoslavia in 1934. Serious people have devoted years of their working life to discussing projects of this kind even though they must have known in advance what the outcome would be.

All this is not to say that democracies are powerless against domestic or international terrorism; but it is certainly true that global collaboration is a chimera and that usually they will not be able to take a decisive action before some damage has been caused. They will have to wait until public opinion becomes fully aware of the danger. In many cases terrorism may not outgrow the nuisance stage, in which case drastic action will not be necessary. There is an inclination to magnify the importance of terrorism in modern society: society may be vulnerable to attack but it is also quite resilient. A plane is hijacked, but all others continue to fly. A bank is robbed, but the others continue to function. Oil ministers are abducted and yet not a single drop of oil is lost. Describing the military exploits of his Beduin warriors, Lawrence of Arabia once noted that they were on the whole good soldiers but for their unfortunate belief that weapons were dangerous and destructive in proportion to the noise they created. Present-day attitudes toward terrorism in the Western world are strikingly similar: terrorism makes a tremendous noise, but compared with other dangers threatening mankind, it seems almost irrelevant for the time being.

Paradoxically, terrorism may in certain circumstances have side effects that are not altogether negative, precisely in view of its provocative nature. True, there is the danger of overreaction and of marshaling the efforts in the wrong direction. But in the absence of a better demonstration effect, terrorism directed against democratic societies reiterates some useful general lessons which are only too easily forgotten — that freedom is under attack and cannot be taken for granted, that appeasement does not work, and that decisive action has its uses. Such daring propositions are, of course, disputed, but it is precisely in the context of terrorism that the advocates of surrender face an uphill struggle. For terrorism is blackmail, and the victim of blackmail is less likely to forget and to forgive than the victim of almost any other crime: he feels a special sense of outrage because it is not just his life or property that has been affected. He is humiliated, his elementary human rights, his dignity and his self-respect are violated. To argue that this counts for little, to rationalize surrender to blackmail, to maintain that one should always be guided by expediency is asking too much of human nature, all the more so if the expediency is highly dubious.

PERSPECTIVES

The frequent invocation of the "steady growth of terrorism" to be found not only in the popular literature, is not borne out by facts and figures. If, in this respect, a mistaken impression has prevailed, the dramatic character and the enormous publicity given to individual terroristic exploits have caused it, as has, on the other hand, the indiscriminate use of the term "terrorist." Many forms of political violence, ranging from government repression to civil war and rural guerrilla war, are indiscriminately lumped together under the heading "terrorism" in various research programs and statistics as if terrorism was a synonym for political violence in general.* That there

*All statistics on terrorism are suspect — partly because there are genuine difficulties of definition; it is not always easy to establish, whether, for instance, the hijacking of a plane or a kidnapping was politically motivated or not. On occasion the term

has been a great deal of political turbulence in many parts of the world is not in doubt, nor is there any reason to assume that there will be fewer coups d'état, insurrections, civil wars, or local wars in the years to come. Not a global threat now, terrorism could become one as a result of technological developments.

Professor Bernard Feld, a leading American physicist once discussed the nightmarish consequences of the disappearance of twenty pounds of plutonium from government stocks. What if the mayor of Boston received a note to the effect that a terrorist group had planted a nuclear bomb somewhere in central Boston — accompanied by a crude diagram which showed that the bomb would work? Professor Feld stated that he would advise surrender to blackmail rather than the destruction of his hometown. Such fears in one form or another have been expressed for almost a century, albeit with less justification. If Most and some of his Anarchist contemporaries hailed dynamite as the ultimate weapon, a panacea for the solution of all political and social problems, such joy was not universally shared. Thus a British police officer in the 1890s said:

> Murderous organizations have increased in size and scope; they are more daring, they are served by the more terrible weapons offered by modern science, and the world is nowadays threatened by new forces which, if recklessly unchained, may some day wreak universal destruction. The Orsini bombs were mere children's toys compared with the later developments of infernal machines. Between 1858 and 1898 the dastardly science of destruction has made rapid and alarming strides. . . .[4]

With the use of poison gas in the First World War, fears were voiced that millions of people would die in gas bomb attacks. Musprath wrote in the 1920s that with the help of certain chemicals unlimited areas could be destroyed in a very short time. Lord Halsbury who

---

terrorism is used in such a vague way as to make comparisons virtually meaningless. Thus, for instance, reference is frequently made to the killing of four U.S. ambassadors between 1968 and 1976 "by terrorist action," whereas in reality the ambassadors to Cyprus and Lebanon were actually killed during a civil war, which, of course, is not quite the same. A RAND study on 63 major kidnapping operations between 1968 and 1974 reached the conclusion that there has been an 87 percent probability of success in attempts to seize hostages and a 79 percent chance that all members of the terrorist team would escape punishment or death. Such figures may accurately reflect a certain trend in one part of the world at a given time, they are quite misleading with regard to other times and places.

had been chief of the explosives department of the British ministry of war told the House of Lords in 1928 that forty tons of diphenylcyanarsin (a poison gas of the Blue Cross type) were sufficient to destroy the whole population of London. But the quantity of the poisonous material needed was such that it was generally assumed that only a modern army would be capable of using these lethal weapons. There had been talk in Irish extremist circles in the United States in the 1880s about the use of poison gas, but this had been sheer fantasy at the time. Bacteriological warfare including the poisoning of water reservoirs was first discussed as a practical possibility in the First World War. According to one report "Anarchist elements" had been hired toward the end of the war to carry cholera bacilli from a neutral state to the territory of one of the belligerents.[5] The neutral country was apparently Switzerland, and the "Anarchist elements" were to smuggle the bacilli in fountain pens to Russia. There is reason to doubt the authenticity of the report, nor is it certain that the scheme would have been practical. But in the 1920s the danger was taken seriously, and a study commission on bacteriological warfare was established by the League of Nations. In 1936 a first nerve gas (GA-tabun) was synthesized in Germany, to be followed by the discovery of even more toxic agents — sarin (GB) in 1938, and soman in 1944, all of them fatal within minutes. They all belong to the organophosphates (OPA), a substance first discovered as far back as 1854; but its toxic properties were then unknown. Considerable quantities of these and other gases were produced by the belligerents in the Second World War but not used. In 1944 a germ warfare center was established in the United States; there were similar establishments in other countries. Even before the first nuclear device had been exploded, scientists and statesmen in the United States voiced the fear that some insane people or agents of a hostile power could smuggle a bomb wherever they wanted — "twenty thousand tons of TNT can be kept under the counter of a candy store."[6] The possibility of such a threat has been discussed and investigated ever since. During the last seven years there have been 175 cases of threatened violence at nuclear facilities; in 1973 a group of ERP terrorists attacked a nuclear plant near Buenos Aires which was not, however, operating yet; a fire was started in 1975 at a nuclear plant at Fessenheim, France, allegedly by the Meinhof-Puig Antich group. With the growth of the civil nuclear industry, the establishment of new reactors all over the world and the declassification of technical information the danger has grown that technically competent people having stolen a sufficient quantity of plutonium could build a primitive nuclear device. The plutonium needed could either be stolen while in transport or smuggled out from a plant. Nor were the theft of a nuclear device or the emergence of a black market in plutonium ruled out. However stringent the means of control employed, it was assumed that they could not possibly be totally effective. Various official and private reports concluded that a sufficiently determined and able group could perform acts of sabotage endangering not only nuclear plants but also the safety of the public living in its vicinity. Another study stated that the acquisition of special nuclear materials by a terrorist group was a threat to be taken very seriously.[7] If the United States faced such danger, they existed, *a fortiori*, in other countries in which supervision was less effective and terrorism more active. Yet another study argued that while INW (illicit nuclear weapon) production was both plausible and feasible, the probability for success was low. Assuming that SNM (special nuclear material) had been acquired in sufficient quantity, an effort by a sizable group of people would be needed over a lengthy period. There was low probability that such a group would have the skills, motivations, resources and opportunities to make the venture a success.[8] The fuel delivered to atomic plants has characteristics which make it nearly impossible to convert to nuclear weapons. The terrorist group would have to steal a number of centrifuges to produce high enrichened uranium from stolen low enrichened or natural uranium. The popular idea of a nuclear device produced in a garage and transported on a tricycle seems to belong for the time being to the realm of fantasy. Technical details are classified; it is believed however that the weight of an effective device would be at least one ton, possibly twice as much. Various other means of nuclear sabotage have been mentioned, such as the disposal of plutonium powder. All these possibilities have to be taken seriously, and the danger will undoubtedly increase in future even though the risks involved for nuclear terrorists are formidable. According to some estimates there is a 50 percent death risk in stealing nuclear material, and about 30 percent in bomb manufacture. But terrorist groups ready to make use of nuclear devices or poisonous substances cannot be measured by rational standards in any case, and it is also true that the technical obstacles would be greatly reduced if the terrorists could count on the help of a friendly government which had nuclear reactors and the facilities to produce plutonium or uranium-235. All this may take longer than some experts assume but there is little reason to doubt that "if present trends continue, it seems only a question of time before some terrorist organization exploits the possibilities for coercion which are latent in nuclear fuel."[9] In the meantime certain safeguards — sensors for instance — may be developed which at the present do not exist. But there is no reason to assume that there will ever be totally effective safeguards.

Most attention has focused on the potential of nuclear blackmail because it is the most dramatic threat; but modern technology has provided other, equally lethal weapons more frequently discussed in the scientific literature than in popular writing.[10] This refers to various poisons such as the OPA's which include the nerve gases of which mention has already been made and the monofluoro-alipathic compounds as well as BTX (botulinum toxin) which is physiologically effective however it enters the body. In addition there are a great many other potential biological weapons capable of spreading contagions ranging from anthrax to bubonic plague, from certain forms of encephalitis to psittacosis.[11] Some bacteria are difficult to cultivate or to disseminate, but the list of those that could possibly be used is still uncomfortably long. Most of the biological pathogens (like most of the highly poisonous substances) have been available for many decades but there have been several important technological developments since the Second World War. These include the continuous culture of micro-organisms, the production of monodisperse aerosols and the stabilization of organisms to maintain their viability in aerosol dissemination.[12] At the same time modern society has become more vulnerable as the result of rapid communication, central ventilation, central water storage systems and in many other respects.[13] Biological pathogens are more easily available than special nuclear material; transport and dissemination might be undertaken by very small groups of people, possibly even single individuals. On the other hand, it is precisely the almost unlimited destructive character of biological pathogens which makes them less suitable as a terrorist weapon, not only because nuclear terrorism has the greater publicity value, but mainly because a threat to use biological pathogens would be less credible. A terrorist group could prove that it is capable of carrying out a nuclear threat by exploding a device in a sparsely inhabited area, whereas a "trial epidemic" is impossible to launch. A crude fission bomb of, say, 0.1 kiloton, would have a limited effect — that of a bomb of 100 tons of high explosive or more. It could destroy a big factory, or several blocks of buildings. An epidemic, on the other hand, could spread to all parts of the globe, which makes it impractical for international terrorism. A weapon of this kind is more likely to be used by a madman, rather than by political terrorists.[14] For these and other reasons the use of biological weapons despite their greater availability seems less likely than the use of chemical agents, such as the OPA substances, some of which are commercially available in any case. But chemical agents like homemade nuclear devices involve high risks for those engaged in their preparation and their effectiveness is not guaranteed. By the mid-1970s there had been reports of the theft of mustard gas from German ammunition bunkers allegedly by the Baader-Meinhof Gang; a quantity of nerve gas (stolen by criminals) had been recovered by the Austrian police; there had been unconfirmed reports that the Baader-Meinhof Gang and a Spanish terrorist group had enlisted the services of chemists and microbiologists; that an Arab Pharmaceutical Congress had pledged support to the PLO urging training in biological warfare.[15] But there has not been as yet a single attempt at terror on the grand scale.

It can be taken for granted that most of the terrorist groups existing at present will not use this option, either as a matter of political principle or because it would defeat their purpose. If weapons of this kind were used in Ulster, for instance, Catholics and Protestants alike would be the victims. But some groups might well opt for the weapons of superviolence because their aim is not political change but the total destruction of the enemy.

Various scenarios based on the spread of unconventional weaponry have been developed, such as the use, or threat of use, of arms of mass destruction by poor Third World countries against the "rich" industrial states. Others have envisaged the emergence of two types of states — those of nations in the traditional sense, with boundaries, capital cities and national armies, and those of groups which are not nations, do not always have precisely defined national territory, but possess some sort of armed force of their own.[16] Such scenarios, while not *a priori* impossible, seem a little farfetched; "surrogate warfare" of this kind would lead sooner or later to full-scale war. A discussion of these scenarios leads in any case beyond the confines of a study which is not concerned with state terrorism. It seems possible, in theory, that the weapons of superviolence would endanger totalitarian rule as much as democratic societies. But the means of control on which totalitarian rule rests makes this much less likely; there may be the necessary determination on the part of the enemies of the regime, but opportunity will be far less than in an open society.

Credible threats of the use of arms of mass destruction would face governments with agonizing choices. The advocacy of surrender (as suggested by Professor Feld and others) seems natural enough, but it would not, of course, answer the challenge. For according to experience, one case of successful blackmail leads to another and yet another; a left-wing nuclear threat would sooner or later be countered by a similar threat from the extreme right; and there would be conflicting threats of nuclear terror or biological or chemical warfare by nationalist separatist groups. This would lead to constant tyranny by small groups of people or, more likely, total anarchy and possibly widespread destruction, unless, of course, society learns to face blackmail. Society may be spared the dilemma, but if the emergency arose countermeasures could involve a degree of state control and repression hitherto unknown in any democratic society except at a time of war. In the long run it could result in the surrender of sovereign rights thought unthinkable at the present. But then it would be a situation at least as dangerous as full-scale war and if a choice has to be made between survival and a restriction of civil liberty and sovereign rights there is no doubt what the response would be. Whether preventive measures could forestall an emergency of this kind is a moot question, but if it came to it, greater clarity about the roots and the character of terrorism would be needed to face the threat without panic and hysteria.

The debate on whether or not one should compromise with terrorist has lasted a long time. Concessions may be advisable in some exceptional cases; consistent conciliation of terrorism on the other hand is bound to claim a higher toll in human life in the long run than resisting it. But while terrorism is on a relatively small scale it is not really that important what kind of is taken; societies facing a determined terrorist onslaught will opt for a hard-line policy in any case. But what is true with regard to a period in which terrorism is no more than a nuisance does not, of course, apply to an age in which mankind may be threatened by weapons of superviolence. There is the certainty that society would not be able to satisfy the grievances real or imaginary, the demands justified or unjustified of all its members in the foreseeable future. There is equally the certainty that some individuals will have at some future date the skill and the determination to dictate their wishes to society. Such action would, of course, be irrational, leading sooner or later to destruction without precedent. But is this likely to deter individuals or small groups of people convinced that the whole world ought to be punished if their demands, whatever they might be, are not met?

If these are the more distant dangers, there is reason for concern also for the near future. Attempts have already been made by terrorist groups to use precision guided weapons, such as the Soviet SA-7 or the American Redeye, against civilian aircraft. This does not necessarily add a new dimension to the technology of modern terrorism, but it could lead sooner or later to war between nations. For country X, the victim of such an attack, would assume, rightly or wrongly, that the terrorists were acting on behalf of country Y, which financed and trained them and provided the weapons. It could retaliate by bombing the capital or the oil fields of that country or in some other way. The assumption underlying the policy of the sponsors of international terrorism that they will escape retaliation cannot be taken for granted. Precisely in view of its international character international terrorism, in contrast to the purely domestic species, can easily lead to war, but it must be taken that those sponsoring it will not desist until a disaster has befallen one of them.

If these are the future perspectives, they are far removed indeed from the origins of political terrorism inasmuch as they were rooted in the struggle against despotism and in tyrannicide. Terrorism appeared in the secret societies and revolutionary organizations of the nineteenth century fighting a tyranny against which there was no legal redress. It was adopted by national movements against foreign oppressors, but also by some movements of the extreme left and right. Circumstances still vary from country to country and what is said about one is not necessarily true with regard to another. By and large, however, there has been an essential change in the character of terrorism with the shedding of restraints on the one hand, the growing practice of indiscriminate murder on the other, the emergence of multinational, remote-controlled terror and, above all, the failure or unwillingness to challenge effective dictatorships. Once it was the strategy of the poor and weak used against ruthless tyrants; today its more prominent representatives are no longer poor, and modern technology is giving them powerful weapons. Some present-day terrorist groups have quite clearly acquired the characteristics once attributed to tyranny, *atrox et notoria iniuria;* the tyrant wanted to impose his will on society and to keep it at ransom and so do terrorists. Others genuinely believe in their liberating mission, yet if their actions have any effect at all it is that of unwitting pacemakers of a new breed of tyrants. The wheel has come full circle: modern terrorism from its beginnings could challenge only nonterrorists, that is, governments or groups which would stop short at using their own weapons. It first appeared on the scene under the banner of freedom and democracy and at a time when it was thought that these ideas would prevail all over the world. These hopes have not come true and nondemocratic regimes, unlike the democracies, suffer from no inhibitions in dealing with political opponents. If the power of democratic societies shrinks so does the sphere in which terrorism can operate.

Notes

CHAPTER ONE: THE ORIGINS

1. *Dictionnaire, Supplément* (Paris, an VII [1798]), 775.
2. *Le Néologiste Français*, quoted in Aulard, *Paris pendant la réaction ther-midorienne et sous le Directoire* (Paris, 1902), V, 490. See also F. Brunot, *Histoire de la langue française des origines à 1900* (Paris, 1937), IX, 871.
3. James Murray, *A New English Dictionary on Historical Principles* (Oxford, 1919). It also had a different meaning for a while — an alarmist or scaremonger.
4. Thomas de Quincey, "On Murder Considered as One of the Fine Arts," in *The English Mail Coach and Other Writings* (Edinburgh, 1862), 52.
5. The main sources are M. Hengel, *Die Zeloten* (Leiden, 1961), 47–51; Cecil Roth, in *Journal of Semitic Studies* (1959), 332–355; S. Kleinfelder, "Sicarius," in Pauly-Wissowa, *Real Lexicon;* S. G. E. Brandon, *Jesus and the Zealots* (Manchester, 1967), 56–57; Josephus Flavius (Thackeray ed.), 2 vols. (London, 1956); Y. Yadin, *Megilat Bne Or ubne Khoshekh* (Jerusalem, 1957); R. Laqueur, *Der Jüdische Historiker Flavius Josephus* (Giessen, 1920).
6. B. Lewis, *The Assassins* (London, 1967), 47; see also M. G. S. Hodgson, *The Order of Assassins* (The Hague, 1955), and the articles in *Speculum*, 27 (1952), by Lewis and Prawer.
7. Both *sicarii* and Assassins have made a contribution to the terminology of modern terrorist groups. The *Sikarikin* (and the *Biryonim*) were precursors of the "dissident terrorists" in Mandatory Palestine and the term *fida'i* was, of course, adopted by the Palestinian Arab terrorists. Abba Achimeir, a Revisionist ideologist, wrote in a pamphlet on the *sicarii* in the 1930s asserting that they were unknown heroes who chose as victims central figures of the establishment: "... what mattered was not the action but the purpose behind it." Avraham Stern in one of his poems called Jerusalem "the city of prophets and biryonim" *(ir nevi'im vebiryonim).*
8. The main sources are Sleeman's writings, and most recently George Bruse, *The Stranglers* (London, 1968), 111.
9. The most recent survey of Chinese secret societies is Jean Chesneaux, ed., *Popular Movements and Secret Societies in China 1840–1950* (Stanford, 1972).
10. On the Mafia in politics see V. Frosini, *Mitologia e sociologia della Mafia* (Milan, 1969); G. C. Maino, *L'opposizione mafiosa 1870–1882* (Palermo, 1964); M. Pantelone, *The Mafia and Politics* (New York, 1966).

11. Charles C. Alexander, *The Ku Klux Klan in the Southwest* (University of Kentucky Press, 1965), 254.
12. *Pamiatnaya Knizhka Sotsialista — Revolutsionera* (Paris, 1914), 8 *et seq.* These figures do not include terrorist operations carried out by other political groups, but they accurately reflect the general trend.
13. St. Christowe, *Heroes and Assassins* (New York, 1935), 50 *et seq.* There is no history of the IMRO, but see D. Kosev, *Istorija na makedonskoto natsionalno-revoliutsonno dvizhenie* (Sofia, 1954), and *Makedonia, minalo i novi borbi* (Sofia, 1932).
14. On the terrorist operations among Polish socialists see T. Jablonski, *Zarys Historii PPS* (Warsaw, 1946), and Kwapinski, *Organisacia Bojowa* (London, 1943); also Georg W. Strobel, *Die Partei Rosa Luxemburgs* (Wiesbaden, 1974), 288–294; for a local survey on Lodz, where terrorist operations were very frequent, *Zródia do dziejów revolucii 1905–1907 w okregu lódzkim* (Warsaw, 1957), *passim.* For the history of Indian terrorism see Nirajan Sen, *Bengal's Forgotten Warriors* (Bombay, 1945); B. Hardass, *Armed Struggle for Freedom* (Poona, 1958); H. Mukerjee, *India's Struggle for Freedom,* 3 vols. (Bombay, 1962), and other literature quoted below.
15. E. A. Vizetelly, *The Anarchists* (New York, 1912), 293.
16. Wayne G. Broehl, Jr., *The Molly Maguires* (New York, 1966), 350.
17. For an excellent bibiliography on Spanish anarchism see J. Romeo Maura, "The Spanish Case," in David E. Apter and James Joll, *Anarchism Today* (London, 1971). The most important recent studies are those by John Brademas and Gerald H. Meaker; see below.
18. David Rock, *Politics in Argentina 1830–1930. The Rise and Fall of Radicalism* (Cambridge, 1975), 163 *et seq.*
19. P. Wurth, *La répression internationale du terrorisme* (Lausanne, 1941); see also the *Journal Officiel de la SDN,* 1934–1935.
20. Jawaharlal Nehru, *An Autobiography* (London, 1936), 175.
21. Ibid., 482.
22. Abdel Fatah Ismail, "How We Liberated Aden," in *Gulf Studies* (April 1976), 9.
23. Urban terrorism had in fact played a part of some significance in Castro's campaigns, but its importance has always been played down in official Cuban historiography.

CHAPTER TWO: THE PHILOSOPHY OF THE BOMB

1. For a recent summary of ancient and medieval writings on tyrannicide, see Roland Mousnier, *L'Assassinat d'Henri IV* (Paris, 1964), 47–90. Oliver Lutaud traces the discussions on tyrannicide throughout the seventeenth and eighteenth centureies, *Des révolution d'Angleterre à la révolution Française* (The Hague, 1973).
2. J. W. Allen, *A History of Political Thought in the Sixteenth Century* (London, 1960), 320.
3. N. A. Morozov, *Povest moei zhizni* (Moscow, 1965), II, 420. N. A. Morozov, *Terroristicheskaya Borba* (London, 1880), *passim.*
4. *Della Tirannide, Opere di Vittorio Alfieri* (Piacenza, 1811), XX, 252. Paul Sirven, *Vittorio Alfieri* (Paris, 1938), III, 257 *et seq.*
5. P. Buonarroti, *History of Baboeuf's Conspiracy for Equality* (London, 1836), 244; Richard Cobb, *The Police and the People* (London, 1970), 195.
6. A. Spitzer, *Old Hatreds and Young Hopes* (Cambridge, Mass., 1971), 293; Pierre Mariel, *Les Carbonari: idealisme et la révolution* (Paris, 1971), *passim.*

7. Bartoldi, *Memoirs of the Secret Societies of the South of Italy* (London, 1821), 176–177.
8. Vicomte d'Arlincourt, *L'Italie Rouge* (Paris, 1850), 4 *et seq.*
9. Bartoldi, op. cit., 30.
10. A. Ottolini, *La Carboneria, dalle origini ai primi tentativi insurrezionali* (Modena, 1946); A. Falcionelli, *Les Sociétés secrètes italiennes* (Paris, 1969); P. Mariel, *Les Carbonari* (Paris, 1971)
11. *Della guerra nazionale d'insurrezione per bande* (Italy, 1830), I, 235. See W. Laqueur, *Guerrilla* (Boston, 1976), chapter 3, *passim.*
12. G. Mazzini, *Scritti editi ed inediti* (Imola, 1931) LIX, 331–332.
13. J. K. Bluntschli, *Die Kommunisten in der Schweiz* (Zürich, 1843), 106–113.
14. *Garantien der Harmonie und Freiheit* (Hamburg, 1849), 221, 225, 236.
15. The article was first published in the monthly *Die Evolution* in Biel, Switzerland. See C. F. Wittke's Heinzen biography, *Against the Current* (Chicago, 1945), 74–75. The article was reprinted many times, for instance in Most's *Die Freiheit* about which more below. As a result of yet another publication, after the assassination of President McKinley, Most got a year's prison sentence on Blackwell's Island, even though Most's attorney, Morris Hillquit, drew the attention of the court to the fact that the author of the article had been dead for a long time and that, in any case, it had been directed against European kings, not American presidents. In actual fact, Most's article was a paraphrase on the Heinzen essay, not a reprint.
16. *Perezhitoe i Peredumannoe* (Berlin, 1923).
17. E. H. Carr, *Michael Bakunin* (London, 1961), 128.
18. Quoted from a pamphlet published in Geneva in 1869. The theme also occurred in Bakunin's letters to his friends and it appears in M. Confino's and Arthur Lehning's recent studies.
19. M. Bakunin, *Sobranie sochinenii i pisem* (Moscow, 1935), IV, 172–173.
20. Originally published in *Pravitelstvenni Vestnik*, July 1871, it has been translated and republished, usually incomplete, many times since. It is quoted here from M. Confino, *Violence dans la violence* (Paris, 1973), 97 *et seq.*
21. V. I. Burtsev, *Za sto let* (London, 1897), 40–46; for the literature on the Zaichnevski circle see F. Venturi, *Roots of Revolution* (London, 1960), 763.
22. Venturi, 336–337; for the literature on the Ishutin "organization" see Venturi, 768–769.
23. N. I. Sheveko, *Khronika sotsialisticheskovo dvizheniya v Rossii, 1878–1887* (Moscow, 1906), 19; these are the internal annual reports of the Ministry of the Interior.
24. G. V. Plekhanov, *Sochineniya* (n.d.), IX, 20.
25. P. 19. The brochure is quoted here from the 1920 Petrograd reprint. Kravchinski-Stepniak subsequently became the best-known chronicler of the Narodnaya Volya. His *Podpolnaya Rossia* (Underground Russia) appeared in many languages.
26. N. A. Morozov, *Povest moei Zhizni* (Moscow, 1965), II, 48.
27. S. S. Volk, *Narodnaya Volya* (Moscow, 1966), 89.
28. O. V. Aptekman, *Obshestvo Zemlya i Volya* (Moscow, 1966), 89.
29. Burtsev, op. cit. 149, 154.
30. Felix Kon quoted in S. S. Volk, loc. cit., 234.
31. Plekhanov, *Sochineniya*, II, 350.
32. Nikolai Morozov, *Terroristicheskaya Borba* (London, 1880); Romanenko's pamphlet was published under the pen name V. Tarnowski — *Terrorism i rutina* — in Geneva in the same year. Articles in favor of terrorism had appeared in the Russian emigré press even before, notably by Kaspar Turski in Tkachev's *Nabat*. But Tkachev was a Blanquist who would not accept a single-minded concentration on terrorist acts.

33. Morozov, *Povest*, II, 418.
34. Morozov, *Terroristicheskaya Borba*, 7 *et seq.*
35. V. Tarnovski [G. Romanenko], *Terrorism i rutina* (Geneva, 1880), 18 *et seq.*
36. This pamphlet appeared in 1884; it was hectographed, not printed. It was not accessible to me and I have quoted from Z. Ivianski, "Individual Terror as a phase in Revolutionary Violence in the late 19th and the Beginning of the 20th Century" (in Hebrew). Doctoral Dissertation, Jerusalem, 1973.
37. M. P. Dragomanov, *Terrorism i Svoboda* (Geneva, 1880), *passim;* see also his subsequent *La tyrannicide en Russie et l'action de l'Europe Occidentale* (Geneva, 1883).
38. *Literatura partii Narodnoi Voly* (Moscow, 1907), 451 *et seq.*
39. L. Deitch, *Delo Pervovo Marta 1881 goda* (Moscow, 1906), 412.
40. Venturi, op. cit., 597.
41. *Sotsial Demokrat* I, 1.
42. *Podpolnaya Rossiya*, quoted from the most recent edition (Moscow, 1960), 201.
43. *Podgotovitelniya Raboti Partii Narodnoi Volny* (St. Petersburg, 1892).
44. A. I. Ulianova-Elizarova, *A. I. Ulianov i Delo I Marta 1887* (Leningrad, 1927); A. I. Ivanski, *Zhizn Kak Fakel* (Moscow, 1960); B. C. Henberg and A. Y. Cherniak, *Zhizn A. Ulianova* (Moscow, 1966).
45. An even earlier brochure by Alisov on terrorism (1893) was not accessible to me.
46. V. I. Burtsev, *Doloi Tsaria* (London, 1901), 22.
47. *Nasha zadacha* (1902).
48. "Terroristicheskii element v nashei programme," in *Revoliutsionnaya Rossia*, June 7, 1902.
49. *Iskra*, May 1, 1902.
50. Alexander Gerassimoff, *Der Kampf gegen die erste russische Revolution* (Berlin, 1933), 205.
51. L. Tikhomirov, *Vospominaniya*, op. cit., 104–105.
52. Manfred Hildermeier, "Sozialstruktur und Kampfmethode der Sozial-Revolutionären Partei," in *Jahrbücher für Geschichte Osteuropas* (December 1972), 539–540.
53. *Protokoly Pervovo sezda partii Sotsialistov — Revoliutsionerov* (n.p., n.d.), 314.
54. G. Nestroev, *Iz dnevnika Maksimalista* (Paris, 1910), 153.
55. "Vopros o Terrore," in *Sotsial Revoliutsioner* (Paris, 1910), II, 1–52. This is an abridged version of the main speeches and the discussion at the May 1909 meeting. Further contributions in the journal *Znamya Truda* throughout 1909–1912.
56. P. Avrich, *The Russian Anarchists* (Princeton, 1971), 48 *et seq.*
57. Paul Avrich, ed., *The Anarchists in the Russian Revolution* (London, 1973), 54.
58. Boris Savinkov, *Erinnerungen eines Terroristen* (Berlin, 1929), 29.
59. V. Dedijer, *The Road to Serajevo* (New York, 1966), 178, 205.
60. William L. Langer, *The Diplomacy of Imperialism 1830–1902* (New York, 1956), 156 *et seq.*
61. Louise Nalbadian, *The Armenian Revolutionary Movement* (Berkeley, 1963), 168–173.
62. Avetis Nazarbeck, *Through the Storm* (London, 1899), 212.
63. *St James Gazette*, August 29, 1896; *Foreign Relations of the United States 1895* (Washington, 1896), 1416.
64. *La Verité sur les massacres d'Armenie*, Par un Philarmene (Paris, 1896), *passim.*
65. *Bal Ganjadhar Tilak. His Writings and Speeches* (Madras, n.d.).
66. Dhanonjay Keer, *Veer Savarkar* (Bombay, 1950), 41.
67. S. Wolpert, *Tilak and Gokhale: Revolution and Reform in the Making of Modern India* (Berkeley, 1962), 81.
68. *Source Material for a History of the Freedom Movement in India* (Bombay, 1958), II, 978 *et seq.*

69. Valentine Chirol, *Indian Unrest* (London, 1910), 71.
70. The book was first published in Holland in 1909; a French edition came out a year later.
71. D. Keer, *Veer Savarkar,* 401; J. C. Jain, *The Murder of Mahatma Gandhi. Prelude and Aftermath* (Bombay, 1961), *passim.*
72. Bipan Chanda, "The Revolutionary Terrorists in Northern India in the 1920s," in B. R. Nanda, ed., *Socialism in India* (Delhi, 1972), 165 *et seq.*
73. *Peaceful and Legitimate,* quoted in Bipan Chanda, 181.
74. Bipan Chanda, loc. cit., 183.
75. The document was clandestinely distributed in various parts of India in late January of 1930 and is now exceedingly rare. I am grateful to Professor Bipan Chandra of Jawaharlal Nehru University of New Delhi who obtained a copy for me.
76. *Young India,* January 2, 1930.
77. *Speeches and Writings of M. K. Gandhi* (Madras, n.d.), 231.
78. *The Philosophy of the Bomb, passim.*
79. Ibid.
80. Ibid.
81. Virendra Sandhu, *Yugdrastha Bhagat Singh* (Delhi, 1968); Gopal Thakur, *Bhagat Singh* (New Delhi, 1957); *Lahore Conspiracy Case* (exhibits).
82. Secretary of State for India, *Terrorism in India* (1933), 328.
83. R. C. Majumdar, *History of the Freedom Movement in India* (Calcutta, 1963), II, 529.
84. George Woodcock, *Anarchism* (London, 1962), 308.
85. *Bulletin de la Fédération Jurassienne,* December 3, 1876.
86. David Stafford, *From Anarchism to Reformism. A study of the political activities of Paul Brousse 1870–1890* (London, 1971), 76 *et seq.*
87. *Bulletin, 31,* August 5, 1877, in J. Guillaume, ed., *L'Internationale, documents et souvenirs 1864–1878* (Paris, 1910), II, 224; according to Guillaume, IV, 206, the expression was first used in a speech in Geneva by Andrea Costa on June 9 of that year. The era of "propaganda by deed" is exceedingly well documented. The following are of particular interest: R. Hunter, *Violence and the Labor Movement* (New York, 1914), chapter III; Andrew R. Carlson, *Anarchism in Germany* (New York, 1972), chapter VIII; Richard Hostetter, *The Italian Socialist Movement* (New York, 1958), chapters XIV and XV; E. Semicoli, *L'Anarchia,* vol. I: *La propaganda di fatto* (Milan, 1894); Zoccoli, *L'Anarchia* (Torino, 1907), 43 *et seq.;* as well as the histories of anarchism by Nettlau, Maitron *et al.,* mentioned below.
88. *Le Révolté,* December 25, 1880; Guillaume, op. cit., II, 96.
89. *Le Révolté,* October 18, 1879.
90. Kropotkin to Georg Brandes, *Freedom,* October 1898: P. A. Kropotkin, *Selected Writings on Anarchism and Revolution* (London, 1973), 20–23.
91. Max Nettlau, *Anarchisten und Sozialrevolutionaere* (Berlin, 1919), 217–218.
92. *Le Révolté,* July 23, 1881.
93. *L'Internationale* (London), May 1890.
94. *La Dynamite et l'anarchie* (Geneva, n.d.); many quotations, some of doubtful provenance, appear in Felix Dubois, *Le Péril anarchiste* (Paris, 1894), *passim.*
95. J. Maitron, *Histoire du mouvement anarchiste en France (1880–1914)* (Paris, 1955), 211; E. V. Zenker, *Anarchism* (London, 1895), 262.
96. Maitron, loc. cit., 196; similar suggestions had been made by Colonel de Wüst and other eighteenth-century theoreticians of the *petite guerre* — but had been rejected as outdated at the time. Laqueur, *Guerrilla,* op. cit., chapter 3, *passim.*
97. Maitron, op. cit., 197.
98. George Woodcock, *Anarchism* (London, 1962), 326.
99. Prolo, *Les Anarchistes* (Paris, 1912), 55.

100. *Le Révolté,* September 1886, quoted in Maitron, 245.
101. *Le Révolté,* March 18, 1891.
102. Gerald Brenan, *The Spanish Labyrinth* (Cambridge, 1960), 251.
103. Romero Maura, "Terrorism in Barcelona and its impact on Spanish politics 1904–19," *Past and Present* (December 1968); Gerald H. Meaker, *The Revolutionary Left in Spain, 1914–1923* (Stanford, 1973), 173–175.
104. Quoted in H. David, *History of the Haymarket Affair* (New York, 1936), 121: Samuel Yellen, *American Labor Struggles* (New York, 1936), *passim.*
105. David, op. cit., 122.
106. Ibid., 343. See also H. Karasek, ed., *1886, Haymarket. Die deutschen Anarchisten von Chicago* (Berlin, 1975), 65 *et seq.*
107. A. Berkman, *Prison Memoirs of an Anarchist* (New York, 1970), 5.
108. Ibid., 7.
109. Emma Goldman, *Living My Life* (New York, 1970), I, 97.
110. *Freiheit,* May 17, 1879.
111. *Freiheit,* September 18, 1880.
112. *Freiheit,* March 19, 1881; March 4, March 11, 1882.
113. *Freiheit,* March 8, 1884; November 15, 1884.
114. *Freiheit,* March 8, 1884.
115. *Freiheit,* March 14, 1885.
116. Ragnar Redbeard, *Might is Right* (1921), 70. (First published in Chicago, in 1903.) An earlier edition of the same work was published under the title *Survival of the Fittest* (1896). The idea that might is right has occurred in terrorist manifestoes with surprising frequency. Thus Black September after the Munich massacre in 1972: *Le monde ne respecte que les forts . . . , Problèmes politiques et sociaux,* May 30, 1975. A reprint of Redbeard's book was published in New York in 1972.
117. Ibid., 60.
118. Ibid., 39.
119. *Freiheit,* June 7, 1884.
120. *Freiheit,* February 16, 1884.
121. *Freiheit,* May 5, May 26, 1883.
122. Andrew R. Carlson, *Anarchism in Germany* (New York, 1972), 255.
123. *Freiheit,* May 5, 1883: *Revolutionaere Kriegswissenschaft,* 69–71.
124. *Freiheit,* September 13, 1884.
125. *Freiheit,* April 16, 1887.
126. *Freiheit,* October 30, 1886.
127. *Freiheit,* January 12, 1884; September 13, 1884.
128. Carlson, op. cit., 279; Rudolf Rocker, *Johann Most, das Leben eines Rebellen* (Berlin, 1924), 162.
129. *Freiheit,* October 11, 1890.
130. *Freiheit,* July 30, 1887.
131. *Freiheit,* April 24, 1886.
132. Wisnitzer, "Marx und Engels und die irische Frage," *Archiv für Geschichte des Sozialismus,* X (1922); Eduard Bernstein, "Fr. Engels und das heutige Irland," *Neue Zeit* (1916).
133. Gustav Mayer, *Friedrich Engels* (Haag, 1934), II, 256.
134. *Karl Marx, Friedrich Engels i revoliutsionnaya Rossiya* (Moscow, 1967), *passim; Perepiska K. Marksa i F. Engelsa s russkimi politicheskimi deyatelami* (Moscow, 1951).
135. *Perepiska,* loc cit., 294; S. S. Volk, op. cit., 436–437; Mayer, *Engels,* op. cit., 423.
136. *Ireland and the Irish Question. A collection of writings by Karl Marx and Friedrich Engels* (New York, 1972), 149.
137. Ibid., 230.
138. Lenin, *Polnoe sobranie sochineniya,* IX, 130.

139. Ibid., XLIX, 312.
140. Lenin, *Sochineniya*, V, 7.
141. Bolshevik expropriations are described in detail in Boris Souvarine's *Stalin* (Paris, 1939).
142. *Der Kampf*, November 1911.
143. *Przeglad Socyal-demokratyczny*, May 1909.
144. Hsi-huey Liang, *The Berlin Police in the Weimar Republic* (Berkeley, 1970), *passim*.
145. Thomas N. Brown, *Irish American Nationalism* (New York, 1966), 67.
146. P. J. P. Tynan, *The Irish Invincibles* (New York, 1894), 488.
147. Tynan, op. cit., 490.
148. *Devoy's Post Bag* (ed. W. O'Brien and D. Ryan) (Dublin, 1953), II, 41.
149. *Irish World*, March 3, 1876.
150. Tom Corfe, *The Phoenix Park Murders* (London, 1968), 31, 138.
151. *Frankfurter Zeitung*, May 9, 1931.
152. W. Kube, ed., *Almanach der nationalsozialistischen Revolution* (Berlin, 1933), 107.
153. J. Goebbels, *Knorke, Ein neues Buch Isidor* (Munich, 1929), 18; J. Goebbels, *Kampf um Berlin* (Munich, 1941), 62–63
154. Renzo de Felice, *Mussolini, il rivoluzionario* (Turin, 1965), 120.
155. Hermann Okrass, *Hamburg bleibt rot* (Hamburg, 1934), 198; Wilfrid Bade, *Die SA erobert Berlin* (Munich, 1937), 83.
156. J. Goebbels, *Kampf um Berlin*, loc. cit.: "there were 85 injured; everything went as planned, before we were a small *Verein*, now we got publicity. . . ."
157. Thor Goote, *Kameraden die Rotfront und Reaktion erschossen*, Berlin 1934, 231.
158. *Abwehrblätter*, October 1931, 182.
159. Gabriele Krüger, *Die Brigade Ehrhardt* (Berlin, 1932), *passim*.
160. Ernst von Salomon, *Die Geaechteten* (Berlin, 1932), *passim*.
161. M. Lacko, *Arrow-Cross Men, National Socialists* (Budapest, 1969), 43.
162. Eugen Weber, in H. Rogger and E. Weber, *The European Right* (Berkeley, 1963), 531.
163. E. Weber, loc. cit., 537; see also Corneliu Zelea Codreanu, *Pentru Legionari* (Bucharest, 1936), *passim*.
164. O. Tanin and E. Yohan, *Militarism and Fascism in Japan* (London, 1934), 125, 219.
165. R. Storry, *The Double Patriots* (London, 1957), 70, 192.
166. Friedrich Berg, *Die weisse Pest* (Vienna, 1926), 32.
167. Carl Schmitt, *Der Begriff des Politischen* (Munich, 1932), *passim*.
168. On the *Landvolk;* Herbert Volck, *Rebellen um Ehre* (Berlin, 1932), 278 *et seq.;* Rudolf Heberle, *Landbevoelkerung und Nationalsozialismus* (Stuttgart, 1965), *passim*.

CHAPTER THREE: THE SOCIOLOGY OF TERRORISM

1. *United Irishman*, February 14, 1885.
2. Jim Devoy, *Recollections of an Irish Rebel* (Shannon, 1969), 211–212.
3. J. Remak, *Sarajevo* (London, 1959), 56.
4. Michael St. John Paeke, *The Bombs of Orsini* (London, 1957), 293 *et seq.*
5. Louis Adamic, *Dynamite* (New York, 1935), 196.
6. Gerald W. Meaker, *The Revolutionary Left in Spain 1914–23* (Stanford, 1974), 173 *et seq.*
7. Bernard B. Fall, *Last Reflections on a War* (New York, 1967), 219–220.
8. *Etudes polémologiques* (July 1974), 78–95.

9. Ivianski, Dissertation, loc. cit., *passim*.
10. R. C. Majumdar, *History of the Freedom Movement in India* (Calcutta, 1963), 480.
11. Vladeta Milicevic, *Der Königsmord von Marseille* (Bad Godesberg, 1959), 44.
12. Wilhelm Herzog, *Barthou* (Zürich, 1938), 256.
13. *The Times* (London), April 19, 1976.
14. Michael Baumann, *Wie alles anfing* (Munich, 1975), 117–118.
15. *The Sunday Press* (Dublin), February 15, 1976.
16. A. Gerassimoff, *Der Kampf,* 211.
17. F. J. Klein, *Sturm 138* (Leipzig, 1937), 98.
18. Major Arthur Griffith, *Mysteries of Police and Crime* (London, 1898), II, 459.
19. *The New York Sun,* November 29, 1885.
20. D. Kantor, "Dynamit Narodnoi Volyi," in *Katorga i Sylka* (1929), 8–9, 119–128. Nobel was a radical both in religious and political matters and his biographers note that there can be no doubt that his attitude had been affected by the Russian milieu in which he had grown up. H. Schück and R. Sohlma, *The Life of Alfred Nobel* (London, 1929), 217. See also the most recent biography, St. Tjerneld, *Nobel — En biografi* (Stockholm, 1972), *passim*.
21. J. Most, *Revolutionäre Kriegswissenschaft,* 39.
22. Jack London, *The Assassination Bureau Ltd.* (London, 1964), 6.
23. W. D'Arcy, *The Fenian Movement in the United States 1858–1886* (Washington, 1947), 406.
24. Victor Drummond, British chargé d'affaires in Washington to James G. Blaine, Secretary of State, July 28, 1881. In the *Annual Report of the American Historical Association for the year 1941* (Washington, 1942), 146.
25. Ivianski, op. cit., 190.
26. Nikolajewski, *Asew,* 177.
27. J. Bowyer Bell, "The Thompson Submachine Gun in Ireland, 1921," *The Irish Sword,* VIII, 31.
28. *Terrorist Activity.* Committee on the Judiciary, United States Senate, 94th Congress (1975), Hearings, part 7, 524.
29. R. Clutterbuck, *Living with Terrorism* (London, 1975), 75 *et seq.*, for a fuller discussion of bombing techniques used.
30. Interview in *New York Herald,* February 10, 1889; the exploits of Le Caron are described in his autobiography and in Sir Robert Anderson, *Sidelights on the Home Rule Movement* (London, 1907), *passim*.
31. Lucien de la Hodde, *Histoire de sociétés secrètes* (Paris, 1850).
32. L. Andrieux, *Souvenirs d'un préfet de police* (Paris, 1885).
33. Many revealing facts about the activities of the West European police forces were listed in a speech by August Bebel, delivered in Berlin in 1898, later published as a brochure, *Attentate und Sozialdemokratie* (Berlin, 1905), *passim*.
34. A. T. Vasilyev, *The Okhrana* (London, 1930), 53.
35. For Azev and similar cases see Jean Longuet and Georges Silber, *Terroristes et policiers* (Paris, 1909); Nikolayevski's Azev biography, *supra,* and the memoirs by high Okhrana officials such as Spiridovich, Vasilyev, Gerassimov et al.
36. Stephan Lukashevich, "The Holy Brotherhood," in *American Slavonic and East European Review* (1959), 502 *et seq.*
37. T. D. Williams, *Secret Societies in Ireland* (Dublin, 1973), 105.
38. An excellent account of the psychology of an informer is given in Liam O'Flaherty's famous novel.
39. Anderson, *Sidelights,* 89.
40. "Degayevshina," in *Byloe* (April 1906).
41. Alexander Bekzadian, *Der Agent Provocateur* (Zürich, 1913), deals mainly with the legal aspects of the phenomenon. See also Gary T. Marx, "Thoughts on a Neglected Category of Social Movement Participant: The Agent Provocateur

and the Informant," in *American Journal of Sociology* (September 1974), 402–442.

42. Christo Silianoff, "Briefe and Beichten," in *Deutsche Rundschau* (September 1928), 173.
43. David C. Rapoport, *Assassination and Terrorism* (Toronto, 1971), *passim*.
44. Louis Adamic, *Dynamite*, 147.
45. Carol E. Baumann, *The diplomatic kidnappings: a revolutionary tactic of urban terrorism* (The Hague, 1973), *passim*.
46. Clara E. Lida, *Anarquismo y Revolución en la España del XIX siglo* (Madrid, 1972), 254. Clara E. Lida, "Agrarian Anarchism in Andalusia. Documents on the *Maño Negra,*" JRSH (1969), 315–352.
47. *Der Weg zum Nationalsozialismus* (Gaupresseamt Berlin-Fürstenwalde, n.d.), 319.
48. Major Carlos Wilson, *The Tupamaros* (Boston, 1974), 147.
49. E. Faller, Gewaltsame Flugzeugentführungen (Berlin, 1972); James A. Arey, *The Sky Pirates* (New York, 1972), *passim*; La Documentation française, *problèmes politiques et sociaux: "La piraterie aérienne,"* March 22, 1974; S. K. Agrawala, *Aircraft Hijacking and International Law* (Dobbs Ferry, 1973); Nancy D. Joyner, *Aerial Hijacking as an International Crime* (Dobbs Ferry, 1974); Edward McWhinney, *The Illegal Diversion of Aircraft and International Law* (Leiden, 1975). There were 35 successful hijackings throughout the world in 1968; the figure rose to 87 in 1969 and 83 in 1970; there were 58 such cases in 1971, 62 in 1972, followed by a sharp decrease to 22 in 1973.
50. Camilo Cataño, "Avec les guerrillas de Guatemala," *Partisans* (July 1967), 150.
51. Jacques Duchêne, *Histoire du F.L.N.* (Paris, 1962), 263; Abdul Fatah Ismail, "How we liberated Aden," *Gulf Studies* (April 1976), 6.
52. *Jerusalem Post*, May 18, 1976.
53. Quoted in D. D. Egbert, *Social Radicalism and the Arts* (New York, 1970), 254.
54. *Le Monde*, May 12, 1976.
55. *Parliamentary Papers, Turkey, No. 6* (1898), 103, 171.
56. [Rowlett], *Report of the Committee appointed to investigate revolutionary conspirators in India* (1918), Cmd. 9190, 4.
57. Dr. Mark F. Ryan, *Fenian Memoirs* (Dublin, 1949), 40 *et seq*.
58. J. Plumyène and R. Lassiera, *Les Fascismes français* (Paris, 1963), 84–86; G. Warner, "France," in S. J. Woolf, ed. *European Fascism* (London, 1968), 270.
59. La Lutte Internationale contre le Terrorisme, *La Documentation française* (May 30, 1975), 31–66.
60. Max Nomad, *Aspects of Revolution* (New York, 1959), 207.
61. "The bombs exploding in Havana gave Washington the impression that the Machado regime was in a permanent crisis. It was only when President Roosevelt's decision to ease him out of office became known in Cuba that the internal opposition against Machado grew strong enough to overthrow him." Ernst Halperin, *Terrorism in Latin America*, Washington Papers 33 (Beverly Hills, 1976), 7–8.
62. Adrian Lyttleton, *The Seizure of Power* (London, 1973), 61.
63. L. Venturi, op. cit., 563.
64. De la Hodde, 14 *et seq*.
65. Ivan Avacumovic, "A statistical approach to the revolutionary movement in Russia," *The American Slavic and East European Review* (April 1959), 183.
66. A. C. Porzecanski, *Uruguay's Tupamaros* (New York, 1973), 30 *et seq*. Halperin, loc. cit. 37 *et seq*.
67. E. Wasiolik, *The Notebook for the "Possessed"* (Chicago, 1968), *passim*; A. Volynski, *Kniga velikovo gneva* (St. Petersburg, 1904), *passim*.
68. B. Savinkov, *Erinnerungen eines Terroristen* (Berlin, 1927), 73.

69. Manfred von Killinger, *Ernstes und Heiteres aus dem Putschleben* (Munich, 1934), 15.
70. Wayne G. Broehl, Jr., *The Molly Maguires* (New York, 1966), 20.
71. See, for instance, Hermann Reisse, *Sieg Heil SA* (Berlin, 1933), 100; W. Kube, ed., *Almanach der nationalsozialistischen Revolution* (Berlin, 1933), 117 *et seq.*
72. *Rote Fahne,* June 26, 1923.
73. S. Kravchinski, *Podpolnaya Rossiya,* 42 *et seq.*
74. Emma Goldman, "The Psychology of Political Violence," in *Anarchism and Other Essays* (New York, 1910), 113.
75. Nestroev on Sokolov, *Iz Dnevnik Maksimalista,* 64, 75.
76. S. S. Volk, op. cit. 468.

CHAPTER FOUR: INTERPRETATIONS OF TERRORISM — FACT, FICTION AND
POLITICAL SCIENCE

1. Emma Goldman, "The Psychology of Political Violence," in *Anarchism and Other Essays* (Port Washington, 1960), 89.
2. Ibid., 113.
3. C. Lombroso and R. Laschi, *Le crime politique et les révolutions* (Paris, 1892), *passim.*
4. R. Garraud, *L'Anarchie et la répression* (Paris, 1895), *passim.*
5. C. Lombroso, *Les Anarchistes* (Paris, 1896), 184 *et seq.*
6. E. V. Zenker, *Anarchism* (London, 1895), 262.
7. Lucian Pye, in H. Eckstein, ed., *Internal War* (New York, 1964), 162.
8. *Encyclopaedia of the Social Sciences* (New York, 1934), vol. 14.
9. Edward E. Gude, in J. C. Davies, ed., *When Men Revolt and Why?* (New York, 1971), 252.
10. P. M. Cobbs and H. Grier, Foreword to Jerome H. Skolnick, *The Politics of Protest* (New York, 1969), XII.
11. John Dollard et al., *Frustration and Aggression* (New Haven, 1939).
12. E. F. Durbin and John Bowlby, *Personal Aggressiveness and War* (London, 1938), 28.
13. T. R. Gurr, *Why Men Rebel* (Princeton, 1970), *passim;* T. R. Gurr, "The Calculus of Civil Conflict," *Journal of Social Issues,* I (1972), 29.
14. Douglas P. Bwy, "Political Instability in Latin America: The Cross-Culture Test of a Causal Model," in *Latin American Research Review* (Spring 1968).
15. Lloyd A. Free, in Davies, *supra,* 258.
16. Ivo K. Feierabend and Rosalind I. Feierabend, "Aggressive Behaviors within Politics, 1948–1962," in *Journal of Conflict Resolution,* vol. X, no. 3, 269.
17. Betty Nesvold, "A Scalogram Analysis of Political Violence," in Gillespie and Nesvold, loc. cit., 171 *et seq.*
18. Gurr, *Calculus,* 34.
19. Ibid.
20. Feierabend, supra, 269
21. Gurr, *Calculus,* 44.
22. Harry Eckstein, "On the Etiology of Internal Wars," in *History and Theory,* 2 (1965); Idem., *The Study of Internal Wars* (Princeton, 1969); Erich Weede, "Unzufriedenheit, Protest und Gewalt, Kritik an einem makropolitischen Forschungsprogramm," in *Politische Vierteljahresschrift* (September 1975).
23. Gurr and Duval, "Civil Conflict in the 1960s," in *Comparative Political Studies,* 6 (1973), *passim.*
24. D. A. Hibbs, *Mass Political Violence* (New York, 1973), *passim.*

25. Lodhi and Tilly, "Urbanization, Crime and Collective Violence in 19th century France," *Journal of Sociology*, 2 (1972), 297; Snyder and Tilly, "Hardship and Collective Violence in France 1830–1960," *American Sociological Review* (October 1972), 520.

26. Egbal Ahmad, in N. Miller and R. Aya, *National Liberation* (New York, 1971), 137 *et seq.*

27. In David E. Apter and James Joll, *Anarchism Today* (London, 1971), 65.

28. T. R. Gurr, *Civil Strife in the Modern World: A Comparative Study of Its Extent and Causes* (Princeton, 1969); State Department Conference on Terrorism, December 29, 1969.

29. Paul Wilkinson, *Political Terrorism* (London, 1974), 129.

30. E. V. Walter, *Terror and Resistance* (New York, 1969).

31. Thomas P. Thornton, "Terror as a Weapon in Political Agitation," in H. Eckstein, *Internal War* (New York, 1964), 71 *et seq.*

32. Brian Crozier, *The Rebels* (London, 1960), *passim;* Paul Wilkinson, op. cit., 126.

33. R. Moss, *The War for the Cities* (New York, 1972), 24 *et seq.;* Z. Ivianski, "Individual Terror as a phase in Revolutionary Violence in the late 19th and the beginning of the 20th Century" (in Hebrew), Doctoral Dissertation (Jerusalem, 1973), 71; P. Wilkinson, *Political Terrorism* (London, 1974), *passim.*

34. H. Arendt, "On Violence," in *Crisis of the Republic* (Harmondsworth, 1973), 83 *et seq.*

35. Feliks Gross, *Violence in Politics* (The Hague, 1972), 94.

36. H. Eckstein, *On the Etiology . . . ,* supra, 153.

37. Richard Blackmur, *The Art of the Novel: Critical Prefaces by Henry James* (New York, 1946), 59.

38. Malcolm Brown, *The Politics of Irish Literature* (London, 1972), 278.

39. J. L. Borges, *Labyrinths, Selected Short Stories and Other Writings* (New York, 1964), 72–75.

40. *The Works of R. L. Stevenson* (London, 1911), V, 130.

41. G. K. Chesterton, *The Man who was Thursday* (London, 1908).

42. *Times* (London, March 17, 1881, quoted in W. H. Trilley, *The Background of the Princess Casamassima* (Gainesville, Florida, 1960), 19.

43. Emile Zola, *Les trois villes. Paris* (Paris, 1898).

44. John Henry Mackay, *Die Anarchisten* (Berlin, 1893), 240–244.

45. Pio Baroja y Nessi, *Aurora Roja,* part three of *La lucha por la vida* (Madrid, 1904).

46. Ibid., 358.

47. Published first in Prague in 1921 in the journal *Kvety.*

48. On Libertad and his group Jean Maitron, 420 *et seq.*, and Victor Serge's autobiography, *Memoirs of a Revolutionary 1901–1941* (London, 1963); *Namesti Republiky* was republished in Czechoslovakia under the Communist regime with some major ideological adjustments.

49. The play was performed in Paris in 1897; its premiere in the original Norwegian did not take place until two years later.

50. Bertold Brecht, *Die Massnahme,* first performed in Berlin in December 1930; see also B. Brecht, *Anmerkungen zur Massnahme,* in *Schriften zum Theater,* vol. 2 (Frankfurt, 1963).

51. First performed in Paris in December 1949; see also Camus, *L'homme revolté* (Paris, 1951).

52. See V. Gebel, *Shestidesyatye Gody* (Moscow, n.d.), and the biographical studies by P. Kowalowski, Leonid Grossman, B. M. Drugov and V. Setschkareff.

53. *Podpolnaya Rossiya.* The book was first published in Italian in Milan (1882); the most recent Russian edition of 1960 is quoted here.

54. Sophia Kovalevsky, *Vera Barantzova* (London, 1895), 281; the author is better remembered as a distinguished mathematician.

55. Stepniak, *The Career of a Nihilist (Andrei Kozhukhov)* (London, 1889), 320; the Russian version was published in Geneva in 1898.

56. The book was first published in two parts in 1908. It is now exceedingly rare; the Library of Congress, for instance, has only the Hebrew translation, *Lehavot* (2 vols., Naharia, 1939–1940). The book exercised a powerful influence on the left-wing Jewish youth movement in Poland *Habent sua fata libelli*. I have used a more recent Polish edition (2 vols., Cracow, 1946–1947). A French translation exists.

57. V. L. Burtsev, *Borba za svobodnuyu Rossiu* (Berlin, 1923), I, 183 *et seq.;* see also Cz. Milosz, *Czlowiek wsrod skorpionow* (Paris, 1962), 84–107.

58. V. Ropshin, *Kon Blednyi (The Pale Horse)* (St. Petersburg, 1909), 124; first published in the journal *Russkaya Mysl,* January 1909.

59. First published in installments in the journal *Zavety,* 1912; there was an English edition in 1916 or 1917: *What Never Happened.* Cf. G. Plekhanov, in *Sovremennyi Mir,* 2 (1913); Chonov in *Zavety,* 8 (1912); and A. Amfiteatrov in *Zavety Serdtsa* (Moscow, 1909).

60. There is yet another Azev novel by Roman Gul, *General B.O.* (London, 1930), and Rebecca West has also written about the subject *(The Birds Fall Down* [London, 1966]).

61. *Borstal Boy* (London, 1958), 11.

62. Donald Davie, "The Young Yeats," in Conor Cruise O'Brien, *The Shaping of Modern Ireland* (London, 1960), 143.

63. Sean O'Casey, *Drums under the Windows* (New York, 1960), 423.

64. Liam O'Flaherty, *Civil War;* Sean O'Casey, *The Plough and the Stars* (London, 1926).

65. O'Casey, *Collected Plays* (London, 1949), I, 156.

66. Conor Cruise O'Brien, "An unhealthy intersection," in *The New Review* (July 1975); see also W. A. Armstrong, "History, Autobiography and 'The Shadow of a Gunman,'" in *Modern Drama,* 2 (1960).

67. Liam O'Flaherty, *The Martyr* (London, 1933); see also Liam O'Flaherty, *The Assassin* (London, 1928), *passim.*

68. Régis Debray, *L'indésirable* (Paris, 1976), 77.

69. *Izbrani Proizvedeniya* (Sofia, 1953), 150.

70. A. Stern, *Bedamai lead tikhi* (Tel Aviv, 1976), 18; his friend Y. Ratosh dedicated an untranslated (and perhaps untranslatable) poem *Argaman* (Purple) to the solitude of Yair's life and the ultimate futility of his death.

71. Gyorgy Kardos, *Avraham's Good Week* (New York, 1975).

72. E. von Salomon, *Die Geächteten* (Berlin, 1935).

73. Ibid., 302.

74. Hanns Johst, *Schlageter,* in Günther Rühle, *Zeit und Theater* (Berlin, 1975), III, 28. The play was first performed on Hitler's birthday, April 20, 1933.

75. Arnold Bronnen, *O/S* (1929); *Rossbach* (1930); Hans Fallada, *Bauern, Bonzen, Bomben* (1931).

76. M. Djilas, *Memoirs of a Revolutionary* (London, 1973), 132 *et seq.*

77. Michael Baumann, *Wie alles anfing* (Munich, 1975), 130.

78. Omar Seyfeddin, *Bomba* (Constantinople, 1913); Ion Dragumis, *Martiron Ke iroon ema* (Athens, 1907).

79. Two of Khanafani's novels were made into films, *Les Dupes* and *Le Couteau,* both produced in Syria; the Algerians produced a terrorist "action" film *(Sana'ud* [*We Shall Return*]) which was, however, criticized for lack of political content and for making too many concessions to Wild West style.

80. Alfred Faraj's play *Al nar valseitun (The Fire and the Olive Tree);* Suheil Idris' *Sahra min Dam (Flower of Blood);* Abdul Rahman al Sharqawi's *Watani Akka (Acre, My Homeland);* Moen Basisu's *Shamshun va Dalila.* See Sasson Somekh

in *New Outlook* (January 1972), and Shimon Ballas, "The Ugly Israeli in Arab Literature," *New Outlook* (November 1974), as well as the same writer's series of articles in *Ha'olam Hasen* (July 9, 16, and 23, 1975).

81. Meri Franco-Lao, *Basta* (Paris, 1967).

82. *No znaem, kak znal ty rodymyi,*
chto skoro iz nazhikh kostei
rodymetsya mstitel surovy
I budet on nas posilnei.

83. *Terrorism Part 2*, Hearing before the Committee on Internal Security, House of Representatives (Washington, 1974), p208.

CHAPTER FIVE: TERRORISM TODAY

1. Alex Schubert, *Stadtguerrilla* (Berlin, 1974), 3–22.
2. Of 161 Palestinian terrorists arrested between 1968 and 1973 for acts of terror in third countries, all but two of those who had actually committed murder were set free. Paraguay was the one exception: it imposed a three-year prison sentence on two Palestinians who had killed the wife of an Israeli diplomat. *Times* (London), July 5, 1976. According to other statistics 267 individuals who had engaged in multinational terrorism were arrested between 1970 and 1975. Of these 39 were released without punishment, 58 escaped by getting safe conduct to another country, 16 were freed from confinement on the demand of fellow terrorists, 50 were released after serving their sentence, and 104 were still in jail in September 1975. The average sentence meted out to terrorists who actually stood trial was eighteen months. *International and Transnational Terrorism, Diagnosis and Prognosis* (Washington 1976), 22–23.
3. Fritz René Allemann, *Macht und Ohnmacht der Guerilla* (Munich, 1974), 133; Luigi Valsalice, *Guerriglia e Politica, L'Esemplo del Venezuela 1962–1969* (Florence, 1973); Robert J. Alexander, *The Communist Party of Venezuela* (Stanford, 1969), *passim;* Norman Gall, *Teodoro Petkoff*, Field Staff Reports, No. 1 (1972).
4. For a short summary of Latin American guerrilla doctrine in the early 1960s and bibliographical references see Laqueur, *Guerrilla* (Boston, 1976), chapter 8.
5. The literature on the subject is so large that a stage has been reached in which bibliographies of bibliographies are needed. See A. Thomas Ferguson's valuable essay in Sam C. Sarkesian, ed., *Revolutionary Guerrilla Warfare* (Chicago, 1975), 617–623. To this the following two bibliographies should be added: Russell, Miller and Hildner, "The Urban Guerrilla in Latin America," *Latin American Research Review* (Spring 1974); *Bibliografia: Guerra Revolucionaria y Subversión en el Continente* (Washington, 1973).
6. The literature on the Tupamaros is vast. Among the most important the following should be mentioned: *Actas Tupamaros* (Buenos Aires, 1971); M. E. Gilio, *The Tupamaro Guerrillas* (New York, 1970); A. Mercader and J. de Vera, *Tupamaros, Estrategia y Acción* (Montevideo, 1969); A. Porcecanski, *Uruguay's Tupamaros* (New York, 1973); Alain Labrousse, *The Tupamaros* (London, 1973); *Generals and Tupamaros*, Latin American Review of Books (London, 1974); Régis Debray, *La Critique des armes*, vol. 1 (Paris, 1974); Major Carlos Wilson, *The Tupamaros* (Boston, 1974); Ernesto Mayans, ed., *Tupamaros, Antologia documental* (Cuernavaca, 1971); as well as a source book, J. Kohl and J. Litt, eds., *Urban Guerrilla Warfare in Latin America* (Cambridge, Mass., 1974).
7. Primary sources on urban terror in Brazil and Argentina are difficult to come by. See Vannia Bambirra, ed., *Diez Años de Insurrección en America latina*, 2 vols. (Santiago, 1971). The best descriptive account is F. R. Alleman, *Macht und Ohn-*

macht der Guerilla (Munich, 1974). On the early phase, the articles by Hector Suarez in *Granma*, Havana, should be mentioned, December 13 and 27, 1970, January 3 and 17, 1971, and in *Punto Final*, 122–125. The main sources are *Punto Final* (Chile under Allende), *Tricontinental Bulletin*, *Bohemia* and *Granma* (Havana), *Prensa Latina*, *Latin America*. The Montoneros published a (legal) newspaper, *La Causa Peronista*, which was shut down in 1974; the ERP issued various illegal newsheets such as *Estella Roja*, *El Combatiente*, *Liberación*. On the ERP: *Resoluciones del Vᵒ Congreso y de los comité central y comité ejecutivo posteriores*. (The resolutions of the PRT Congress in which the creation of an armed organization was officially decided; there is reason to believe that the organization existed well before.) Marighela's writings have been translated — *For the Liberation of Brazil* (London, 1973); see also João Quartim, *Dictatorship and Armed Struggle in Brazil* (New York, 1971); and *Pan de Arara, La Violencia Militar en el Brasil* (Mexico, 1975).

8. João Quartim, *Dictatorship and Armed Struggle in Brazil* (New York, 1971), *passim*.

9. R. D. Evans, *Brazil, the Road back from Terrorism*, Conflict Studies, 47 (July 1974).

10. John William Cooke, *La lucha por la liberación nacional* (Buenos Aires, 1973); Donald C. Hodges, *Philosophy of the Urban Guerrilla* (New York, 1973), 9–12.

11. R. Lamberg, *Die Guerilla in Lateinamerika* (Stuttgart, 1972), 217.

12. Patrick O'Donnell, *The Irish Faction Fighters of the Nineteenth Century* (Dublin, 1975), 63.

13. Among recent histories of the IRA and the struggle in Ulster the following deserve mention: Tim Pat Coogan, *The IRA* (London, 1970); J. Bowyer Bell, *The Secret Army* (London, 1970); M. Dillon and D. Lehane, *Political Murder in Northern Ireland* (London, 1973); Liam de Paor, *Divided Ulster* (London, 1970); Maria McGuire, *To Take up Arms* (London, 1973).

14. Altogether there were 153 such "third-country operations" between 1967–1975; the record number was in 1973 (50), falling to 7 in 1975. In these operations 210 individuals were killed, 80 percent of them were citizens of countries other than Israel. Sixteen countries were affected altogether. In the same period of nine years 2,670 Arabs and 502 Jews were killed in clashes in Israel or on its borders; the highest number of Jewish victims was in 1969–1970, after which there was a steady decline in the number of both Arabs and Jews killed, simply because there were far fewer such operations.

15. *Al Ahram*, June 28, 1976.

16. The basic documents issued by Palestinian organizations appear in the Beirut quarterly, *Journal of Palestinian Studies*, published since 1972. For the earlier period see L. S. Kadi, ed., *Basic Political Documents of the Armed Palestinian Resistance Movement* (Beirut, 1969); and R. N. Rayes and D. Nahas, *Guerrillas for Palestine* (Beirut, 1974); as well as Y. Harkabi, *Fedayeen Action and Arab Strategy*, Adelphi Papers, 53 (London, 1968). For Palestinian terrorist practice see R. Tophoven, *Fedayin, Guerilla ohne Grenzen* (Munich, 1975); Z. Schiff and R. Rothstein, *Fedayeen* (London, 1972); E. Yaari, *Strike Terror* (Jerusalem, 1970); Edgar O'Ballance, *Arab Guerrilla Power* (London, 1973); Christopher Dobson, *Black September* (London, 1974); Leila Khaled, *My People Shall Live* (London, 1973); John Cooley, *Green March, Black September* (London, 1973); John Laffin, *Fedayeen* (London, 1973); and innumerable other books, mostly on a popular level.

17. Quoted in John Gerassi, *Towards Revolution* (London, 1971), I, 231.

18. S. de Madariaga, *Spain* (London, 1942), 179.

19. Gustave Morf, *Terror in Quebec* (Toronto, 1970), *passim;* Arnold Hottinger, *Spain in Transition*, Washington Papers, 19 (1974), 47–52.

20. U.N. General Assembly, 27th Session, A/C.6 1389, December 13, 1972; Leon Romaniecki, "The Soviet Union and International Terrorism," *Soviet Studies* (1974), 417 *et seq.*
21. G. Mirski, "Arabskie narody prodolzhayut borbu," in *MEMO*, March 1968, 120 and other writings of the same author, for instance, *New Times*, June 26, 1968 and October 2, 1968; see also L. Steidin, "Imperialisticheski Zagovor na Blizhnem Vostoke," *Kommunist*, XI (July 1967), 107 *et seq.*
22. Luis Carlos Prestes, in *Tribuna Popular*, January 12 and 13, 1973.
23. The shift in strategy is reflected in many articles in *Tricontinental* throughout 1969–1970.
24. *Le Point*, June 21, June 28, 1976.
25. Resolution on Latin America, *Intercontinental Press*, July 14, 1969, 720–721.
26. See the polemics between American Trotskyites and the British *Red Mole;* Joseph Hansen in *International Information Bulletin*, April 1971; the resolution of the French *Ligue Communiste* on Munich in *Rouge*, September 23, 1872; *Red Mole* on Ireland, January 1, 1971.
27. *Rouge*, September 30, 1972.
28. Report on Armed Struggle in Latin America by Roman, *International Information Bulletin*, August 1974, 17 *et seq.*
29. Counterreport by Joseph Hansen, *International Information Bulletin*, August 1974, 23 *et seq.*
30. See, for instance, Ernest Germain and Martine Knoeller in *International Information Bulletin*, January 1971, and Ernest Mandel, "In Defence of Leninism," ibid., April 1973.
31. American congressional committees have paid inordinate attention to Trotskyite attitudes toward terrorism — and very little to Communist links. See for instance *Trotskyite Terrorist International*, Hearings before the Subcommittee to Investigate the Administration of the Internal Security Act and Other Internal Security Laws. Committee on the Judiciary, United States Senate Ninety-fourth Congress, July 24, 1975. These documents are of value to students of the byways of the extreme left but they create a mistaken impression inasmuch as there were forces at work infinitely more powerful than the "United Secretariat."
32. *Punto Final*, August 29, 1972.
33. Letter to the PRT (Combatiente) by Ernest, Livio, Pierre, Sandor, Tariq, Delphin, *International Internal Discussion Bulletin*, June 1973, 22 *et seq.*
34. Frantz Fanon, *The Wretched of the Earth* (London, 1967), 74.
35. A first attempt to describe New Left politics and culture in historical perspective is Klaus Mehnert's *Jugend im Zeitbruch* (Stuttgart, 1976).
36. Alex Schubert, *Stadtguerilla*, op. cit., 117.
37. On West German terrorism see Alex Schubert, *Stadtguerilla*, op. cit.; Kollektiv RAF, *Über den bewaffneten Kampf in Westeuropa* (Berlin, 1971); M. Müller-Borchert, *Guerilla im Industriestaat* (Hamburg, 1973); M. Baumann, *Wie alles anfing* (Munich, 1975); Peter Brückner et al., *Gewalt und Solidarität* (Berlin, 1974); *Sozialistisches Jahrbuch 5* (1973); *Stadtguerilla und soziale Revolution* (Haarlem, 1974); Günter Bartsch, *Anarchismus in Deutschland, Band II* (Hanover, 1973); *Holger, der Kampf geht weiter* (n.p., 1974); *Bewaffneter Kampf. Texte der RAF* (Verlag Rote Sonne, 1974 [?]).
38. Literature on the United Red Army and other Japanese terrorist groups is not available in languages other than Japanese. On its origins see Takashi Tachibara, *Chukaku us kakumaru*, 2 vols. (Tokyo, 1975); on its ideology, the symposium *Uchi Geba no Ronri* (*The logic of the inner struggle*, Geba = Gewalt) (Tokyo, 1974); of particular interest are the essays on the aesthetics of assassination (57 *et seq.*) the philosophy of murder (77) and the philosophy of hatred (147); a docu-

mentary record is *Sekigun* by the Sasho Henshu committee, Tokyo, 1975, with a detailed bibliography (361–484).

39. Literature on Weatherman and Black Panther party is abundant: *Prairie Fire* (n.p., 1974); Harold Jacobs, ed., *Weatherman* (Berkeley, 1970); J. Raskin, ed., *The Weather Eye* (New York, 1974); Kirkpatrick Sale, *S.D.S.* (New York, 1974); as well as *Liberation News Service, The Guardian, The Berkeley Barb* and congressional publications such as *The Weatherman Underground*, January 1975. On black terrorism: Philip S. Foner, *The Black Panther Speaks* (New York, 1970); as well as the writings by Eldridge Cleaver, Stokely Carmichael, David Hilliard, George Jackson, Huey Newton, Bobby Seale *(Seize the Time)* and others; the periodical *Black Panther;* and the periodicals of the Cleaver faction.

40. George Jackson, *Blood in My Eye* (London, 1975), 65.

41. Of one thousand bombings in the United States in 1975, only forty-six were attributed to organized terrorist groups.

42. M. Ram, "The urban guerrilla movement in Calcutta," *Institute for Defence Studies and Analyses Journal* (January 1972), 288–301.

43. Research Study: *International and Transnational Terrorism: Diagnosis and Prognosis* (Washington, April 1976), 26.

44. The following two examples should suffice: according to an unnamed Israeli source, quoted in Brian Jenkins, *International Terrorism*, the total cost in men and money to Israel in combatting Arab terrorism between 1967 and 1972 was forty times that of the Six Days' War in 1967. But the war of 1967 cost Israel at least a billion dollars; multiplied by forty this adds up to a sum exceeding the total Israeli GNP during the period. American observers noted with considerable alarm that $40 million had to be spent in 1976 to protect American diplomatic personnel all over the globe. But this is considerably less than the projected cost of a single B-1 bomber.

CONCLUSION

1. Interview with Colonel Khadafi, *Der Spiegel,* July 26, 1976.

2. Comments by Robert H. Kupperman, chief scientist of ACDA, at a conference in Santa Margherita, May 1976 (unpublished).

3. This refers to the Tokyo convention of September 1963 concerning offenses committed aboard an aircraft; the Hague Convention of December 1970 on the unlawful seizure of aircraft; the Montreal Convention of September 1971 also concerned with suppressing unlawful acts against the safety of civil aviation; the OAS convention of February 1971 on preventing and punishing acts of terrorism; the U.N. convention of December 1973 on the prevention and punishment of crimes against diplomats — which has not yet come into force; the Luxembourg Resolution of the European Community of July 1976 on measures to combat international terrorism.

4. Major Arthur Griffith, *Mysteries of Police and Crime* (London, 1898), II, 469.

5. Norman Angell, ed., *What Would Be The Character of a New War* (New York, 1933), 388.

6. Edward Condon, quoted in Dexter Masters and Katherine Way, eds., *One World or None* (New York, 1946), 40.

7. Sandia Report (Washington, 1976); Mitre Report (McLean, Va., 1976).

8. S. J. Berkowitz et al., *Superviolence* (Adcon Report) (1972).

9. M. Willrich and Theodore Taylor, *Nuclear Theft, Risks and Safeguards* (Cambridge, Mass., 1974), 115. See also V. Gilinsky, in B. Boskey and M. Willrich, *Nuclear Proliferation* (New York, 1970); E. M. Kinderman et al., *The Unconven-*

tional Nuclear Threat (Stanford Research Institute, Menlo Park, 1969); and many other studies.

10. For a short survey on chemical and biological weapons see SIPRI, *Arms Uncontrolled* (Cambridge, Mass., 1975), 93–107 and a more detailed report in Berkowitz, op. cit.

11. J. H. Rothschild, *Tomorrow's Weapons* (New York, 1964).

12. Berkowitz, op. cit., chapters 8 and 9, *passim.*

13. C. G. Heden "Defenses Against Biological Warfare," in *Annual Review of Microbiology* (1967), 639.

14. Even in dictatorships, attempted assassinations by individuals have been far more difficult to detect than those undertaken by groups. It should be recalled that the attempt against Hitler's life which came nearest to success prior to the conspiracy of 1944 was made by Georg Elser, a carpenter, who put the bomb in the Munich *Hofbräuhaus* in November 1939. He acted entirely on his own and, in all probability, would never have been caught but for the foolish attempt to cross the border into Switzerland. See Peter Hoffmann, *Die Sicherheit des Diktators* (Munich, 1975), 119 *et seq.*

15. Roberta Wohlstetter, "Terror on a Grand Scale," in *Survival* (May-June 1976), 102.

16. Brian Jenkins, *High Technology Terrorism and Surrogate War* (Santa Monica, 1975), 24; see also David M. Rosenbaum, "Nuclear Terror," in *International Security* (Winter 1977), 140 *et seq.*

Abbreviations

AAA	Argentine Anticommunist Alliance	Argentina
ALN	*Açāo Libertadora Nacional*	Brazil
	Bewegung 2. Juni	West Germany
	Black September *(Fatch?)*	Palestinians
CAL	*Comandos Armados de Liberación*	Puerto Rico
ELF	Eritrean Liberation Front (two factions)	
ELN	*Ejercito de Liberación National*	Peru, Colombia, Bolivia
ELS	Southern Liberation Army	Mexico
EOKA	*Ethniki Organosis Kypriakou Agoniston* (National Organization of Cypriot Fighters)	Cyprus
EPL	*Ejercito Popular de Liberación*	Colombia
ERP	*Ejercito Revolucionario del Pueblo*	Argentina, also San Salvador
ETA	*Euzkadi ta Askatasunc* (two factions)	Basque Spain
FALN	*Fuerzas Armadas de Liberación Nacional*	Venezuela
FAR	*Fuerzas Armados Rebeldes*	Guatemala
FARC	*Fuerzas Armadas Revolucionarias de Colombia*	Colombia
Fatah	*Harakat Tahrir Falestin*	Palestinian
FLQ	*Front de Liberation du Quebec*	Canada
FRAP	*Fuerzas Revolucionarias Armadas del Pueblo*	Mexico
FRAP	*Frente Revolucionario Anti-Fascista y Patriota*	Spain

FSLN	*Frente Sandinista de Liberación Nacional*	Nicaragua
HRB	Croatian Revolutionary Brotherhood	
IMRO	Inner Macedonian Revolutionary Organisation	
IRA	Irish Revolutionary Army.	Ireland
IRA-Provisionals		Ireland
Irgun	IZL, *Irgun Zvai Leumi*	Palestinian
LEHI	*Lohame Herut Israel* (Stern Gang) (Fighters for the Freedom of Israel)	Palestinian
MANO	*Movimiento Argentino Nacional Organisación*	Argentina
MANO	*Mano Blanca*	Guatemala
MIR	*Movimiento de la Izquierda Revolucionaria*	Venezuela, Chile, also Peru
MIRA	*Movimiento Independista Revolucionario Armado*	Puerto Rico
MLN	*Movimiento de Liberación Nacional* (Tupamaros)	Uruguay, also in Chile and Guatemala
	Mohamed Boudia Commando (Carlos gang) *Montoneros* (Juan Jose Valle Montoneros)	International Argentina
MR-8		Brazil
MR-13		Guatemala
NOA	*Nueva Organisación Anticomunista* *Nippon Sekigun* (also JRA, Japanese Red Army)	Guatemala International
PDFLP	Popular Democratic Front for the Liberation of Palestine (Hawatme)	
PFLP	Popular Front for the Liberation of Palestine (Dr. Habash)	
PFLP-General Command		Palestine
PRD	*Partido Revolucionario Dominican*	Dominican Republic
RAF	*Rote Armee Fraktion* (Baader-Meinhof Gang)	Germany
Saiqa	Vanguard	Palestinian-Syrian

Siahkal		Iran
SLA	Symbionese Liberation Army	United States
TPLA	Turkish People's Liberation Army	Turkey
UDA	Ulster Defence Association	Ireland
UFF	Ulster Freedom Fighters	Ireland
Ustasha		Croats
UVF	Ulster Volunteer Forces	Ireland
VPR	*Vanguardia Popular Revolucionaria*	Brazil
Weatherman		United States
Zapata	*Frente Urbano Zapatista*	Mexico

Bibliography

The following bibliographical note refers only to certain works of special interest. Historical bibliographies on terrorism do not exist; a standard work such as Venturi's *Roots of Revolution* can, of course, be used as a guide to the main sources. The same applies to Nettlau's works on anarchism, to Zoccoli (the early period of Anarchism), or Maitron (French Anarchism). There is rich documentation on terrorism in Ireland, Latin America, the Middle East, and the New Left and multinational terrorism, but most of the material is not easy to locate and bibliographical aids are virtually nonexistent. A rare exception is Charles A. Russell, James A. Miller and Robert Hildner, "The Urban Guerrilla in Latin America: A Select Bibliography," in *Latin American Research Review* (spring, 1974).

General Literature on Terrorism
(see also footnotes to chapter four)

Y. Alexander, ed. *International Terrorism*. New York, 1976.
M. C. Bassiouni, ed. *International Terrorism and Political Crimes*. Springfield, 1975.
Anthony Burton. *Urban Terrorism*. London, 1975.
B. J. Bell. *Transnational Terror*. Washington, 1975.
R. Clutterbuck. *Protest and the urban guerrilla*. London, 1973.
_____. *Living with terrorism*. London, 1975.
Roland Gaucher. *The Terrorists*. London, 1968.
F. Hacker. *Terror, Mythos, Realität, Analyse*. Vienna, 1973.
International Terrorism. U.S. House Committee on Foreign Affairs. Washington, 1974.
Hans Langemann. *Das Attentat*. Hamburg, 1957.
J. Malin, ed. *Terror and Urban Guerrillas*. Coral Gables, 1971.
W. Middendorff. *Der politische Mord*. Wiesbaden, 1968.
Robert Moss. *Urban Guerrillas*. London, 1972.
Political Kidnappings. Committee on Internal Security, House of Representatives. Washington, 1973.
David C. Rapoport. *Assassination and Terrorism*. Toronto, 1971.
Terrorism. Parts 1–4, Committee on Internal Security, House of Representatives. Washington, 1974.

Terrorism. Staff study, Committee on Internal Security, House of Representatives. Washington, 1974.
Terrorist Activity. Parts 1–8, Committee of the Judiciary, House of Representatives. Washington, 1974–1975.
Jerzy Waciorski. *Le Terrorisme Politique.* Paris, 1939.
Paul Wilkinson. *Political Terrorism.* London, 1974.
Lester Sobel. *Political Terrorism.* New York, 1975.

Tyrannicide, Secret Societies

J. Althusius. *Politica metodice digesta.* 1603.
M. Ballestreos-Gaibrois. *Juan de Mariana, cantor de Espana.* 2 vols. Madrid, 1938–1939.
J. Boucher. *De iusta Henrici III.* . . . 1589.
G. Buchanan. *De jure Regni apud Scotos.* . . . 1579.
P. Buonarroti. *Conspiration pour l'égalité dite de Babeuf.* 1828.
A. Blanqui. *Textes Choisis.* Paris, 1955.
L. Daneau. *Politicae Christianae libri VII.* 1596.
M. Dommanget. *Pages Choisies de Babeuf.* Paris, 1935.
Duplessis-Mornay. *Vindiciae contra Tyrannos.* 1579.
T. Frost. *The secret societies of European revolution.* 2 vols. London, 1876.
O. Jaszi and D. Lewis. *Against the tyrant.* New York, 1957
R. M. Johnston. *Napoleonic Empire in Southern Italy.* 2 vols. London, 1904.
M. I. Kovalskaia. *Dvizhenie Karbonartsev v Italii 1808–1821.* Moscow, 1971.
La Boetie. *De la servitude volontaire au contru'un'.* 1578.
P. Liman. *Der politische Mord im Wandel der Geschichte.* 1912.
O. Lutaud. *Des révolutions d'Angleterre à la révolution française.* Paris, 1973.
J. de Mariana. *De rege et regis institutione.* 1599.
R. Mousnier. *Assassinat d'Henri IV.* Paris, 1964.
W. Platzhoff. *Die Theorie von der Mordbefugnis der Obrigkeit im 16. Jahrhundert.* 1906.
C. Rossaeus. *De iusta Rei publicae Christianae.* 1590.
E. Sexby. *Killing no murder* . . . . 1657.
G. Sencier. *Le Babouvisme après Babeuf.* Paris, 1912.
John of Salisbury. *Policraticus.* 1595.
F. Schoenstedt. *Der Tyrannenmord im Spätmittelalter.* 1938.
D. Spadoni. *Sette, cospirationi e cospiratori.* Turin, 1904.
G. Weill. *Le Parti Républicain en France 1814–1870.* Paris, 1900.

Bakunin and Nechaev

M. Bakunin. *Izbrannie Sochineniia.* 5 vols. Petrograd, 1919–1921.
――――. *Gesammelte Werke.* 3 vols. Berlin, 1921–1924.
E. H. Carr. *Michael Bakunin.* London, 1937.
M. Confino. *Violence dans la violence.* Paris, 1973.
H. E. Kaminski. *Bakounine: La vie d'un révolutionnaire.* Paris, 1938.
A. Lehning. *Michel Bakounine et ses relations avec Sergej Necaev.* Leiden, 1971.
M. Nettlau. *Michael Bakunin: eine Biographie.* 3 vols. London, 1896–1900.
Y. M. Steklov, *M. A. Bakunin, yevo zhizn i deatelnost. 1814–76.* 4 vols. Moscow, 1926–1927.

Terrorism in Russia (1870–1920)

The most important sources for the study of Russian terrorism are the journals of Narodnaya Volya and the Socialist Revolutionaries as well as Burtsev's *Byloe* and the periodicals of the early Soviet period such as *Katorga i Sylka*.

Paul Avrich. *The Russian Anarchists.* Princeton, 1971.
V. Bogucharski. *Aktivnoe Narodnichestvo.* Moscow, 1912.
V. Burtsev. *Za sto let.* London, 1897.
_____. *Doloi Tsarya.* London, 1901.
_____. *Borba za svobodnuyu Rossiu.* Berlin, 1924.
V. M. Chernov. *Pered Burei.* New York. 1953.
M. Confino. *La violence dans la violence.* Paris, 1973.
Da zdravstvuyet Narodnaya Volya. Paris, 1907.
V. I. Debogori-Mokrievich. *Vospominaria.* St. Petersburg. 1906.
Vera Figner. *Memoirs of a Revolutionist.* New York, 1927.
David Footman. *Red Prelude.* London, 1943.
B. S. Itenberg. *Dvizhenie Revoliutsonovo Narodnichestva.* Moscow, 1965.
A. I. Ivianski, ed. *Zhizn kak Fakel.* Moscow, 1966.
Jan Kucharzewski. *Od Bialego Caratu do Czerwonego.* 7 vols. Warsaw, 1926–1935.
T. G. Masaryk. *Zur russischen Geschichts- und Religionsphilosophie.* Jena, 1913.
N. Morozov. *Povest moei Zhizni.* Moscow, 1947.
"Narodovoltsi." Moscow, 1931.
G. Nestroev. *Iz Dnevnik Maksimalista.* Paris, 1910.
B. Nikolajewski. *Asew.* Berlin, 1932.
Padenie tsarkovo rezhima. 3 vols. Moscow, 1920–1925.
B. Savinkov. *Erinnerungen eines Terroristen.* Berlin, 1927.
A. Spiridovich. *Histoire du terrorisme russe.* Paris, 1930.
I. Steinberg. *Spiridonowa.* London, 1935.
S. Stepniak- Kravchinski. *Podpolnaya Russia.* Moscow, 1960.
L. Tikhomirov. *Vospominania.* Moscow. 1927.
L. Venturi. *Roots of Revolution.* London, 1966.
L. Volin. *Nineteen Seventeen.* London, 1954.
S. S. Volk. *Narodnaya Volya.* Moscow, 1966.

Ireland and Ulster

Tom Barry. *Guerrilla Days in Ireland.* New York, 1956.
P. S. Beaslei. *Michael Collins and the Making of a New Ireland.* London, 1926.
R. Bennet. *The Black and Tans.* London, 1959.
D. Boulton. *The UVF 1966–1973.* Dublin, 1973.
J. Bowyer Bell. *The Secret Army.* London, 1970.
Andrew Boyd. *Holy War in Belfast.* London, 1969.
D. Breen. *My Fight for Irish Freedom.* Kerry, 1964.
Thomas N. Brown. *Irish-American Nationalism.* New York, 1966.
Tim Pat Coogan. *The IRA.* London, 1970.
Tom Corfe. *The Phoenix Park Murders.* London, 1968.
Devoy's Post Bag. Ed. by W. O'Brien and D. Ryan. 2 vols. Dublin, 1953.
J. Devoy. *Recollection of an Irish Rebel.* Shannon, 1969.
O. D. Edwards and F. Pyle, eds. *The Easter Rising.* London, 1968.
M. Harmon. *Fenians and Fenianism.* Dublin, 1968.

Ireland and the Irish Question. A collection of writings by Karl Marx and Friedrich Engels. New York, 1972.
F. X. Martin, ed. *Leaders and Men of the Easter Rising.* New York, 1967.
Jeremy O'Donovan Rossa. *My Years in English Jails.* New York, 1967.
Desmond Ryan. *The Phoenix Flame.* London, 1937.
————. *The Rising.* Dublin, 1957.
————. *James Connolly.* Dublin, 1924.
M. F. Ryan. *Fenian Memoirs.* Dublin, 1945.
Mac Stiofain. *Revolutionary in Ireland.* London, 1975.
C. Tansill. *American and the Fight for Irish Freedom.* New York, 1957.
P. J. P. Tynan. *The Irish Invincibles.* New York, 1894.
T. D. Williams. *Secret Societies in Ireland.* Dublin, 1973.

Terrorism and the Police Counterterror

Sir Robert Anderson. *Sidelights on the Home Rule Movement.* London, 1907.
L. Andrieux. *Souvenir d'un préfet de police.* Paris, 1885.
A. Bekzadian. *Der Agent Provocateur.* Zürich, 1913.
H. Le Caron. *Twenty Five Years in the Secret Service.* London, 1892.
A. Gerassimoff. *Der Kampf gegen die erste russische Revolution.* Berlin, 1933.
R. Garraud. *L'anarchie et la répression.* Paris, 1885.
Lucien de la Hodde. *Histoire de sociétés secrètes.* Paris, 1850.
Maurice Laporte. *Histoire de l'Okhrana.* Paris, 1935.
Jean Longuet et G. Zilber. *Les dessous de la police russe,* Paris, 1909.
A. P. Vasilief. *Police russe et révolution.* Paris, 1936.

India

U. S. Anand. *Savarkar.* London, 1967.
Anon. *The Philosophy of the Bomb.* N.p. 1930.
V. Chirol. *Indian Unrest.* London, 1910.
Manmathnat Gupta. *History of the Revolutionary Movement in India.* Delhi, 1960.
Dhananjang Keer. *Veer Savarkar.* Bombay, 1966.
R. C. Majumdar. *History of the Freedom Movement in India.* 3 vols. Calcutta, n.d.
B. R. Nanda. *Socialism in India.* New Delhi, 1972.
Report of the Commission of Inquiry into the Conspiracy to Murder Mahatma Gandhi. 6 vols. New Delhi, 1970.
J. N. Vajpeyi. *The Extremist Movement in India.* Allahabad, 1974.
Yashpal. *Singhavalokan.* 3 vols. Lucknow, 1951–1952.

Doctrine and Sociology
(see also notes to chapter four)

E. H. Carr. *Michael Bakunin.* New York, 1961.
Gérard Chaliand. *Mythes révolutionnaires du Tiers Monde.* Paris, 1976.
David Caute. *Fanon.* London, 1970.
James Connolly. *Revolutionary Warfare.* Dublin, 1968.
H. Eckstein, ed. *Internal War.* New York, 1964.
Frantz Fanon. *The Wretched of the Earth.* New York, 1963.
Emma Goldman. *Anarchism and Other Essays.* New York, 1910.

Feliks Gross. *Violence in Politics*. The Hague, 1972.
Abraham Guillen. *Philosophy of the Urban Guerrilla*. New York, 1973.
P. A. Kropotkin. *Selected Writings*. Cambridge, Mass., 1973.
A. Lehning. *Bakunin et ses relations avec S. Nechaev*. Leiden, 1971.
Emilio Lussu. *Théorie de l'insurrection*. Paris, 1971.
C. Marighella. *Mini Manual of the Urban Guerrilla*. London, 1971.
Johann Most. *The Beast of Property*. New Haven, ca. 1885.
_____. *Revolutionäre Kriegswissenschaft*. New York, ca. 1884.
N. Morozov. *Terroristicheskaya Borba*. London, 1880.
George Plechanov. *Anarchism and Socialism*. Minneapolis, n.d.
D. C. Rapoport. *Assassination and Terrorism*. Toronto, 1971.
V. Tarnovski. *Terrorism i Routina*. London (Geneva), 1880.

Middle East
(see also notes to chapter 5)

1. Palestine 1938–1948

J. Banai. *Hayalim Almonim*, Tel Aviv, 1958.
Y. Bauer. *Diplomacy and Resistance*. New York, 1970.
M. Begin. *The Revolt*. London, 1964.
Lohame Herut Israel. 2 vols. Tel Aviv, 1959
D. Niv. *Ma'arakhot ha'irgun hazvai haleumi*. 5 vols. Tel Aviv, 1977.
N. Yalin-Mor. *Lohamei Herut Israel*.

2. Terror and the Arab-Israeli Conflict

N. Aloush. *Al thawra al filistiniya*. Beirut, 1970.
G. Chaliand. *The Palestine Resistance*. London, 1972.
J. Cooley. *Green March, Black September*. London, 1973.
G. Denoyan. *El Fath parle*. Paris, 1970.
Y. Harkabi. *Fedayeen Action and Arab Strategy*. London, 1968.
_____. *Palestinians and Israel*. Jerusalem, 1974.
L. Kadi. *Basic political documents of the Armed Palestinian Resistance Movement*.
    Beirut, 1969.
W. Kazziha. *Revolutionary Transformation in the Arab World*. London, 1975.
L. Khaled. *My people shall live*. London, 1973.
G. Khorshid. *Dalil Harakat al muqawama al filistiniya*. Beirut, 1971.
J. Laffin. *Fedayeen*. London, 1973.
Z. Schiff and R. Rothstein. *Fedayeen*. London, 1972.
R. Tophoven. *Fedayin. Guerilla ohne Grenzen*. Munich, 1975.
E. Yaari. *Strike Terror*. Jerusalem, 1970.

Anarchism

David Apter and James Joll, eds. *Anarchism*. London, 1971.
Alexander Berkman. *Prison Memoirs of an Anarchist*. New York, 1912.
Andrew Carlson. *Anarchism in Germany*. New York, 1972.

April Carter. *The Political Theory of Anarchism*. London, 1971.
Richard Drinnon. *Rebel in Paradise*. Chicago, 1961.
Felix Dubois. *Le péril anarchiste*. Paris, 1894.
Emma Goldman. *Living My Life*. New York, 1931.
Daniel Guérin. *L'anarchisme*. Paris, 1965.
J. Guillaume. *L'Internationale*. Paris, 1910.
I. L. Horowitz, ed. *The Anarchists*. New York, 1964.
Richard Hostetter. *The Italian Socialist Movement*. Princeton, 1958.
James Joll. *The Anarchists*. London, 1964.
P. A. Kropotkin. *Selected Writings*. Cambridge, Mass., 1973.
Cesare Lombroso. *Les anarchistes*. Paris, 1894.
Jean Maitron. *Histoire du mouvement anarchiste en France 1880–1914*. Paris, 1955.
M. A. Miller. *Kropotkin*. Chicago, 1976.
Max Nettlau. *Anarchisten und Sozialrevolutionäre*. Berlin, 1914.
Max Nomad. *Aspects of Revolt*. New York, 1959.
_____. *Rebels and Renegades*. New York, 1932.
Vernon Richards, ed. *Enrico Malatesta*. London, 1965.
Rudolf Rocker. *Johann Most*. Berlin, 1924.
_____. *The London Years*. London, 1956.
Victor Serge. *Memoirs of a Revolutionary*. London, 1963.
E. Sernicoli. *L'Anarchia*. 2 vols. Milan, 1894.
E. A. Vizetelly. *The Anarchists*. New York, 1912.
George Woodcock. *Anarchism*. London, 1962.
E. V. Zenker. *Anarchism*. London, 1895.
Hector Zoccoli. *Die Anarchie und die Anarchisten*. Leipzig, 1909.

Terrorist Groups in Various Countries, 1870–1939

Louis Adamic. *Dynamite*. New York, 1934.
Wayne G. Broehl. *The Molly Maguires*. New York, 1966.
C. Z. Codreanu. *Pentru Legionari*. Bucharest, 1937.
C. Christowe. *Heroes and Assassins*. New York, 1935.
V. Dedijer. *The Road to Sarajevo*. New York, 1966.
Den Doolard. *Quatre mois chez les Comitadjis*. Paris, 1932.
M. Fatu and Ion Spalatelu. *Garda de Fier*. Bucharest, 1971.
E. Gumbel. *Vier Jahre politischer Mord*. Berlin, 1922.
R. Hunter. *Violence and the Labor Movement*. New York, 1914.
H. Karasek, ed. *Haymarket, 1886, die deutschen Anarchisten in Chicago*. Berlin, 1975.
M. Lacko. *Arrow-Cross Men*. Budapest, 1969.
L. Nalbandian. *The Armenian Revolutionary Movement*. Berkeley, 1963.
A. Nazabek. *Through the Storm*. London, 1899.
M. S. Packe. *The Bombs of Orsini*. London, 1957.
C. Papanace. *La genesi ed il martirio del Movimento Legionario Rumeno*. N.p., 1959.
J. Perrigault. *Bandits de l'Orient*. Paris, 1931.
E. von Salomon. *Die Geächteten*. Berlin, 1932.
C. Sburlati. *Codreanu, il Capitano*. Rome, 1970.
R. Storry. *The Double Patriots*. London, 1957.
J. et J. Tharaud. *L'envoyé de l'archange*. Paris, 1939.

Latin America
(see also footnotes to chapter 5)

Actas Tupamaros. Buenos Aires, 1971.
F. R. Allemann. *Macht und Ohnmacht der Guerilla.* Munich, 1974.
V. Bambira et al. *Diez años de insurrección en America Latina.* 2 vols. Santiago, 1971.
R. Debray, *La critique des armes*, 2 vols. Paris, 1973–1974.
———. *Revolution in the Revolution.* New York, 1967.
C. Detrez. *Les mouvements révolutionnaires en Amerique Latine.* Brussels, 1972.
F. Gèze and Alain Labrousse. *Argentine, révolution et contrerévolution.* Paris, 1975.
M. E. Gilio. *The Tupamaro Guerrillas.* New York, 1972.
Boris Goldenberg. *Kommunismus in Latein Amerika.* Stuttgart, 1971.
Ernesto Ché Guevara. *Guerrilla Warfare.* London, 1969.
E. Halperin. *Terrorism in Latin America.* Washington, 1976.
Donald C. Hodges. *The Latin American Revolution.* New York, 1974.
INDAL. *Movimientos Revolutionarios en America Latina.* Louvain, 1973.
James Kohl and John Litt. *Urban Guerrilla Warfare in Latin America.* Cambridge, 1974.
Robert Lamberg. *Die Guerilla in Lateinamerika.* Stuttgart, 1972.
Alan Labrousse. *Les Tupamaros.* Paris, 1970.
C. Marighella. *For the Liberation of Brazil.* London, 1971.
Ernesto Mayans. *Tupamaros, antologia documental.* Mexico, 1971.
A. C. Porzecanski. *Uruguay's Tupamaros.* New York, 1973.
Joãs Quartim. *Dictatorship and Armed Struggle in Brazil.* New York, 1973.
Hugh Thomas. *Cuba.* London, 1970.
Luigi Valsalice. *Guerriglia e Politica, l'esemplo del Venezuela.* Florence, 1973.
Luis Mercier Vega. *Guerrillas in Latin America.* London, 1969.

Spain
(see also footnotes to chapter 2)

B. Bolotten. *The Grand Camouflage.* New York, 1961.
S. J. Brademas. *"Revolution and social revolution."* Dissertation (Oxford, 1953).
Gerald Brenan. *The Spanish Labyrinth.* Cambridge, 1943.
H. M. Enzensberger. *Der kurze Sommer der Anarchie.* Frankfurt, 1972.
Clara E. Lida. *Anarquismo y revolucion en la España del XIX, siglo.* Madrid, 1972.
Cesar M. Lorenzo. *Les anarchistes espagnois.* Paris, 1969.
G. H. Meaker. *The Revolutionary Left in Spain 1914–1923.* Stanford, 1974.
Angel Pestaña. *Lo que apprendi en la vida.* Madrid, 1933.

Terrorist Groups in Various Countries Since 1945
(see also footnotes to chapter five)

A. Adelson. *S.D.S. A profile.* New York, 1972.
Avner. *Memoirs of an Assassin.* New York, 1959.
E. Bacciocco. *The New Left in America.* Stanford, 1974.
Günter Bartsch. *Anarchismus in Deutschland.* Vol. II. Hannover, 1973.
B. J. Bell. *Transnational Terror.* Washington, 1975.
Richard Clutterbuck. *Protest and the Urban Guerrilla.* London, 1974.
———. *Living with Terrorism.* London, 1975.

Regis Debray. *Revolution in the Revolution.* New York, 1967.
Jacques Duchemin. *Histoire du FLN.* Paris, 1962.
Geoffrey Fairbarn. *Revolutionary and Communist Strategy.* London, 1968.
M. Feraoun. *Journal 1955–1962.* Paris, 1962.
C. Foley and W. Scobie. *The Struggle for Cyprus.* Stanford, 1973.
G. Grivas-Dighenis. *Guerrilla Warfare and 'EOKA' Struggle.* London, 1964.
G. Jackson. *Blood in My Eye.* London, 1975.
Harold Jacobs, ed. *Weatherman.* New York, 1970.
Kollektiv RAF. *Über den bewaffneten Kampf in Westeuropa.* Berlin, 1971.
Jay Mallin, ed. *Terror and Urban Guerrillas.* Coral Gables, 1971.
J. Massu. *La vraie Battaille d'Alger.* Paris, 1971.
K. Mehnert. *Jugend im Zeitbruch.* Stuttgart, 1976.
G. Morf. *Terror in Quebec.* Toronto, 1970.
M. Müller-Borchert. *Guerilla im Industriestaat.* Hamburg, 1973.
Robert Moss. *The War of the Cities.* New York, 1972.
Julian Paget. *Last Post: Aden 1964–67.* London, 1969.
L. Payne and T. Findley. *The Life and Death of the SLA.* New York, 1976.
Prairiefire. N.p., 1974.
J. Raskin. *The Weathereye.* New York, 1974.
R. Rauball, ed. *Die Baader-Meinhof Gruppe.* Berlin, 1973.
Kirkpatrick Sale. *S.D.S.* New York, 1974.
Sasho Henshu, ed. *Sekigun.* Tokyo, 1975.
Alex Schubert. *Stadtguerilla.* Berlin, 1974.
Stadtguerilla und soziale Revolution. Haarlem, 1974.
S. Stern. *With the Weathermen.* New York, 1975.
T. Tachibara. *Chukaku us Kakumaru.* 2 vols. Tokyo, 1975.
R. Tophoven, ed. *Politik durch Gewalt.* Bonn, 1976.
Pierre Vallières. *Nègres Blancs de l'Amerique.* Montreal, 1969.
R. Wassermann, ed. *Terrorismus contra Rechtsstaat.* Darmstadt, 1976.

Index

DATE DUE

5 28 '81	
11 05 '84	
10 02 '85	
3 19 '86	
6 25 '86	
11 26 '86	
7 13 '88	
DEC 1 3 '89	
MAY 23 '90	
JUN 3 '92	
JUN 0 1 '94	
NOV 2 6 1996	
DEC 2 6 1996	
MAY 1 5 2002	

BRODART, INC.   Cat. No. 23-221